A GUIDE TO CONFESSION
LARGE AND SMALL

in the Mexican Language, 1634

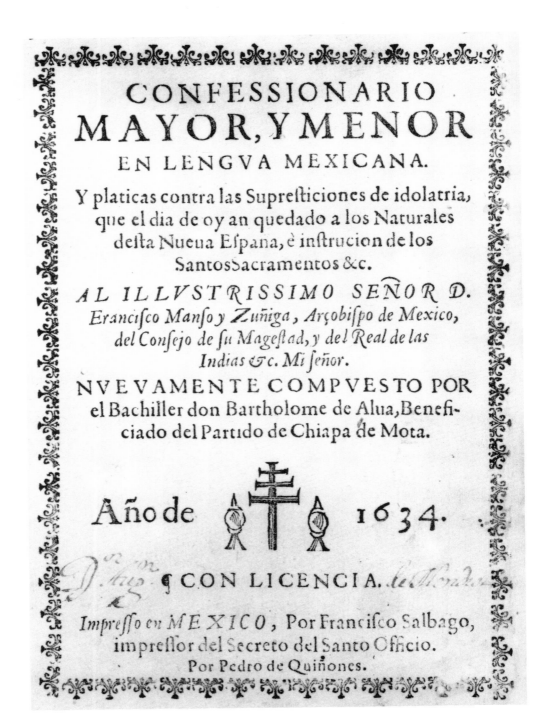

CONFESSIONARIO MAYOR, Y MENOR

EN LENGVA MEXICANA.

Y platicas contra las Suprefticiones de idolatria,
que el dia de oy an quedado a los Naturales
defta Nueua Efpaña, è inftrucion de los
SantosSacramentos &c.

AL ILLVSTRISSIMO SEÑOR D.
Erancifco Manfo y Zuñiga, Arçobifpo de Mexico,
del Confejo de fu Mageftad, y del Real de las
Indias &c. Mi feñor.

NVEVAMENTE COMPVESTO POR
el Bachiller don Bartholome de Alua, Bene-
ciado del Partido de Chiapa de Mota.

Año de ☩ 1634.

¶ CON LICENCIA.

Impreffo en MEXICO, Por Francifco Salbago,
impreffor del Secreto del Santo Officio.
Por Pedro de Quiñones.

Title page of the manuscript of the *Confessionario mayor*.
Courtesy of The John Carter Brown Library, Brown University, Providence, Rhode Island.

A GUIDE TO CONFESSION LARGE AND SMALL

in the Mexican Language, 1634

By Don Bartolomé de Alva

Edited by Barry D. Sell
and John Frederick Schwaller,
with Lu Ann Homza

UNIVERSITY OF OKLAHOMA PRESS : NORMAN

Also by John Frederick Schwaller

Origins of Church Wealth in Mexico: Ecclesiastical Finances and Church Revenues (Albuquerque, 1985)
The Church and Clergy in Sixteenth-Century Mexico (Albuquerque, 1987)

Alva, Bartolomé de, fl. 1634–1641.
　　[Confessionario mayor, y menor en lengva mexicana. Polyglot]
　　A guide to confession large and small in the Mexican language, 1634 / by Don Bartolomé de
Alva ; edited by Barry D. Sell and John Frederick Schwaller, with Lu Ann Homza.
　　　　p.　cm.
　　English, Aztec, and Spanish.
　　Includes bibliographical references (p.　　) and index.
　　ISBN 0–8061–3145–4 (cl. : alk. paper)
　　1. Confession (Liturgy)—Catholic Church—Texts.　2. Catholic Church—Mexico—Liturgy—
Texts.　3. Nahuatl language—Texts.　4. Confession (Liturgy)—Catholic Church—Texts—History
and criticism.　5. Catholic Church—Mexico—Liturgy—Texts—History and criticism.　I. Sell, Barry
D., 1949–　.　II. Schwaller, John Frederick.　III. Homza, Lu Ann, 1958–　.　IV. Title
BX2263.M6A5812　　1999
264´.02086´0972—dc21　　　　　　　　　　　　　　　　　　　　　　　99–18502
　　　　　　　　　　　　　　　　　　　　　　　　　　　　　　　　　　　CIP

Text Design by Ellen Beeler

1　2　3　4　5　6　7　8　9　10

To Miguel León-Portilla and Frances Karttunen

CONTENTS

ACKNOWLEDGMENTS

THIS PROJECT BEGAN many years ago when John Frederick Schwaller was compiling a guide to Nahuatl manuscripts in United States repositories. In the course of that endeavor, funded by a generous grant from the National Endowment for the Humanities, he had the chance to visit the major collections of Nahuatl materials in the United States. A series of short guides were the product of that effort. While working in the Los Angeles area, Jim Lockhart introduced Schwaller to Barry D. Sell who, at that time, was working on a study of early Nahuatl publications from Mexico. The two became close as a result of their common interests. Schwaller went on to spend years on other projects, later moving into academic administration, while Sell continued to work on Nahuatl imprints. A felicitous set of coincidences followed. While Schwaller was working at the Academy of American Franciscan History at the Franciscan School of Theology, he had the opportunity to study daily in the Bancroft Library of the University of California at Berkeley where several Nahuatl manuscripts which he had attributed to Alva were held. Schwaller became more interested than ever in working in greater depth on Alva and the school of Nahua scholars centered around the Jesuit Father Horacio Carochi. This led him inexorably to the *Confessionario*. It was an enlightening rediscovery of the book. During this same period, Sell had been working on similar topics and was about to do a transcription and translation of the *Confessionario*. A brief comment in a casual e-mail exchange revealed that their two paths had happily and productively coincided.

They quickly resolved to collaborate on publishing Alva in a modern edition that would include both the original text and an English translation as well as three introductory essays. They both saw the need to reach outside the field of Latin American history to bring in a Europeanist who would be deeply familiar with the Spanish counterparts of Alva's book. Fortunately Schwaller had met Lu Ann Homza at a meeting of the American Historical Association and was impressed with her research on sixteenth-century Spanish confessional guides. With the enthusiastic support of Sell, he invited her to join the project. She shared their vision of a collaboration between historians studing early modern Latin America and Europe and immediately accepted. Thus was born the book you now hold in your hands.

A collaborative work like this requires the efforts of so many people it would be impractical to name everyone. We offer all of them our heartfelt gratitude for their assistance.

Special mention must be given to the following people and institutions. A one-month fellowship in June 1994 at the John Carter Brown (JCB) Library in Providence, Rhode Island, provided Sell with the time necessary to compare his transcription with the original text and begin the arduous task of translating it. Norman Fiering, director of the library, Daniel Slive, and Van Edwards made his stay there a productive one. Many years earlier Schwaller also had the great pleasure of spending several weeks at the JCB and likewise extends his deep thanks to Director Fiering and his fine staff. Sell completed the work during his one-year fellowship at the University of Calgary (1996–1997) where Christon Archer, Patricia Evans, and Haijo Westra were very helpful and supportive to him. Stafford Poole, C.M., gave generously of his time in providing translations of the Latin text as well as reviewing various versions of the entire manuscript.

We extend our heartfelt gratitude to him. The late Arthur J. O. Anderson meticulously read the entire transcription and translation, smoothing over more than one rough spot. His facility in the three languages of the original, common among the colonial European clerics and Nahuas who wrote such texts, is now so rare that we were fortunate to benefit from his expertise. He will be missed. Charles Faulhaber and the staff of the Bancroft Library in Berkeley deserve special thanks for the assistance they so generously provided Schwaller. The Franciscan School of Theology and the Academy of American Franciscan History were instrumental in providing Schwaller with the time and facilities to make this project possible. John Drayton, Director of the University of Oklahoma Press, made sure that our manuscript saw the light of day. Some years ago Schwaller had the pleasure of serving as a reader for some Nahuatl-related manuscripts submitted to the University of Oklahoma Press and so came to know Drayton, who has an abiding interest in Nahuatl. Consequently, when our manuscript was ready for publication we turned to him for advice, which led to the Press's acceptance of our work. Louise Burkhart assisted us greatly with her incisive comments. We thank her for serving as a reader for the manuscript. Leah Remer, office assistant in the Provost's Office at the University of Montana at Missoula, heroically reformatted the electronic manuscript to meet the requirements of the press. Scholarship is in part the art of the possible and without her very practical assistance all our previous work would have been in vain.

Finally we thank our families and loved ones. Their help was often not as tangible as that of the people mentioned above but their contributions were just as real. Had it not been for them this book simply would not have been possible. Thanks, Anne, Rob, Will, and Mariko.

Barry D. Sell
John F. Schwaller

A GUIDE TO CONFESSION
LARGE AND SMALL

in the Mexican Language, 1634

DON BARTOLOMÉ DE ALVA,
NAHUATL SCHOLAR
OF THE SEVENTEENTH CENTURY

JOHN FREDERICK SCHWALLER

DON BARTOLOMÉ DE ALVA is one of the lesser-known Nahuatl specialists in colonial Mexico. His only publication was the *Confessionario mayor y menor en lengua mexicana* (1634).[1] In recent years other works have been discovered in manuscript, namely three theatrical pieces from the Spanish Golden Age which Alva translated into Nahuatl. The collection includes Pedro Calderón de la Barca's *El gran teatro del mundo*, Antonio Mira de Amescua's *El animal profeta y dichosa patricida*, and Félix Lope de Vega's *La madre de la mejor*. The first translation was dedicated by Alva to Father Jacome Basilio, S.J., and the last was dedicated to Father Horacio Carochi, S.J. Between the first and second play is an *entremés* by an unknown author, a satire on clerical and judicial abuses.[2] One of the few other reasons Alva is known to scholars is that he served as one of the examiners for the publication of Carochi's landmark Nahuatl grammar, *Arte de la lengua mexicana*.[3] These biographical fragments attract our attention and call us to investigate further the life of this seventeenth-century scholar.

Don Bartolomé de Alva was a mestizo, born around 1597. His reputation was almost totally eclipsed by that of his older brother, don Fernando de Alva Ixtlilxochitl.[4] In addition to the difference in their reputations, the age difference between the boys was so great that several scholars

---

1. Bartolomé de Alva, *Confessionario mayor y menor en lengua mexicana y platicas contra las supersticiones de idolatria que el dia de hoy an quedado a los naturales desta Nueva Espana, è instruccion de los Santos Sacramentos* (Mexico: Imprenta de Francisco Salbago, 1634). The only copies of this in the United States seem to be held by the Library of Congress and the John Carter Brown Library. Several others have microfilm copies of the one held in the British Museum.

2. John Frederick Schwaller, *Guías de manuscritos en Nahuatl* (Mexico: Universidad Nacional Autónoma de México, 1987), 55. For a study and modern translation of the Calderón de la Barca piece, see William A. Hunter, "The Calderonian *Auto Sacramental* 'El Gran Teatro del Mundo,'" *Publications*, Tulane University, Middle American Research Institute (1960) 27:105–201. For a general study of all the pieces, see Angel María Garibay, *Historia de la literatura náhuatl* (Mexico: Editorial Porrúa, 1953–55), 2:339–69.

3. Horacio Carochi, *Arte de la lengua mexicana* (Mexico: Juan Ruiz, 1645). A facsimile edition was published in 1983 by the Universidad Nacional Autónoma de México with an introductory study by Miguel León-Portilla.

4. Archivo del Arzobispo de México, Sagrada Mitra, *Ordenes Sacros*, fol. 274. Much of the existing biographical data on Alva comes from the records of his application of 1627 to become the beneficed curate of Zumpahuacan.

have reported don Bartolomé to be don Fernando's son.[5] Nevertheless, the two were brothers and equally proficient at their chosen professions.

Don Fernando and don Bartolomé were children of Juan Pérez de Peraleda and doña Ana Cortés.[6] The two boys had a total of seven brothers and sisters, and it seems that don Fernando was the second oldest of the nine children. The oldest was a brother, don Francisco de Navas y Peraleda.

Although some scholars reported that don Fernando was born in Texcoco after 1570, in all likelihood he was born around 1578, since his older brother, don Francisco, declared himself to be "about 80" in 1655. Their mother was born after 1561 and it is unlikely that she had children before the age of 15.[7] This made don Fernando approximately nineteen years older than don Bartolomé who was probably born around 1597. The children were probably born in San Juan Teotihuacan where their parents had their principal residence and held the bulk of their land. Nevertheless, ecclesiastical records refer to don Bartolomé as a *domiciliario* which implies that he was not born in the archdiocese of Mexico, but rather took up canonical residence there later. When don Bartolomé was born his mother was about thirty-six, and would live for nearly another forty years. His father, Juan Pérez de Peraleda, would die in 1620.

Doña Ana Cortés de Alva Ixtlilxochitl, also known as doña Ana Cortés Ixtlilxochitl, was a descendent of the kings of Texcoco and the *cacica,* or governor, of nearby San Juan Teotihuacan. Although two of her sons would become famous because of their writing, doña Ana was illiterate. Her parents were Juan Grande, a Spaniard, and doña Francisca Verdugo Ixtlilxochitl, also known as doña Francisca Cristina. In turn, doña Francisca's parents were don Francisco Verdugo Quetzalmamalintzin-Huetzin and doña Ana Cortés Ixtlilxochitl. This older doña Ana was the daughter of don Hernando Cortés Ixtlilxochitl who was the son of the famous Texcocan king Nezahualpilli and doña Beatriz Papantzin, a relative of the last Aztec emperor, Cuitlahuac. At the time of doña Ana Cortés's death in 1639, don Bartolomé was her youngest living child: two of his brothers had died previously, leaving the family with three girls and four boys.[8]

By the early seventeenth century the family's claim to hereditary rights over San Juan Teotihuacan had been questioned. A series of lawsuits in the middle of the seventeenth century not only helped to determine the *caciques* of the town but also to clarify relationships among relatives of the family. It is interesting to note that some of the townspeople claimed that the family had lost its claim to the hereditary office because it was no longer Indian but Spanish since both Juan Grande and Juan Pérez de Peraleda were Spanish.

Nevertheless, the family was related to other members of the Indian nobility. Nearly all of these families had ceased to be pure Indian through frequent marriage with Spaniards. Some of the relatives included the Alvarado Montezuma clan, descendants of the caciques of Ixtapalapa. In depositions in 1666, two of the Alvarado Montezumas discussed their ties to the Alvas. Both witnesses were secular priests, Licenciado don Fernando de Alvarado Montezuma and his

5. José Mariano Beristaín y Souza, *Biblioteca septentrional* (Amecameca: Colegio Católico, 1883), 1:58–59. Garibay, *Historia de la literatura náhuatl,* 2:340.

6. Fernando de Alva Ixtlilxochitl, *Obras Históricas,* edited by Edmundo O'Gorman (Mexico: Universidad Nacional Autónoma de México, 1975–77), 2:346–49.

7. Alva Ixtlilxochitl, *Obras históricas,* 1:17.

8. The use of the surnames Cortés and Verdugo reflects a common pattern of the immediate post-conquest era when natives adopted the surnames, and often given names, of their Christian baptismal sponsors or of local notables. The first *encomendero* of San Juan Teotihuacan was Francisco Verdugo.

nephew, Bachiller don Diego de Alvarado Montezuma. The elder referred to don Fernando de Alva as his second cousin, the younger merely called him uncle.[9]

It is unclear how don Fernando and don Bartolomé received their early education. Scholars have attempted to link don Fernando with the famous Colegio de Santa Cruz at Santiago Tlatelolco, run by the Franciscan friars and home to fray Bernardino de Sahagún and his native student assistants. It is unlikely that don Fernando attended the school because he was not a full-blooded native. His mother was in line for succession to the *cacicazgo* of San Juan Teotihuacan, but he was not, since under the laws of Spanish inheritance his older brother, don Francisco, would have precedence. We do know that don Fernando was fully fluent in both Spanish and Nahuatl, for he earned his living as an interpreter in the royal courts. Relatively early in his life don Fernando became fascinated by the history of the natives of Mexico and especially of his home region, Texcoco and Teotihuacan.

In the case of don Bartolomé, we know that he attended the University of Mexico, receiving the bachelor's degree in arts in 1622, and later a licentiate, also in arts.[10] He was awarded the baccalaureate degree for having successfully completed the qualifying exams rather than necessarily having attended university courses, since ecclesiastical records indicate that he received the baccalaureate *por sufficiencia*. From an early age he was probably destined for a career in the Church. Since it seems that none of his other brothers or sisters became priests or nuns, it would not be unusual for him to have been prepared from an early age for a clerical vocation. Certainly by the time of his father's death in 1620, it looked likely that don Bartolomé would enter the priesthood. In his will, Juan Pérez de Peraleda ordered the establishment of a chantry to provide don Bartolomé with sufficient income to become ordained.

In the colonial period certain obstacles were placed in the way of young men wishing to be ordained, to assure that all clerics had sufficient sources of income. In order to be ordained, a young man had to demonstrate how he would support himself after entering the clergy. The very wealthy could simply give their sons sufficient patrimony. Families of more limited means usually established chantries, which consisted of a relatively large sum of money invested in a real estate mortgage. The money generated by the mortgage would provide the young priest with an annual income. He, in turn, was required to perform a specific number of masses for the benefit of the patron who had endowed the chantry and anyone else the patron might indicate. A chantry could also be formed through a gift of land which when rented out would provide a constant income. Lastly, parents could impose a lien on previously clear property and begin to pay the interest. All of these arrangements were in perpetuity, so the income could be passed from one generation to the next as needed within the extended family.[11] Young men who won ecclesiastical benefices in public examinations could use those assignments as the basis for their ordination. Men fluent in the native languages could also receive ordination based entirely on that knowledge, as it would give them a great competitive advantage when it came to seeking a benefice.

Don Bartolomé de Alva's father established a chantry for his son's benefit in case he should choose to enter the clergy. Had don Bartolomé not used the chantry, it could have passed to

---

9. Alva Ixtlilxochith, *Obras históricas* 2:376–78.

10. Ibid., 1:28; 2:359. Don Bartolomé must have received his licentiate sometime between 1641, when he translated the theater pieces, and 1643, when he was referred to as "*licenciado*" in court testimony.

11. John Frederick Schwaller, *The Origins of Church Wealth in Mexico* (Albuquerque, NM: University of New Mexico Press, 1985), 112–21.

another of Juan Pérez de Peraleda's sons or grandsons. The basis of the chantry was two and a half *caballerías* of land which the family held in the Apayango district of Teotihuacan. The land had come to Pérez de Peraleda as part of his wife's dowry. Part of the land was under irrigation, allowing for year-round cultivation. In all, Pérez de Peraleda estimated the land to be worth 2,000 pesos. In 1620 that would have generated between 100 and 140 pesos a year, approximately the same amount as the annual salary of an average parish priest if the principal were invested in a mortgage. As real estate, however, it is difficult to estimate how much annual income it might have produced.

Among the conditions which Pérez de Peraleda imposed on the chantry was that a mass be said on the first Friday of each month for his soul and those of his wife, parents, and grandparents. In addition, the chaplain would have to celebrate a sung mass on the feast of the Immaculate Conception at the altar in the church where Pérez de Peraleda was buried. Other sung masses were ordered for the feasts of Saint Joseph and Saints Peter and Paul. The initial patrons of the chantry were Pérez de Peraleda's wife, doña Ana Cortés, and two of his sons, don Francisco de Navas and don Fernando de Alva.

It is quite possible that don Bartolomé also benefitted from another chantry which the family controlled. Pérez de Peraleda's aunt, Mariana de Navas, left a chantry imposed on some houses she owned in Mexico City. Pérez de Peraleda willed the chantry to his son, don Fernando, should he choose to become a priest. Since don Fernando did not become a priest, but married instead, it is quite possible that this chantry also passed to don Bartolomé.[12]

In her will, doña Ana Cortés left him her residence in the Santa Anna district of Mexico City and certain plots of irrigated land. There was no mention in her will of the chantries established by her husband nor did she establish any chantries herself.

After completing his education don Bartolomé entered the clergy, becoming a secular priest in the archdiocese of Mexico. As it turned out, he did not use the income from his chantries as the basis upon which he would be ordained but rather was ordained due to his fluency in Nahuatl. A candidate for ecclesiastical orders had to present his *título* upon ordination to the subdiaconate. Don Bartolomé did so on June 13, 1623 and on December 23, 1624, was ordained a deacon. It is not clear when he finally entered the priesthood, but in all likelihood that occurred in June 1625.[13]

In order to receive an appointment as a full-time parish priest with a guaranteed income, one had to participate in competitive exams called *oposiciones*. These exams tested the candidates' training and abilities and sought to ensure that the best-qualified priests served the parishes of the archdiocese. Once a priest had been appointed to a parish by the viceroy, confirmed by the archbishop, and canonically installed in his benefice, he could not be easily removed from office. Consequently beneficed clergy tended to remain in a specific parish for quite a long period of time. Not all parish priests, however, were beneficed.[14]

Don Bartolomé is known to have served as a beneficed cleric, or *beneficiado*, in two parishes: Chiapa de Mota and Zumpahuacan. The first competition for which there is evidence of Alva's participation was in the *oposición* for the parish of Zumpahuacan. As it turned out, he was

---

12. Alva Ixtlilxochitl, *Obras históricas*, 2:341.

13. Archivo del Arzobispo de México, Sagrada Mitra, *Ordenes Sacros I*, fols. 230, 240.

14. John F. Schwaller, *The Church and Clergy in Sixteenth-Century Mexico* (Albuquerque, NM: University of New Mexico Press, 1987), 82–85.

successful his first try, receiving a recommendation for appointment to the viceroy on July 15, 1627. The clerics of the examining tribunal noted in their recommendation that Alva was extremely qualified in Nahuatl, although his training in sacraments and moral theology were only of moderate sufficiency. They also noted that he was a descendant of the lords of Texcoco and that as proof of this affiliation he had presented a royal decree issued in favor of his brother, don Fernando, which outlined the family's services to the crown and their descent from Nezahualpilli.[15] Texcoco held great fame as a home to scholars of Nahuatl. The Jesuit Father Antonio del Rincón, author of a famous *Arte* of 1595, was also a descendant of Texcocan royalty and a mestizo.

In 1634, when Alva published his *Confessionario mayor y menor*, he was serving as benefici-ado of Chiapa de Mota. This parish is located to the northwest of Mexico City. The oposición for the benefice took place during the late summer and fall of 1631. On Oct. 14, 1631, Alva received his royal provision to serve the parish as a beneficed curate from the viceroy Marqués de Cerralvo and was canonically instituted into the benefice eleven days later.[16] At this time the town was still an *encomienda* held by the Mota family, the territory having been granted to Jerónimo Ruiz de la Mota, a conqueror and captain of one of the twelve brigantines that partic-ipated in the final assault on Mexico City. By the 1630s, the encomienda was held by Jerónimo's grandson, don Antonio de la Mota y Portugal. While all benefices were supposed to be filled through competitive exams, there are indications that *encomenderos* still exercised some power in selecting the clerics who would serve in their encomiendas. As it turns out, don Bartolomé de Alva's mother had some not insignificant financial ties to the Mota family. In fact the very houses she gave to don Bartolomé had a mortgage on them in favor of don Cristóbal de Mota Osorio, the nephew of don Antonio de la Mota. It was not uncommon for a family to loan out money in the form of mortgages and liens to establish chantries while at the same time borrowing from other families. The family of don Bartolomé also owned land near Chiapa de Mota. In 1566, Juan Grande, don Bartolomé's grandfather, acquired two caballerías of land for sheep raising near the town of Chiapa. The Mota family was still the largest landowner in the district.[17]

Interestingly enough, at the same time don Bartolomé's mother was dying and granting him the houses with the Mota mortgage on them, don Fernando de Alva was appointed special judge to investigate the senior Mota, don Antonio de la Mota, who was at that time the *alcalde mayor*, or local magistrate, of the province of Chalco. Mota and his lieutenant had been accused of improper distribution of Indian labor among the farmers of his district.[18]

The chantry to which don Bartolomé was ordained eventually was inherited by a friend of the family, the famous *savant* of colonial Mexico, don Carlos de Sigüenza y Góngora. The patron of the chantry came to be don Bartolomé's nephew, don Fernando's son don Juan de Alva Cortés. Moreover, the Motas held a mortgage lien on the property at the time of the death of don Juan de Alva Cortés in 1684, which the Motas had received in exchange for money they had loaned to don Bartolomé's mother, or someone before her.[19]

15. Archivo del Arzobispo de México, Sagrada Mitra, *Ordenes Sacros*, fol. 274.

16. Archivo General de la Nación, Bienes Nacionales, 1253, exp. 1, "Provisión real, 14 Oct. 1631;" Bienes Nacionales, 830, exp. 3, fol. 165, "Colación e institución canónica, 25 Oct. 1631."

17. Mario Colín, *Indice de documentos relativos a los pueblos del Estado de México. Ramo de Mercedes del Archivo General de la Nación* (Mexico: Biblioteca Enciclopedia del Estado de México, 1967), 1:#505.

18. Alva Ixtlilxochitl, *Obras históricas*, 2:344–45.

19. Ibid., 2:394.

The assignment of don Bartolomé de Alva to the parish of Zumpahuacan took him far from his home region. Although Chiapa de Mota was not close to San Juan Teotithuacan, both were at least in the general vicinity of Mexico City, one to the northeast, the other to the northwest. Zumpahuacan, on the other hand, was located far to the southwest of Mexico City, directly south of Toluca and west of Cuernavaca. At some point after this assignment, Alva served as an examiner for Carochi's grammar.

Although there are few other details available about the life of don Bartolomé de Alva, we know that his brother don Fernando died in 1650 and was buried in the church of Santa Catalina in Mexico City. His death must have been unexpected because the notation in the burial record of the church indicates that he died intestate. For a man who had worked in the courts most of his life and participated in several lawsuits over land and inheritance it is remarkable that he did not make a last will and testament. This oversight on his part made matters somewhat more difficult for his oldest son, don Juan de Alva Cortés, who was born to his parents sometime around 1635, but before their marriage, and later legitimized.[20]

Records of the cacicazgo of San Juan Teotihuacan indicate that the elder Alva brother don Francisco de Navas died in 1660. Both don Francisco and don Fernando were twenty to twenty-five years older than don Bartolomé, so one might expect don Bartolomé to have lived at least into the 1670s, although don Luis de Alva, the nearest in age of his brothers to Bartolomé, died in 1666.[21]

Don Bartolomé de Alva's legacy is found in the works he composed. Of these the only text to be published in his lifetime was his *Confessionario mayor y menor*. This short work, only fifty-three leaves long, was one of the very few confessional guides written in the seventeenth century. While there was an outpouring of doctrines, catechisms, and grammars being published throught the colonial period, only six confessional guides were printed, in a total of nine editions.

Nevertheless, the market for such guides must have been fairly strong when Alva published his own. In the same year, 1634, fray Francisco de Lorra Baquio, O.P., published his *Manual mexicano de la administración de los santos sacramentos*; in 1638, fray Pedro Contreras Gallardo published the *Manual de administrar los santos sacramentos*; and in 1642 Andrés Sáenz de la Peña published his *Manual de los santos sacramentos*. All four of these works sought to provide parish priests with resources in Spanish and Nahuatl for the administration of the sacraments; Alva's guide specifically focused on the sacrament of penance. One should also consider fray Martín de León's *Manual breve y forma de administrar los santos sacramentos a los indios*, the third edition of which was published in 1640.[22] Although it was written to assist the priest serving in an Indian parish, it was written completely in Latin and Spanish, thus assuming that either the priest would properly translate the texts into Nahuatl or would administer the sacraments in Spanish. León was rightly famous for two other works, both written in Nahuatl: *Sermonario* (1614) and *Camino del cielo* (1611), a very important devotional work. The fact that there were a number of works competing with Alva's indicates a significant demand, mostly by priests, for these guides.

---

20. Ibid., 2:370, 373–78.
21. Guillermo Fernández de Recas, *Cacicazgos y nobiliario indígena de la Nueva España* (Mexico: Universidad Nacional Autónoma de México, 1961), 115.
22. This work went through four editions: 1614, 1617, 1640, and 1669.

The title of Alva's work indicates that, in addition to being a confessional guide, it contains short talks which could be used in the suppression of idolatry among the Indians. In fact, the title is somewhat misleading. The guide consists of short talks, *pláticas*, followed by questions and answers which imitate the confessional dialogue. This dialogue constitutes the bulk of the work.

In his introduction Alva makes reference to the story of Jacob wrestling with the angel in which, at the coming of dawn, the angel blesses Jacob in order to be released. Alva alludes to this story in several ways. His central trope is the play on words between his surname, Alva, or Alba as it was frequently written, and the Spanish word for dawn, *alba*. Bartolomé implies he has labored through the night of Mexican ignorance to spread the light of truth for he is the dawn. Moreover, he has found time to write the book in addition to his normal course of work and despite his shortcomings. Alva is offering the fruit of his labors to the archbishop so that just as Jacob was blessed by the angel, so might Alva's efforts be blessed as well. Alva's guide was examined by three church officials, the Visitor General of the Archdiocese of Mexico, Dr. Jacinto de la Serna, and two Jesuit priests, Fathers Juan de Ledesma and Antonio de Carvajal. All three found the work to be free of error and useful for parochial service. Ledesma went a bit further than the other two, praising Alva's command of Nahuatl.

Alva structured his work around short homilies on various points of Christian doctrine, the Ten Commandments, and the seven Sacraments. Beyond that, Alva attempted to use concrete examples in the confessional itself, referring to specific native deities and practices. The work itself is layed out in two columns: Nahuatl is on the left, Spanish on the right. Frequently Alva also includes marginal notations to describe the context of the examples he used in greater detail. One quickly sees that this is a very complex work despite its relatively short length.

One of the most interesting sections deals with questions to be asked regarding the Ten Commandments. Here one can see Alva attempting to help the parish priest to discern the continuance of pagan beliefs. In the questions concerning the First Commandment, Alva has the penitent respond that he loves the Lord his God with all his heart "but at times I have believed in dreams, herbs, peyote and *ololiuhqui*, and other things."[23] Alva then has the priest ask: "Are you guarding in your home [idols called] 'turquoise children' and 'turquoise toads?' Do you bring them out into the sun to warm them? Do you wrap them in cotton, honoring them?" He further asks if the penitent believes that the stones bring him wealth or other material possessions.[24]

In the middle of these questions Alva inserts one of his homilies refuting the pagan beliefs of the Indians, especially that the jade objects could bring them material wealth and possessions. From that homily Alva then has the confessor begin to determine if the penitent still harbors a belief in the pagan rain deities, the *tlaloques* and *ahuaques*. His questions give us interesting insights into the belief system of the period. Alva has the priest ask: "And do you believe that they [i.e., ahuaques and tlaloques] emerge and come from the mountain Tlaloc and other lofty mountains, when clouds newly form? . . . And as for you: do you think that there are some

---

23. Alva, *Confessionario*, fol. 8v, "Ca quemaca onicnozentlaçotili mochi yca in noyolo, yeçe ca quenmanian, onicneltocac in temictli, in xiuhtzintli in peyotl in ololiuhqui? Yhuan in oc cequi tlamantli." "Si è amado con todo mi coraçon, pero algunas vezes è creido en sueños, en yerbas, en el ololiuqui, y peyote, y otras cosas." *Ololiuhqui* is a plant with seeds that contain a narcotic, the effects of which are similar to peyote.

24. Ibid., fol. 9, "Cuix tiquinpixtica in mochan in chalchiuhcoconeme chalchiuhtamaçoltin? . . . Cuix tonayan tiquinquixtia cuix, tiquintotonia? Cuix tiquimiychcaquimiloa tiquinmahuiztillia?" "Tienes hasta oy algunos idolillos de Chalchihuite? . . . Los sacas al Sol a calentar, emboluiendolos en blandos algodones, con mucha veneracion, y respeto?"

ahuaques who do thus, who first give life to the clouds and rainstorms?"[25] Moreover, to assure the proper action of the tlaloques and ahuaques it was necessary to make offerings to them of candles, bowls, and copal incense. At this point Alva launches into another homily on the futility of these beliefs.

In this curious homily Alva compares the faith of the Mexicans with that of the Japanese. He asks his audience to consider the Japanese, who although newer to the Christian faith have left their Mexican "brothers" behind in terms of acts of faith and firmness of resolve, who having embraced the Christian faith, abandoned their old beliefs once and for all.[26] Alva also pointed to the numerous martyrs who had died in defense of the faith in Japan as a sign of their more deeply rooted acceptance of Christianity. The inspiration for this homily was the 1622 martyrdom of Christians in Nagasaki, which was part of a wave of persecution of Christians in Japan which began in 1597 and continued up to the time when Alva was writing.

In his marginal notes to this same homily Alva declares that its purpose is to dissuade the Indians from their beliefs in the heathen gods of rain and the custom of placing gifts of copal, candles, and *yauhtli* (a plant which smells and tastes of anis and which was burned in place of incense) to the gods Tlaloc and Matlalcueye. These customs had been recently discovered (1631) in Pantitlan, according to the note.[27]

At the close of this homily, Alva returns to questions for the confessor to pose to the penitent, this time inquiring about burial practices. Alva had the confessor ask if when burying a loved one the penitent included a henequen blanket or other grave offerings.[28] These offerings were to insure that the departed would to go the paradise called Ximoayan by the ancients, Alva explains in the following question and marginal note.[29] The other question on burial practices deals with women and the death of a nursing child. The confessor is to ask if they normally buried such a child with a small tube of cane filled with breast milk or if they continued to sprinkle breast milk over the grave.[30] Alva then begins yet another of his brief homilies against super-

---

25. Ibid., fol. 11, "Auh cuix ticneltoca in ca itech, hualquiza, hualehua in tepetl tlaloc, ihuan in oc zequi, huehuecapan tepetl, in iquac iancuican momexotia . . . auh in tehuatl, cuix yuh timomati in acame oncate Ahuaque in iuh quichihua, in yancuican quiyolitia in mixtli, in quiahuitl?" "Y crees, que estos tales, salen, y vienen del serro Tlaloc, y de otros altos, y encumbrados montes, quando al entrar de las aguas, se cubren, y tocan de nuves . . . Y tu estàs muy persuadido, que esto no sucede sino, por medio de los Ahuaquez, y que ellos producen los aguaceros?"

26. Ibid., fol. 11v, "auh xiquimitacan, xiquinmahuiéocan, in tlaneltoquiliztica amote[ic]cahuan Iapon tlaca, yhuan in oc zequintin in quin axcan oquizelique in tlaneltoquiliztli, ca ye tlaneltoquiliztlachihualtica, óamechpanahuique, óamechtlaztiquizque; canel àtle ic quitzotzona quitlacoa in tlaneltoquiliztli ca àmo tlateotoquilizxolopiyotl, ic quineneloa in yuhqui amehuantin ca ye içenmayan oquizentelchiuhque oquiçemixnahuatique in tlateotoquiliztli ipan onenca." "Volved los ojos atras (mejor diria adelante) y mirad a la Nacion de los Iapones, y otras que siendo vuestros hermanos menores en la Fé, y muy modernos, y nuevos en ella, os an dexado muy atras, con actos, y demostraciones que an hecho, siendo muy firmes y constantes: no tienen vuestras supersticiones, y reçabios; porque de una vez dieron de mano, y desterraron de sus coraçones la idolatria en que andaban siegos."

27. Peter Gerhard, *A Guide to the Historical Geography of New Spain*, 2d ed. (Norman, Okla.: University of Oklahoma Press, 1993), lists no place called Pantitlan. Nevertheless, there is a neighborhood in modern Mexico City that bears this name.

28. Alva, *Confessionario*, fol. 12v, "Cuix in, ycuac aca omomiquilli in àço mohuayolqui in àço, oc çe tlacatl, cuix Ayatl, piçietl, mecapalli, cactli, tomin, atl, tlaqualli, oanquihuicaltique, in ipan oanquitocaque, oanquiquimiloque in amo oquima in teopixqui?" "¿Por ventura quando murio alguno, o tu pariente, o otro qualquiera enterrasteslo, echandole en la sepultura manta de Nequen, piciete, mecapal, sapatos, dineros, comida, y veuida, y todo a escusas de vuestro Ministro?"

29. Alva himself makes an error in describing Ximoayan as "the place where all end," since it is more literally "the place where all are flayed."

30. Alva, *Confessionario*, fol. 13r-v, "Cuix in ycuac, omomiquili moconeuh, cuix acatica, otictlallilli in momemeyalo, in mochichihulayo? Cuix ipan otictocac. Cuix noço, in campa toctoc? Cuix ompa tiauh, ticnoquiz ticpipiaçoz, in mochichihualayo." "Si fueren mugeres, se les a de preguntar lo siguiente, que es lo que siempre acostumbran hazer, particularmente en los pueblos. Quando murio tu hijo niño, y pequeñuelo, por ventura pusiste con cañutos tu leche, enterrandole con ellos, o vas a derramarla en la sepultura donde está enterrado."

stitious behavior. In so doing he also describes Christian notions of the afterlife, mentioning purgatory, limbo, heaven, and hell.

As noted earlier, at one point Alva makes reference in a marginal comment to idolatrous behavior which occurred in Pantitlan. In this section, again in the margin, he mentions another outbreak of idolatry in Atlapulco, located between Toluca and Mexico City, which took place in 1631.[31] The parish priest described it all in a report submitted to the Archbishop, Alva explained. It is intriguing that there were so many outbreaks of idolatry at this time. Alva mentions two and we know that other authors of the period were equally concerned. A colleague of Alva's, Hernando Ruiz de Alarcón, wrote an extensive *Treatise on the Heathen Superstitions* in 1629 while beneficiado of the parish of Atenango, located in the south-central part of the archdiocese that lay about halfway between Mexico City and Acapulco.[32] Ruiz de Alarcón did not report any widespread manifestations of apostasy but rather the continuance of practices which had their roots in pre-Columbian beliefs and which detracted from the practice of Christianity as he understood it.

The concern manifested by Alva and Ruiz de Alarcón is found in other observers of the period, notably don Pedro Ponce de León, beneficiado of Zumpahuacan, the same parish Alva would come to serve later in his career.[33] Ponce de León wrote a smaller treatise than did Ruiz de Alarcón, but quite similar in tone and focus.

Parish priests in Peru were launching campaigns to suppress idolatry among the Indians at approximately the same time. Some of the most famous of these occurred in the village of Huarochirí, in the province that neighbored Lima directly to the east.[34] Anti-idolatry campaigns would become a fairly regular feature of the Andean world, but did not become as common in Mexico, despite the efforts of Alva, Ponce de León, and Ruiz de Alarcón.

Alva continues to alternate between questions for the confessor, potential answers by the penitent, and his own brief homilies through the rest of his work. There are references throughout to the idolatry of the Indians, as well as to their other spiritual "shortcomings." The guide ends with a general discussion of the basic Christian prayers: the Nicene Creed, the Lord's Prayer, the Ave María, and the Salve, and their presentation in Nahuatl. In his general introduction to the prayers, Alva points out that they were first translated from Spanish or Latin into Nahuatl by the Franciscan fathers, working in conjunction with Indian nobles of Texcoco and other cities. But because neither group understood the language of the other well, errors of translation occurred. To avoid this problem, early missionaries simply taught the Indians to pray in Latin. Yet Alva found it incongruous that Mexican Indians might pray in Latin, totally ignorant of what they were saying. In that context, Alva explains the specific words he has changed in various prayers.[35]

Alva correctly asserts that previous versions of the Creed had often translated "omnipotentem" as "ixquich ihuilli." He rejects that translation on the grounds that "ixquich" refered to something finite and limited. His contribution used the word "cenhuellitini" which he felt

---

31. Alva, *Confessionario*, fols. 13v–14.
32. Hernando Ruiz de Alarcón, *Treatise on the Heathen Superstitions that Today Live Among the Indians Native to this New Spain, 1629*, translated and edited by J. Richard Andrews and Ross Hassig (Norman, Okla.: University of Oklahoma Press, 1984).
33. Pedro Ponce de León, "Brief Relation of the Gods and Rites of Heathenism," in Ruiz de Alarcón, 211–18.
34. Karen Spaulding, *Huarochirí: An Andean Society Under Inca and Spanish Rule* (Stanford: Stanford University Press, 1984), 253–69.
35. Alva, *Confessionario* , fols. 48-48 [*sic*, 49].

conveyed the idea of infinite and power. Alva also opposed the use of "oquiyocox" to describe the act of creating the heavens and the earth in favor of the reverential form, "oquimochihuilli."[36]

In short, Alva's *Confessionario* is a unique work which deserves greater attention. It marks an important point in the development of Nahuatl as a printed language, and while the work is aimed primarily at non-native speakers, it is composed by a native speaker. The core of the work seeks to reform the spirituality of the Indians through the recognition of the vestiges of their old spirituality still present in their worship and through its destruction, which would result in a purer form of Christianity. The guide clearly shows the concern the clergy had about syncretism and backsliding at the time and as such, it fits well into the contemporary literature. The work shows no sign of the influence of Horacio Carochi, unlike some of Alva's later work.

Alva's other known pieces are his unpublished translations into Nahuatl of the Golden Age Spanish plays mentioned earlier. These works fit into the larger scheme of Alva's work. The *Confessionario* drew upon Alva's knowledge of his native language, Nahuatl, and of the customs and rituals of everyday Indian life. Alva, as a Christian priest, had been trained to perceive these customs and rituals as superstitions and antithetical to proper Christian habits. In translating the comedies Alva moved away from the utilization of language as a tool for religious indoctrination to the transmittal of European cultural values through ostensibly less religious material. Angel María Garibay characterized these works as belonging to the "Vuelo roto," or interrupted flight, a movement among educated Nahuatl speakers to develop their own literature, basing it initially upon European models. In fact these comedies are part of a small corpus of materials written in Nahuatl that were created entirely for recreational reading. Most of the titles deal with Christian didactic themes such as the story of the child-martyrs of Tlaxcala or the lives of various saints.[37] Consequently Alva's comedies stand out even more, since they are not primarily didactic. Among theatrical pieces, they also stand out for their limited emphasis on Christian moral teaching. No theatrical work was published in Nahuatl in the colonial period although we know they enjoyed great success.[38]

The comedies translated by Alva mark a point in the development of the author. The manuscript copy which we have is really a work in process. The three main parts were all copied out in a clean draft, possibly by Alva; additional research might be able to positively identify the handwriting as Alva's own. After the plays were translated into Nahuatl and copied out, a second person, perhaps Alva himself, placed some diacritical markings on the Nahuatl in conformity with the system developed by Horacio Carochi. We known that Alva and Carochi were acquainted with one another, since Alva served as one of the officials who approved Carochi's grammar for publication, and Alva dedicated his translation of the last of the three plays to Carochi. However it is in the second of the three plays where this subsequent process of editing in which diacritics were added is best seen. Throughout the work entitled "Animal propheta y dichosa patricida," or "Animal prophet and happy patricide," one can find the addition of dia-

---

36. Alva, *Confessionario*, fols. 49–50.

37. Among these works are fray Juan de Bautista's *Vida y milagros de San Antonio de Padua* and *Libro de la miseria*, his translation into Nahuatl of Motolinia's *La vida y muerte de los niños de Tlaxcala*; and Francisco Medina's *Vida y milagros de San Nicolás de Tolentino*. All of these works appeared in print between 1601 and 1605.

38. Marilyn Ekdahl Ravicz, *Early Colonial Religious Drama in Mexico: From Tzompantli to Golgotha* (Washington: The Catholic University Press, 1970), 68–72. Fernando Horcasitas lists the three works translated by Alva in his chronology of Nahuatl theatre, but does not include them in the detailed listing: Fernando Horcasitas, *El teatro nahuatl: Epocas novohispana y moderna* (Mexico: Universidad Nacional Autónoma de México, 1974), 79.

critical markings and, in the margins, a commentary on the diacritics. It is this commentary which provides us with many fascinating details of Alva's technique and circle of acquaintances.

In the marginal notations one of the themes is the use of Texcoco as a point of linguistic reference. In the text on the first leaf of the comedy Alva has used two native flowers: "yn tlapa-lyzquixōchitl" and "yn teōcuitlaxochitl."[39] Of the first, the marginal notes says: "Small white and sometimes red tropical fragrant flowers."[40] The second word is glossed as: "Yellow flowers like floripondio but not as large; within they are like what is called the 'Five Wounds'; they are from Texcoco."[41] This is the first of several references to Texcoco within the marginal notes. Clearly the Nahuatl is being glossed from a Texcocan point of view.

The other theme which emerges from the marginal notes is the authority of "don Fernando" de Alva. Well into the play, where the word "yn ēlōtlăpahuacaxtli" appears, the marginal note reads: "D. Fern^do īn ēlopahuaxtli." The discussion seems to be over whether it is a bowl of corn stew or just the corn stew and whether the "a" of "pahuaxtli" is long or short. On the next page the text reads: "cuix àhmo ycnōpilotl yntlacamo niçalli Jesus," while the marginal note reads: "don Fern^do is not satisfied with cuix àmo icnopillahuelilocayōtl."[42] This debate has to do with the use of the word for ingratitude or for wretchedness. But what is important in these cases is that don Fernando is taken as an authority to appeal to in the discussion.

Taken in isolation the textual focus on Texcocan Nahuatl and the references to don Fernando might be considered merely interesting, but in a work translated by don Bartolomé de Alva one might conclude that the don Fernando being referred to here was the writer's brother, don Fernando de Alva Ixtlilxochitl. Furthermore one might assume that don Fernando and don Bartolomé studied similar works and that both either drew on a common set of sources or at least similar sources. Only a more detailed analysis of the works of don Bartolomé, especially one that compares them to the works of his brother, can resolve these questions definitively.

There is at least one other manuscript which has been associated with the family of the Alvas, the work known as the *Codex Chimalpopoca* or the *Anales de Cuauhtitlan* and *Leyenda de los Soles*. The manuscript, which is missing from the library of the Museo Nacional de Antropología e Historia in Mexico, is clearly a seventeenth-century copy of an earlier work. Among the manuscript pages are several sheets written in a very different hand, which detail the genealogy of the Alva family.[43] Yet scholars agree that if don Fernando de Alva was familiar with the codex it was not reflected in his own writings. The handwriting of the *Codex Chimalpopoca* is also consistent with a date sometime in the middle of the seventeenth century as it uses a style which has been called Jesuit because of its occasional recourse to the system of diacritics developed by Carochi.[44] Consequently the manuscript of the *Codex Chimalpopoca* dates from the time don Bartolomé was active and is written in a style, if not the exact hand, that he also used. At

---

39. The diacritical markings are not complete, indicating that this was still an effort in progress. For example "tlapalizquixo-chitl" should be marked "tlapālzquīxōchitl" while "teocuitlaxochitl" would be "teōcuitlaxōchitl." Frances Karttunen, *An Analytical Dictionary of Nahuatl* (Austin, TX: University of Texas Press, 1983), 123, 227, 289, 329.

40. University of California, Berkeley, Bancroft Library, MM 462, "Animal propheta y dichosa patricida," fol.17; "flores de tierra caliente menudas blancas y alguna colorada olorosas."

41. Ibid., "flores amarillos a manera de floripondios no tan grandes y dentro tiene como los cinco llagas danse en Tetzcuco."

42. Ibid., fols. 43v-44v, "no contenta a don Fern^do."

43. Although the original manuscript is missing, a photoreproduction was made and published: Primo Feliciano Velázquez, ed. and trans., *Códice Chimalpopoca, Anales de Cuautitlán y Leyenda de los Soles,* 2d ed. (Mexico: Universidad Nacional Autónoma de México, 1975).

44. John Bierhorst, ed. and trans., *History and Mythology of the Aztecs: The Codex Chimalpopoca* (Tucson, AZ: University of Arizona Press, 1992), 12.

some point the manuscript was associated with the Alva family. Perhaps don Bartolomé and not don Fernando had the *Codex Chimalpopoca* copied in order to study it. Don Bartolomé would have had more interest in the material of the *Anales de Cuauhtitlan* since he served for a time in Chiapa de Mota, only a few leagues away.

Another argument which has been used to connect don Fernando with the manuscript was that don Carlos de Sigüenza y Góngora was familiar with it. Don Carlos became associated with the Alva family in 1682, when he became the principal heir of don Juan de Alva Cortés, the son of don Fernando de Alva. Sigüenza y Góngora also wrote don Juan's will and eventually administered his estate. According to the provisions of the will, the cacicazgo of San Juan Teotihuacan passed from don Juan to his brother, don Diego.[45] Consequently, Sigüenza y Góngora eventually defended the claim of don Diego de Alva Cortés to the cacicazgo. By having served both don Juan and don Diego, Sigüenza y Góngora came into the possession of Alva Ixtlilxochitl's papers. Yet don Carlos also must have had possession, or at least knowledge, of the works of don Bartolomé. Don Carlos served the chantry which had been established for don Bartolomé's ordination and had pursued several suits in order to collect the revenues which had accrued to it. Consequently, although it cannot be proven definitively, the *Codex Chimalpopoca* can logically be associated with don Bartolomé de Alva in many ways better than with don Fernando.

One other manuscript is generally associated with the followers of Carochi. It is titled "Camino del cielo" after a very famous early seventeenth century work by fray Martín de León. Nevertheless, it is very different from León's work, containing a collection of fragments of homilies in Nahuatl, pieces of a confessional guide, possible bits of a *huehuetlahtolli*, or formal speeches from the pre-Columbian period which were adapted by the missionaries and used for evangelization, and other incomplete works. There are two marginal notes of great interest in the manuscript. At one point the marginal note questions the use of the glottal stop: "Don Fern[an]do uses the glottal stop [*saltillo*] in teòcal. I don't know why and I doubt it should be." On the back of one of the fragments, there is also the inscription "To Father Horacio Carochi."[46] The type of works, the fact that they were written in Nahuatl using Carochi diacritics, and the reference to don Fernando all make this manuscript quite similar to the manuscript of the Alva translations of the Golden Age comedies. Finally both were sold in the auction of the José Fernando Ramírez collection in London, in 1880. The "Camino del cielo" was item 510, the Golden Age Comedies, item 515; both items reportedly came from the Library of the Jesuit Colegio de San Gregorio. Nevertheless, the handwriting of the "Camino del cielo" appears to be nearly the same as that of a work attributed to Carochi, the "Bancroft Dialogues" or huehuetlahtolli.[47] Likewise the "Bancroft Dialogues" were also part of the Ramírez sale, item 521. Taking all this information into account, one can thus tentatively associate the "Camino del cielo" to don Bartolomé de Alva.

During his life and even after his death, don Bartolomé de Alva was overshadowed by his older brother. Nevertheless, don Bartolomé can rightly be credited with two very important con-

---

45. Archivo General de la Nación, Bienes Nacionales, 830, exp. 1, "Cuenta de los bienes de don Juan de Alva Cortés."

46. Newberry Library, Chicago, Ayer MS. 1470, "Camino del cielo" [*sic*], B-10, p. 11, "Don Fern^do pone saltillo en teòcal no se porque y dudo que se deva poner," and p. 24, "Al P Oracio Carochi."

47. Frances Karttunen and James Lockhart, eds., *The Art of Nahuatl Speech: The Bancroft Dialogues* (Los Angeles: UCLA Latin American Center, 1987).

tributions to Nahuatl literature, his *Confessionario* and his translation of the Golden Age come-dies. Beyond that, it is quite possible that he was responsible for the copying of the manuscript known as the "Codex Chimalpopoca," and was possibly the author of the collection of Nahuatl fragments known as the "Camino del cielo." In short, don Bartolomé de Alva should rank as one of the leading figures of the study of Nahuatl in the early seventeenth century.

THE CLASSICAL AGE OF
NAHUATL PUBLICATIONS AND
DON BARTOLOMÉ DE ALVA'S
CONFESSIONARIO OF 1634

2

BARRY D. SELL

PUBLICATIONS AND MANUSCRIPTS in Indian languages are one of the enduring lega-
cies of colonial mainland America. They can be found in various European colonies
throughout the western hemisphere. However the greatest concentration, number, and variety of such writings were produced in Mesoamerica, an area encompassing much of what is
now Mexico and northern Central America. This was no accident for there as nowhere else
did American precedent resonate so strongly with European innovation. Long before Spanish
conquest and colonization there had been a Mesoamerican tradition of creating records by
writing/painting[1] on native paper. After the conquest—based on analogies with old practices
and in response to new Spanish demands—Mesoamericans quickly learned to generate
Hispanic-style municipal documentation in alphabetical versions of their own languages.
Hispanics also wrote texts in indigenous languages, usually for the church and often with the
assistance of the same literate natives who acted as notaries. Thus significant amounts of
extant writings were produced by and for such major indigenous groups as the Nahuas
("Aztecs"), Mayas, Zapotecs, Mixtecs, and Tarascans.

Yet even among these documentary riches one part of the extant corpus stands out from all
the rest. In the period preceding Mexican independence in 1821, Nahua notaries and Hispanic
nahuatlatos (experts in Nahuatl, the "Aztec" language) produced more documents than the writings created in all other Mesoamerican languages combined. The over 110 Nahuatl publications
constitute almost 60 percent of extant imprints in such indigenous tongues.[2] The contrast in
publications is even more striking considering the date when Alva's confessional guide left the

---

1. In colonial Nahuatl texts the same verb is used for "to paint" and "to write," regardless of whether the writer is referring to
the period before or after European intrusion. This in itself suggests some perceived sense of continuity between the pre- and
post-conquest ways of keeping records.

2. See Ascensión H. de León-Portilla, *Tepuztlahcuilolli: Impresos en Nahuatl* (México: Instituto de Investigaciones Históricas,
Instituto de Investigaciones Filológicas, Universidad Nacional Autónoma de México, 1988), and Barry D. Sell, "Friars, Nahuas, and
Books: Language and Expression in Colonial Nahuatl Publications" (Ph.D. diss., UCLA, 1993), especially the chart on p. 4.

presses. By 1634 the number of Nahuatl books (at least 44[3]) already had exceeded the combined total for all colonial imprints in the important local vernaculars of Maya, Zapotec, Mixtec and Tarascan.[4]

The relative abundance of Nahuatl publications had a direct impact on how many editions of any one genre were printed[5] and how many genres could be covered. Other well-published indigenous languages might be represented by as many as a dozen or so colonial imprints, all of them ecclesiastical. They could range from a single dictionary and a grammar or two to a small assortment of *doctrinas* (books of Christian doctrine), *confesionarios* (confessional guides), *catecismos* (catechisms), and perhaps a *sermonario* (a collection of sermons). By 1634 the Nahuatl corpus already had covered all these bases and more. Singly or in combination there were two dictionaries, several grammars, various books of Christian doctrine, confessional guides, catechisms, and four thick collections of sermons. During the next two centuries most of these categories would continue to be filled with newly composed works or with reeditions of old ones. Fray Martín de León's eclectic manual for priests of 1611 lists material both typical and atypical of church imprints:

> ACCOUNT of what this book entitled
> *Camino del cielo* (Road of Heaven) contains.
> An entire catechism with all its requirements in order to teach a pagan from the point of his conversion, or any other Christian from the time he has the use of reason, all he must believe and know how to work at and to do in order to save himself.
> ¶   All the prayers in their language, and what they contain from the *persigno* [I cross myself] until the last prayer.
> ¶   The "Articles of the Faith" of Saint Athanasius.[6]
> ¶   Reprobation of idolatry, declaring to them [i.e., the Indians] the falsity of it, and who were the gods that the ancient Indians worshipped, and their evil ends, and the traces that have remained with them of what was past, the worship of fire and their [pre-Hispanic] baptism and other things.
> ¶   The [pre-Hispanic] Mexican calendar.[7]
> ¶   Two confesionarios, large and small.
> ¶   Instruction for taking communion.
> ¶   A way for the Indians to make their testaments.[8]
> ¶   Method of praying the rosary of Our Lady.
> ¶   Some very devout rules in order to better serve God, very easy to understand.
> ¶   Seven meditations about the passion of our Lord Jesus Christ.

---

3. See Sell, "Friars, Nahuas, and Books," Appendix 1, "Extant Colonial Nahuatl Publications, 1547–1819," especially 305–307. The number periodically grows larger as works previously known only through colonial references are found. For example, not included in my count of publications (in part because I have not yet examined them firsthand or in photoreproduction) are fray Alonso de Molina's life of Saint Francis (1577), which was long thought lost, and Francisco de Pareja's *Doctrina christiana . . . en lengua castellana y mexicana* (1578). Copies of both works were recently discovered in Spain (Ascensión H. de León-Portilla, "Algunas publicaciones sobre lengua y literatura nahuas," *Estudios de Cultura Náhuatl*, 1992, 22:467–68).

4. This is based on unpublished research, but much of the raw data can be found in the bibliographic works of José Toribio Medina.

5. The related question of the size of print runs cannot be answered at present.

6. "[Perhaps] this is the same as the Athanasian Creed, which is the only work of Athanasius that I think would have been required of neophytes," Stafford Poole, C.M., personal communication.

7. This item, to a lesser degree than the previous one, and the item below dealing with model testaments are not typical of church imprints.

8. While the copies of this imprint held by The Huntington Library in San Marino, California and the Bancroft Library of the University of California at Berkeley are incomplete and lack this model last will, the relevant pages are included in the copy held by the John Carter Brown Library of Providence, Rhode Island.

§   Ways of helping at mass, in the Dominican usage and according to the Roman usage.[9]

§   Instruction manual for dying properly… [and after death how] to lay out [the body] and carry it to be buried.[10]

Other types of Nahuatl publications find few, if any, printed counterparts in other indigenous languages of the Spanish Indies (colonial Spanish America and the Philippines). Among the most striking publications before 1634 are a Christian songbook, a collection of examples of traditional high oratory, and a layperson's guide to colloquial Nahuatl. The *Psalmodia christiana* (Christian Psalmody) of 1583 contains dozens of songs in Nahuatl keyed to the principal feast days of the Christian calendar. The author of record was the Franciscan nahuatlato fray Bernardino de Sahagún. He is best known today as the hands-on editor of the *Florentine Codex*, a massive manuscript in Nahuatl and Spanish about pre-Hispanic Nahua language, lore, and society. Although he was responsible for many Nahuatl writings, large and small, the only one to be published during his lifetime was the *Psalmodia*.[11] The lone precedent in print for this type of publication seems to be a Christian song in a Mixtec doctrina of 1568.[12] After the *Psalmodia* one has to go all the way to the Philippines to find the only other example of similar printed material in an Indian language. There, in 1610, the Tagalog printer Tomás Pinpin published a grammar in a "romanized phonetic script" to teach Spanish to Tagalog speakers.[13] Included in his language lessons are Christian songs in Tagalog.[14]

Apparently alone in its category anywhere in the Spanish colonies is the *Huehuetlahtolli* of 1600 of fray Juan Bautista and the trilingual (Latin/Nahuatl/Spanish) Nahua teacher Agustín de la Fuente. In the main it is a revised version of material written down in the 1540s. The book illustrates many of the modalities of the polite upper-class metaphorical Nahuatl known as *huehuetlahtolli*, variously translated as "the old word," "the speeches/admonitions of the elders," or "ancient discourse." Its characteristics include "extreme formality, floridness, ceremoniousness, effectiveness in command of figures of speech and recourse to parallelism, balance, and repetition."[15] More than just a kind of "rhetorical device that embellished a number of different kinds of social or political occasions," the huehuetlahtolli was also "an important . . . way of bringing up the young and fitting them properly and with the least friction into Nahua society."[16]

In stark contrast to the *Huehuetlahtolli* of Bautista and de la Fuente is the Berlitz-style *Manual vocabulario en las lenguas castellana y mexicana* of the small businessman Pedro de Arenas. Arenas wrote the Spanish portion of the text and had a professional interpreter provide

---

9. "Readers . . . may not know that until recent times the Dominicans had their own special ceremonies for mass," Stafford Poole, C.M., personal communication.

10. See Sell, "Friars, Nahuas, and Books," 33–34; the original citation is from fray Martín de León, *Camino del cielo* (México: Diego López Dávalos, 1611), preliminary leaf, unnumbered.

11. It has recently been made available in a modern critical edition with a transcription and English translation by Arthur J. O. Anderson, co-translator and co-editor along with Charles E. Dibble of the Nahuatl/English edition of the *Florentine Codex*.

12. See Sell, "Friars, Nahuas, and Books," 102, n. 5.

13. Vicente L. Rafael, *Contracting Colonialism: Translation and Christian Conversion in Tagalog Society Under Early Spanish Rule* (Ithaca: Cornell University Press, 1988), 55. Pinpin's work recently has been the subject of a dissertation by Damon Woods, "Tomás Pinpin and Librong pagaaralan nang manga Tagalog nang uicang Castila: Tagalog Literacy and Survival in Early Spanish Philippines" (UCLA, 1995).

14. For some examples, see Rafael, *Contracting Colonialism*, 60–62.

15. Fray Bernardino de Sahagún, *Florentine Codex. Book 6—Rhetoric and Moral Philosophy*, trans. and ed. Charles E. Dibble and Arthur J. O. Anderson (Salt Lake City and Santa Fe, N.M.: University of Utah Press and School of American Research, Santa Fe, 1969), 1, n. 1.

16. Arthur J. O. Anderson, "Old Word-New Word: *Huehuetlatolli* in Sahagún's Sermons," *Current Topics in Aztec Studies*, ed. Alma Cordy-Collins and Douglas Sharon, San Diego Museum Papers 30 (San Diego: San Diego Museum of Man, 1993), 86.

a translation. The Nahuatl of the marketplace and everyday activities, not that of flowery rhetoric, is the focus of this practical guide. It first appeared in 1611 and went through at least eight more editions before 1821, easily becoming the single most reprinted Nahuatl publication of the colony. This too appears to be unique in its genre among indigenous-language imprints of Spanish America.

The Hispanics and Nahuas who wrote these books ensured that their quality often matched their numbers and variety. This was especially true during the first hundred years of publishing (1540s to 1640s) when the majority of the most authoritative, germinal, original, and unusual works left the presses. This golden age of Nahuatl imprints included the authors mentioned above as well as such distinguished figures as the sixteenth-century Franciscan lexicographer fray Alonso de Molina and his trilingual Nahua collaborator Hernando de Ribas and the early seventeenth-century Augustinian nahuatlato fray Juan Mijangos and again Agustín de la Fuente. The period closes shortly after Alva's guide to confession of 1634 with the unequaled grammar of 1645 by the Jesuit expert Father Horacio Carochi and the first Nahuatl account of the Guadalupan apparition by the secular cleric Bachiller Luis Lasso de la Vega in 1649.[17] By the next century Hispanic nahuatlatos would look back on the pre-1650 era as the time when the "most eminent and classical authors of the discipline" wielded their pens to write books and manuscripts.[18]

Alva stood in good company not only in Mesoamerica but also in the two other major Indian regions of the worldwide Spanish empire. In the Philippines Fray Francisco Blancas de San José was the "most highly esteemed" colonial grammarian of Tagalog; his grammar first appeared in 1610.[19] In the same year the language lessons by Tomás Pinpin were published for Tagalogs wishing to learn Spanish (see above). Pinpin printed the Dominican's grammar as well as many other early colonial Philippine books. Also from the same general period are two rare notarial documents of 1613 and 1625 in the pre-Hispanic Tagalog syllabary *baybayin*.[20]

This period also constitutes an especially noteworthy time for texts in Quechua, the key language of Andean South America. Among the books published in the region were the most sophisticated colonial grammar (1607) and dictionary (1608) of Quechua, both bearing the name of Father Diego González Holguín, S.J. Manuscripts in the language are particularly rich, and include a very rare cache of notarial records covering the years 1605–08, Santa Cruz Pachacuti Yamqui's account of the "antiquities" of Peru written circa 1615, the secular cleric Juan Pérez Bocanegra's text of 1622 on pre-Hispanic ritual, and the Huarochirí manuscript of the early seventeenth century about Andean "myth" which has recently been made available in a new transcription and translation.[21]

---

17. Stafford Poole, C.M., *Our Lady of Guadalupe: The Origins and Sources of a Mexican National Symbol, 1531–1797* (Tucson and London: University of Arizona Press, 1995), is the most recent and thorough (if admittedly anti-apparitionist) survey of this and all the other colonial Nahuatl- and Spanish-language sources concerning the appearance of Our Lady of Guadalupe to the Nahua Juan Diego.

18. See Sell, "Friars, Nahuas, and Books," 114, 215 n. 1; the original citation is from Father Ignacio de Paredes's *Promptuario manual mexicano* (México: Biblioteca Mexicana, 1759), preliminary leaf, unnumbered. To mention just two other outstanding writers of Alva's time: the *Monarquia indiana* of fray Juan de Torquemada was printed in Sevilla in 1615 and the greatest Nahua annalist of the colonial period, Chimalpahin, was active during the first third of the seventeenth century.

19. Rafael, *Contracting Colonialism*, 26.

20. Ibid., 49.

21. For a brief summary of these texts see Bruce Mannhein, *The Language of the Inka Since the European Invasion* (Austin: University of Texas Press, 1991), 142–46. The latest version of the Huarochirí manuscript is by Frank Salomon and George L. Urioste, *The Huarochirí Manuscript* (Austin: University of Texas Press, 1991).

Shortly before Alva's work appeared Spain was itself experiencing its own golden age: 1585–1617 was the era of Cervantes and Lope de Vega.[22] Looking beyond the world under Spanish rule this was also the time when Shakespeare and others were active in England. At any rate, in a number of areas where Spanish culture was officially dominant there was a climate that favored writing and publishing in the major local vernaculars or at least writing about the peoples who spoke them.

Alva's manual thus came on the heels of—or was contemporary with—a great many texts of significance for those interested in the indigenous peoples of Mexico, South America, and the Philippines. Interest in his book is only heightened by the fact that he was literally a part of the two traditions embodied in publications written in alphabetical versions of indigenous languages: biologically he was a mestizo (i.e., of mixed Indian and European ancestry) and by upbringing he knew both "New World" Nahuatl and "Old World" Spanish as first languages.

While Alva was equally at home in both languages and societies the same cannot be said of modern scholars studying colonial Mexico. Many investigators are adept in modern Spanish and so have easy access through Spanish-language documentation to the Hispanic world of Alva's day. Access to Nahuas through documents in their language is a very different matter. The number of those competent in colonial Nahuatl still remains quite small so that direct entry to the Nahua world of the early seventeenth century—even though this was a widely spoken and well-documented language—remains closed to most. As a consequence, even though great advances in our understanding of colonial Nahuas have been made in the last twenty years, the breadth and depth of the interpretive literature on Hispanics still far outweighs that for any indigenous people. What follows is an analysis focused on the Nahuatl side of the *Confessionario* of 1634.

The three clerical nahuatlatos who examined the confessional manual on behalf of the viceroy and the archbishop placed special stress on the author's linguistic expertise. Two of them speak of his superior command of the language and the other of how "the mysteries of our holy faith are faithfully translated with purity and propriety" into Nahuatl.[23] Their formulaic praise is hardly to be taken at face value for it is the hyperbole expected of such approvals.[24] Formulas notwithstanding, Alva's competence is partially confirmed just by his background and by his role as an official examiner of Carochi's highly sophisticated grammar of 1645.[25] Even more convincing proof of the authenticity of his usage is provided by comparing the *Confessionario* to other classical publications and to the Nahuatl notarial record. This also helps clarify certain aspects of style and tone.

The Nahuatl of Alva's work is overwhelmingly in agreement with that of his predecessors and contemporaries despite his protestations to the contrary at the end of the *Confessionario* (see

---

22. Ramón Menéndez Pidal, *La lengua de Cristóbal Colón* (Madrid: Espasa-Calpe, 1978), 82. For a much fuller treatment of the Castilian printing boom in vernacular texts see Sara T. Nalle, "Literacy and Culture in Early Modern Castile," *Past and Present*, 1989, 125:65–96.

23. Alva, *Confessionario*, vi.

24. A late seventeenth-century grammar that was reprinted in the eighteenth century was not only highly derivative but second-rate at best. Yet the examiner of record goes so far as to say that the author was bringing the "Mexican language" out into the light from the darkness [of ignorance] in which it had been; see Antonio de Vázquez Gastelu, *Arte de la lengua mexicana* (Puebla: Francisco Javier Morales y Salazar, 1726), preliminary leaf, unnumbered. This sort of exaggerated praise bordering on adulation would not have deceived any but the totally uninitiated, however it was such common practice as to constitute a standard feature of the preliminary material in any colonial Nahuatl imprint. For various reasons almost all colonial examiners hyped the quality of the texts they were asked to review, and publishers eager to sell books were surely pleased with such glowing testimonials to their wares.

25. Father Horacio Carochi, *Arte de la lengua mexicana* (México: Juan Ruiz, 1645), preliminary leaves, unnumbered.

48r–50r). In the area of lexicon, for example, the complex of Christian terms built around *teotl* "god/God" is well within colonial standards, the ubiquitous if minor pre-Hispanic supernatural being called a *tlacatecolotl*, "man-owl", is the term used since the 1540s for the devil, and deity titles like *Ilhuicahua Tlalticpaque* "Master of Heaven and Earth" can be found in non-ecclesiastical as well as church texts.[26] Of some interest in the area of differences is Alva's use of *miac*, "very much, many", for the church-standard *miec*, betraying what appears to be a dialectical variation due to his Tetzcocan background.[27] Overall the text lacks most of the more complex and (to modern scholars) sometimes baffling lexical and syntactic features of the huehuetlahtolli genre mentioned above. Like the majority of its secular and ecclesiastical counterparts it is strong on a relatively direct mode of expression, placing greater emphasis on imparting factual meaning than on creating an impressionistic effect and making heavy use of the indicative and command modes.[28]

Typical of classical authors like Alva and certain post-classical imitators is the use of selected features of pre-Hispanic oral traditions like the huehuetlahtolli. A very common rhetorical device in the *Confessionario* that is taken from such precedents is the use of two items in set expressions, either by joining synonyms to heighten an obvious meaning or by pairing two words to create a metaphorical doublet. Examples of the former include the little used *moyolia maniman*, "your spirit, your soul" (ubiquitous in many other texts), and the frequent duo *axcaitl tlatquitl*, "goods, property."[29] Metaphors include *quiahuatl ithualli*, "entrance + patio = household;" *tetl quahuitl*, "stone(s) + stick(s) = punishment;" *ihiyotl tlatolli*, "breath + words = fine speech;" *teuhtli tlaçolli*, "dust + garbage = sin;" *iztlactli tenqualactli*, "drool + saliva = lies;" and *eztli tlapalli*, "blood + dye = offspring."[30] Worthy of separate mention is the Nahuatl term *ixtli*, "eye, face, surface," which here as elsewhere often appears in constructions dealing with various aspects of one's inner self.[31] These and other garden-variety idioms certainly raise the tone of Alva's questions and speeches in a manner entirely appropriate to his station and purpose, but his use of them is sparing compared to other classical writers like Bautista, de la Fuente, and Mijangos.[32]

---

26. *Ilhuicahua Tlalticpaque* had long been used in various books and manuscripts associated with the church (Sell, "Friars, Nahuas, and Books," chart on p. 344) and appears to be one of a number of deity epithets from the pre-Hispanic period appropriated by the early friars for the Christian god. See also the 1560 petition of the municipality of Huexotzinco to the Spanish king in James Lockhart, *We People Here: Nahuatl Accounts of the Conquest of Mexico* (Berkeley and Los Angeles: University of California Press, 1993), 290.

27. On *a*-raising see George Whittaker, "Aztec Dialectology and the Nahuatl of the Friars," *The Work of Bernardino de Sahagún: Pioneer Ethnographer of Sixteenth-Century Aztec Mexico*, ed. J. Jorge Klor de Alva, H. B. Nicholson, and Eloise Quiñones Keber, Studies on Culture and Society, 2 (Albany: Institute for Mesoamerican Studies, The University of Albany, State University of New York, 1988), 326–30. For examples in this text, see "anmiaquintin" (fol. 9r); "miac" (fols. 18v, 32r, 33v, 37v, 38r); "miacpa" (fols. 33r, 36v, 37v, 38r–v); and "miacan" (fols. 43v, 44r).

28. While the differences between secular and church texts are not pertinent to this discussion they also can affect style and tone. For example, Alva's guide is typical of heavily Hispanicized writings (like those produced by or under the supervision of clerics) in coming close to expressing Nahuatl in a model built on the "word" and "sentence" while the majority of secular documents were produced by Nahua notaries who thought more in terms of the "syllable" and the "phonological phrase"; see James Lockhart, *The Nahuas After the Conquest: A Social and Cultural History of the Indians of Central Mexico, Sixteenth Through Eighteenth Centuries* (Stanford: Stanford University Press, 1992), 338–39.

29. Alva, *Confessionario*, 4v for the former; for the latter, ibid., fols. 3v, 9v, 20v, 25v, 34v, 38v, 42v–43r.

30. Ibid., fols. 9r, 27v; 17v; 20v, 46v; 47v; 30r; 22v, respectively. For the purposes of presentation the description of these metaphors is considerably abbreviated.

31. For varying (e.g., in tense and person) examples of the common metaphor *ixtzinco icpactzinco nemi* "to live in his/her face, on top of his/her head = to offend him/her" see *Confessionario*, fols. 2r, 20r, 28v, 44v, 45v, 48r. Also note "xictlapo in mix in moyollo" (fol. 13r) and "macamo quen xicmochihuili in mix in moyollo" (fol. 4v).

32. For one of many instances see fray Juan de Mijangos, *Sermonario . . . en lengua mexicana* (México: Juan de Alcázar, 1624), 39–40. In a passage replete with Nahuatl metaphors this Augustinian nahuatlato describes the installation of kings in biblical times.

The observant reader will quickly notice that Spanish loanwords and phrases are an occasional but persistent feature of the Nahuatl text. By my count there are 64 such items in the *Confesionario* proper with 260 total occurrences. These items can be somewhat arbitrarily divided into 47 ecclesiastical loans (occurring a total of 217 times) and 17 mundane ones (43 times). The expected church bias in such borrowings is even more pronounced when the 11 most frequently used loans and their frequencies are listed: *Dios*, "God" (75); *misa*, "mass" (19); *Jesucristo*, "Jesus Christ" (16); *sacramento*, "sacrament" (12); *domingo*, "Sunday" (10); *santa iglesia*, "holy church" (10); *cristiano*, "Christian" (8); *pascua*, "Easter" (7); *sacramentos*, "sacraments" (7); *cuaresma*, "Lent" (6); and *santo*, "[male] saint" (6). Ten of the 11 (excluding the time measurement *domingo*) can be clearly assigned to the church domain. As is common in specialized Nahuatl writings of all types a small core of items compose the bulk of such loans[33]: *Dios* alone accounts for almost 30 percent of all occurrences, all 11 for 68 percent.

These borrowed nouns are treated no differently than any others in the native lexicon. They can be found possessed and bearing the reverential suffix -*tzin*[*tli*] ("*i*Missat*zin* Dios" = His-mass-*REV*, God/God's mass), with the instrumental suffix -*tica* ("juramento*tica*" = with/through/by means of an oath), in verbless constructions ("niGouernador, Nalcalde" = I [*am a*] governor, I [*am an*] alcalde), incorporated as modifiers ("*vino*namacoyan" = *wine*-place where selling goes on/place where wine is sold, tavern), with the Nahuatl verbalizing suffix -*ti* ("otitestigo*ti*c" = you *became* a witness/you testified), and so on.[34]

The most striking and significant feature of loanword usage in the *Confessionario* is its very conservative nature. Almost without exception the loans are common and proper nouns, predictably the kinds of items first and most easily exchanged between Nahuatl and Spanish.[35] Even here Alva was cautious: fifty-nine percent of the 260 loanword occurrences can be confirmed in notarial documents written before 1550 and fully 89 percent of them in records generated before 1560, long before he was born.[36] A loanword comparison of the contemporary Nahua annalist Chimalpahin with Alva shows an astounding 92 percent coincidence, while one between the *Confessionario* and earlier church texts shows a 97 percent

---

33. Sell, "Friars, Nahuas, and Books," 71.

34. Alva, *Confessionario*, fols. 18v, 19v; 15v; 6r; 30v; 33r, respectively.

35. The one exception is Spanish "voto a Dios" (I swear to God) on fol. 31r which Alva puts into the mouths of Nahua parishioners who swear false oaths. The problem here is that this phrase (perhaps simply an unanalyzed string of words) contains the Spanish verb *votar* "to vow, swear" correctly inflected (by Spanish standards) for the first person singular in the present tense, indicative mode. In addition the particle *a* is also used correctly (again by Spanish standards). Nahuas all over central Mexico were beginning to borrow Spanish verbs and particles but used a different strategy for borrowing verbs (adding the Nahuatl verbalizing suffix -*oa* to the infinitive) and this is much too early in the adaptation of Nahuatl to Spanish for the widespread and idiomatic use of *a*.

Quite possibly Alva is referring to highly Hispanicized bilingual Nahuas who gave secular and religious authorities a lot of grief (from the Hispanic administrative perspective) because of their familiarity with the Spanish-speaking world and its regulations. Decades before Alva's *Confessionario* appeared fray Juan de Bautista wrote disapprovingly (*Advertencias para los confesores de los naturales*, México: Melchor Ocharte, 1600, 1:f. 14v) about what he considered to be the marked tendency of Hispanicized Nahuas to give false testimony. In the following century an Augustinian nahuatlato would refer to something similar; see fray Manuel Pérez, *Farol indiano, y guía de curas de indios* (México: Francisco Rivera Calderón, 1713), 178 and passim.

36. The primary sources used were: Fray Alonso de Molina, *Ordinanças* (Ms. M-M 455, 1552, in the Bancroft Library, University of California at Berkeley); Luis Reyes García, ed., *Documentos sobre tierras y señoríos en Cuauhtinchan*, Colección Científica, Fuentes, Historia Social (México: Centro de Investigaciones Superiores, Instituto Nacional de Antropología e Historia, 1978); and Eustaquio Celestino Solís, Armando Valencia R., and Constantino Medina Lima, eds., *Actas de cabildo de Tlaxcala, 1547–1567* (México: Archivo General de la Nación, 1985); see also the loanword list, based on primary sources, in Frances Karttunen and James Lockhart, *Nahuatl in the Middle Years: Language Contact Phenomena in Texts of the Colonial Period*, University of California Publications in Linguistics 85, (Berkeley and Los Angeles: University of California Press, 1976), especially 54–9.

correspondence.[37] His reluctance to innovate in either language also is made clear in another way. New types of loans like Spanish verbs and particles were making their presence felt by the 1620s and 1630s but he fails to use even one of them.[38]

The twentieth-century notion that complete originality is an essential component of good writing is inappropriate when applied to Alva's work. Usages established over time, propounded by acknowledged experts, and enshrined in previous authoritative writings are the rule in Alva's guide to confession just as they are in the vast majority of colonial Nahuatl publications.[39] This holds especially true for ecclesiastical texts, printed or manuscript, where carefully crafted formulations were prized because they were attempting to express most clearly and accurately the official version of Christianity presented to Nahuas.[40]

This sort of continuity and sameness is exemplified by Alva's explanation of the host, especially the effective analogy he makes between the presence of Jesus Christ in each of the consecrated wafers and that of an image in every piece of a shattered mirror.[41] One does not have to turn even to local Latin- or Spanish-language sources to find the immediate source of his inspiration. Mijangos, in his sermonario of 1624, included a piece by the celebrated Jesuit nahuatlato Tovar which dealt with the same subject. Evidently even accomplished nahuatlatos had been having difficulty in correctly phrasing and expressing church doctrine on this point:

> The most sagacious Father Juan de Tovar preached this sermon at my intercession because I wanted to know how I might properly speak about the [external] appearances of [consecrated] bread and wine. And for the same reason I had it printed among these [sermons] of mine so that everyone could take advantage of them and their [good] doctrine.[42]

---

37. For the annalist I used: Domingo Francisco de San Antón Muñon Chimalpahin Quauhtlehuanitzin, *Die Relationen Chimalpahin's zur Geschichte México's*, Günter Zimmermann, ed. (Hamburg: Cram, De Gruyter & Co., 1965), 2:37–146; Chimalpahin's "Exercicio Quotidiano" in fray Bernardino de Sahagún, *Adiciones, apéndice a la postilla y ejercicio cotidiano*, Arthur J. O. Anderson, trans. and ed. (México: Universidad Nacional Autónoma de México, 1993), 146–202; and Karttunen and Lockhart, *Nahuatl in the Middle Years*, 65–66 under "c. 1607–1629"; for the church writings: *Doctrina cristiana en lengua española y mexicana* (México: Juan Pablos, 1548); fray Bernardino de Sahagún, *Sermonario* (manuscript # 1485 in the Newberry Library, Chicago, 1548); fray Pedro de Gante, *Doctrina cristiana en lengua mexicana*, photoreproduction of the 1553 edition with an introduction by Ernesto de la Torre Villar (México: Centro de Estudios Históricos Fray Bernardino de Sahagún, 1981); fray Domingo de la Anunciación, *Doctrina cristiana . . . en lengua castellana y mexicana* (México: Pedro Ocharte, 1565); fray Alonso de Molina, *Confesionario mayor en lengua mexicana y castellana*, photoreproduction of the 1569 edition with an introduction by Roberto Moreno (México: Instituto de Investigaciones Filológicas, Instituto de Investigaciones Históricas, Universidad Nacional Autónoma de México, 1984); fray Juan de la Anunciación, *Doctrina cristiana en lengua castellana y mexicana* (México: Antonio de Espinosa, 1575) and *Sermonario . . . en lengua mexicana* (México: Antonio Ricardo, 1577); fray Juan de Gaona, *Coloquios de la paz y tranquilidad cristiana en lengua mexicana* (México: Pedro Ocharte, 1582); fray Bernardino de Sahagún, *Psalmodia christiana* (México: Pedro Ocharte, 1583); fray Juan de Bautista, *Huehuehtlahtolli* (México: [Melchor Ocharte?], 1600) and *Sermonario . . . en lengua mexicana* (México: Diego López Dávalos, 1606); León, *Camino* [1611]; and Mijangos, *Sermonario*, [1624].

38. For what has been termed "Stage 3 Nahuatl" see Lockhart, *The Nahuas After the Conquest*, 304–18.

39. Three exceptions to this general rule can be found in Barry D. Sell, "Change and the Consciousness of Change: Later Colonial Observations About Nahuatl and Nahuas," paper given at the joint meeting of the Pacific Coast Council on Latin American Studies and the Rocky Mountain Council on Latin American Studies, Las Vegas, March 1995.

40. There is another possible reason for the generally conservative Nahuatl of church writings. Acting on experience priests would tend to pitch their message in terms that were accessible to the greatest number in mixed audiences of monolingual (Nahuatl) and increasingly bilingual (Nahuatl/Spanish) Nahua parishioners. In practical terms this would mean avoiding using the latest linguistic innovations that bilingual speakers were bringing into the language. While I find this hypothesis logically appealing it may be impossible to demonstrate empirically.

41. Alva, *Confessionario*, fols. 43r–45v; for the mirror analogy, see 44r.

42. "ESTE SERMON PREDICO EL SApientissimo Padre Ioan de Tobar, á intercession mia, con desseo de saber yo como diria bien accidentes de Pan, y Vino, y por el mismo caso lo hize imprimir entre estos mios, por que todos se aprouechen del, y de su doctrina" (Mijangos, *Sermonario*, 212). This introduction in Spanish and the Nahuatl sermon which follows will appear in complete translation and transcription, with commentary by Barry Sell and Larissa Taylor, in *Estudios de Cultura Náhuatl* (1996) 26:211–44.

It is hard to imagine any other source for Alva's later, more abbreviated remarks than this explanation by Tovar:

> It [i.e., the presence of Jesus Christ in each consecrated host] is as it appears in a mirror when you look at yourself, see yourself there, for there your image enters in, shows itself, and makes its appearance. And though you break the mirror, even though in many places of the mirror fragments are your eyes and in other places your nose or your lips, your image is not divided up; rather it is the mirror that is divided up, and in one mirror fragment can [even] be your entire image! Such is this angelic bread: if they repeatedly break it up in very many places, right in each one of the pieces of bread is the precious body of our Lord Jesus Christ.[43]

Adherence to accepted practice does not mean that Alva and other classical writers lacked distinctive styles, vigor, or range of expression. The individual touch is evident even in something as formulaic as the Nahuatl version of the Ave Maria. Undoubtedly with reference to the Latin but not to Nahuatl version(s) of the prayer, clerical nahuatlatos of the sixteenth, seventeenth and eighteeenth centuries all produced their own variations on a common orthodox theme.[44] Established convention set boundaries, but within those limits experts like Alva could selectively draw on Nahuatl's many expressive resources.

Not all nuances of Alva's style and tone successfully survive the transition from Nahuatl to English. One feature that does relatively well is the scathing indignation he pours into his denunciations of non-Christian beliefs and rites. His strong feelings are to be expected. Professional motives, loyalty to church and state, and profoundly held personal convictions made for a potent combination when Alva and other priests condemned idolatry. Adding fuel to the fire were the basic conventions of the "anti-idolatry" genre itself: a sharp tone was an inescapable requirement for any priest writing this type of text. The earlier *Camino del cielo* (see above) pairs condemnation with argumentation in this Nahuatl passage:

> All the gods your fathers and grandfathers used to worship—Huitzilopochtli, Copil, Quetzalpatzactli, Toçancol, Quetzalcohuatl, Tepuztecatl, and still very many others they fashioned out of stone and adored—some were just people, all have died already and are suffering in hell. But when they were still living on earth they used to get ill and tired, they used to weep and become disturbed. . . . They could not help themselves [so] how could they aid those who sought help from them? Since it is all an idle joke and fable it comes to nothing.[45]

Many other examples could be cited from sources in both Nahuatl and Spanish.[46]

---

43. "In yuh tezcatitech neci, in ihquac timotezcahuia, in ompa tommotta, ca oncan maqui monezcayotia, hualneci in mixiptla. Auh intlanel xictlapana in tezcatl, in manel mieccan tezcatlapactli itech yetiuh in mixtelolo, auh oc ceccan in moyac, ahnoço in moten, ça ce ahmo xexelihui in mixiptla ça yehuatl in tezcatl xèxelihui, auh itech centetl tezcatlapactli ompa cenyetiuh in mixiptla. Yuhqui inin Angelotlaxcalli, intla huel mieccan quitlàtlapanacan, çan cecenyaca itech in tlaxcallapactli cecenyetiuh itlaçonacayotzin toTecuiyo Iesu Christo" (Mijangos, *Sermonario*, 219–20). An abbreviation in the original was resolved.

44. I compared the versions of the Ave Maria found in the following representative imprints: Anonymous, *Doctrina* (1548), fol. 5r; Gante, *Doctrina*, 79v–80r; Anunciación, *Doctrina* (1565), fols. 71v–72r; Anunciación, *Doctrina* (1575), 232–33; Sahagún, *Psalmodia* (1993) 22–23; León, *Camino*, fol. 87r; Alva, *Confessionario*, fol. 51v; and Father Ignacio de Paredes, *Catecismo mexicano* (México: Biblioteca Mexicana, 1758), 35. The only obvious case of copying is that of Paredes of León (although the versions are not identical by any means).

45. "In izquintin in inteteohuan, in amottàhuan, in amocolhuan, in quimoteotiaya, in huitzilopochtli, copil, quetzalpatzactli, toçancol, quetzalcohuatl, tepuztecatl, yhuan huel oc miequintin tetica quiximaya quimoteotiaya, cequintin ça çan tlacame, ye o moch mímioque, Mictlan tlayhiyohuia, auh "cuac oc nemia tlalticpac, mococoaya, ciahuia, chocaya, mamanaya . . . àmo huel monòmapalehuiaya, quenin quinpalehuizque, in intech mopalehuilania? canel moch ahuilli, camanalli, çaçanilli, àtle ipan pouhqui" (León, *Camino*, fol. 12r). Abbreviations have been resolved.

46. Among printed materials see especially Bautista, *Advertencias*, vol. 1, fols. 105v–112v (descriptions only) as well as León, *Camino*, (first half); among manuscripts nothing surpasses Hernando Ruiz de Alarcón, *Treatise on the Heathen Superstitions that Today Live Among the Indians Native to this New Spain, 1629*, trans. and ed. J. Richard Andrews and Ross Hassig, (Norman, Okla.: University of Oklahoma Press, 1987).

Potential readers of Alva's guide are alerted right on the title page that the war against the "superstitions of idolatry" will be an especially prominent feature of this particular confessional manual. Unmentioned there but equally prominent and deserving of top billing is the topic of "Indian drunkenness." The importance of the subject in Alva's eyes is indicated by his sweeping assertion that "in order to commit any sin they intentionally get themselves drunk," inebriation thus becoming the "door and entry" for "all types of vices and sins."[47] The attention given here to intoxication is not surprising. Beginning in the later sixteenth century clerics began ratcheting up the rhetoric against drunkenness and continued hammering on the theme throughout the seventeenth and eighteenth centuries.

If written sources are any indication clerics ministering to Nahua parishes assailed alleged drunkenness with a fervor typically seen only in their assaults on idolatry. Bautista, in his sermonario of 1606, assails the evils of alcoholism as strongly as Alva does in his guide to confession of 1634. In one of many memorable passages he describes how excess drinking makes one lose all semblance of humanity, the face swelling up and turning very red or white, the eyes becoming inflamed and eventually unable to see, and all the other senses being seriously affected. Eventually many drunkards can no longer distinguish whether it is wine or "cauallo yaxix" (horse urine) with which their cups are filled.[48]

The above sentiments are echoed in León's sermonario of 1614. He accuses Nahuas of neglecting their souls instead putting all their care into what they are drinking: "aic tle huel amotechcopa mìtoz, omolcauh in octli, achtopa molcauaz in tlein mocuaz, canel çan octli in cenca itech antlacuauhtlamàti" (it can never be said of you [that] pulque is forgotten; first what is eaten will be forgotten, since it is just on pulque that you [so] very strongly rely).[49] He later adds what from a priest's perspective were the social pressures behind so much imbibing: if someone tries to abstain "anquicuicuitlahuiltia, anquimamauhtia, anquilhuia xiqui, cuix tiSanto intlacamo tiquiz ic timitzixatequizque, auh ca imauhcacopa in coni, tlahuana, yhuinti" (You goad and frighten him, saying: Drink! Are you a saint? If you do not drink we will throw water on your face! And because of his fear he drinks it, gets drunk and lightheaded).[50] On occasion Nahua administrators also condemned excessive drinking.[51]

Nahua idolatry and drunkenness would appear to be conveniently complementary targets of clerical ridicule and condemnation. Alva himself draws them securely together when he describes how in pre-Christian times the "blindness and mockery of the devil" were imbibed along with alcohol by their ancestors during their drunken sprees.[52] This surely was a match made not in Heaven but in hell. From here it is but a short step for this unholy union to extend into Christian times.

Yet Alva clearly separates the two in one of his most stirring talks. Shaming his Nahuatl-speaking parishioners before "even the Blacks, the Chinese, or the Japanese," he prods them to good behavior by asserting that what is especially shocking is that their pagan forebears were

---

47. Alva, *Confesionario*, fol. 17v (see marginalia in footnote).
48. See Bautista, *Sermonario*, fol. 80.
49. See León, *Sermonario*, fol. 105v. Abbreviations here and elsewhere resolved.
50. Ibid.
51. Selections from the town council minutes of Tlaxcala are very revealing in this regard. See the entries in James Lockhart, Frances Berdan, and Arthur J. O. Anderson, eds., *The Tlaxcalan Actas: A Compendium of the Records of the Cabildo of Tlaxcala (1547–1627)* (Salt Lake City: University of Utah Press, 1986), 80–84 (for the year 1553) and 92–94 (for 1555).
52. Alva, *Confesionario*; see fol. 13v.

very different: "prudent, wise, fearful, and honoring and respecting each other." The Nahuas of his day had been brought low by their "drunkenness and inebriation" which had destroyed the "ingenuity and living light [of reason] that God" had given them. The priest continues with what are (on paper at least) devastating follow-up blows: even though their ancestors drank "it was just with moderation…as do your neighbors the Spaniards."[53] And unlike colonial Nahuas who supposedly lived under a more permissive regime, when the ancients saw a drunkard they forthwith killed him.

Alva the secular cleric was hardly alone in his admiration for certain aspects of pre-Hispanic Nahua society. In a Dominican sermonario of the early seventeenth century a condemnation of colonial Nahua alcoholism is prefaced by the statement that "in tlateotoquilizpan, miquiztica quintlatzacuiltiaya in tlahuanque, quinyolloquixtiaya" (in the time of idolatry they used to punish drunkards with death [by] removing their hearts).[54]

An earlier Franciscan work is even more explicit. A sermon urging the leaders of the *altepetl* (city, realm) to stand firm with their priests against meddling outsiders is tied into alleged rampant alcoholic excess:

> And if a Spaniard or a miserable little mestizo wants you to verify and be a witness to their false accusations and complaints against your spiritual fathers who help you and because of you consume themselves like moths in a flame,[55] nonetheless he will be able to do it, no need thereby to be worried—for he has his instrument of making people talk, he has his instrument of false accusations—it is the leather wine bag, leather wine bag, leather wine bag, the leather wineskin, leather wineskin, leather wineskin.[56] It makes you talk, it makes you giddy, in this way it makes you a brutish animal.[57] O woe are you here in New Spain, especially you [fill in the name]! For long ago in the time of the idolatry of your grandfathers and great-grandfathers [i.e., your ancestors], wine was hardly imbibed, no one got drunk, no one got inebriated. Wherefore they splendidly led their altepetls and the lords and rulers enlarged their reed mats and seats of authority [i.e., their realms], made them reach there "Towards the Place of Women" (*to the south*) and "Towards the Place of the Dead" (*the north*). But now everyone drinks, now everyone gets drunk, and those who overdrink and get drunk are without number. Wherefore you dishonor yourselves with it [i.e., wine] and with it you are dishonored, with it you mistreat yourselves, with it you make yourselves little children. Because of it you lead and govern badly, because of it you thereby mistreat the poor commoners, because of it you do not deserve and merit governance and leadership.[58]

The message is reinforced by the accompanying marginalia: *"The good government of the ancients, because there were hardly any drunkards."*[59]

---

53. For all citations in this paragraphs see Alva, *Confessionario*, fol. 17r.

54. Fray Martín de León, *Sermonario . . . en lengua mexicana* (México: Imprenta de Diego López Dávalos por C. Adriano César, 1614), fol. 142v.

55. Sahagún, *Florentine Codex*, 225, has an entry pertinent to "motlepapalochihua" in the original. Included under "Notlepapalochiuhtiuh" [sic] (I fly into the fire like a moth/butterfly) is the following: "It is as if he fell into the fire. The fire moth comes up to it thinking that perhaps the fire does not kill one. When it has gone to fall into the fire, it at once dies there. Just so is one who is to wrangle with one. Perhaps he goes to fall into the hands of others, or he will be put to death there." See also Rémi Siméon, *Diccionario de la lengua nahuatl o mexicana* (México: Siglo Veintiuno, 1988), 704, where "tlepapalochiua" is defined literally as "to plunge into the fire like a butterfly" and figuratively as "to place oneself in danger."

56. The pair of triple repetitions appear in the original.

57. Bautista, *Sermonario*, 12, has "vida mas brutal" as marginalia for "in çan yuhqui mamaça yc nemi" in the text.

58. Ibid., 49. The glosses (in parentheses and italics) are by the most renowned Nahua Latinist of colonial Mexico, don Antonio Valeriano. The translation (slightly modified) is taken from Sell, "Friars, Nahuas, and Books," 174; a transcription of the original Nahuatl text is in ibid., 173.

59. *"El buen gouierno de los antiguos, porque apenas auia borrachos"* (Bautista, *Sermonario*, 49).

Other facets of pre-conquest life could be favorably noted too. Molina, in his doctrina of 1578, attacks many pagan beliefs and practices yet mentions approvingly that in the olden days, before the Nahuas knew the Christian god, they regarded adultery as such a serious crime that they punished transgressors by smashing their heads.[60] Similar statements concerning adultery and drunkenness can be found in colonial Spanish-language sources as well.[61]

Many educated Christians acknowledged with pride that part of their heritage had its origins in Latin and Greek pagan antiquity. Since more than one colonial writer saw parallels between the pre-Christian Nahuas and the ancient Latins and Greeks, the admiration Alva and others felt for certain features of Nahua heathendom is not surprising in and of itself. Yet such favorable treatment would seem more suitable—and safer—for inclusion in Spanish-language texts destined only for clerics and other members of the "informed" reading public. To simultaneously extol and condemn pre-Hispanic Nahuas in mainstream church texts aimed directly at the ordinary Nahuatl-speaking parishioner might, in theory, muddy the doctrinal waters, leading to uncertainty about what were acceptable and unacceptable native traditions. Why then did Alva and others include both praise and blame of Nahua "antiquity" in their works?

The answers to this question lie in developments in both Mesoamerica and Europe and have been broached elsewhere in some detail.[62] Of particular relevance to this discussion is the impact Nahuas themselves had on Hispanic perceptions of the Nahua past. A reorientation in perspectives that casts a more positive light on that past is especially evident during the crucial second half of the sixteenth century. The key players on the Nahua side were the literate trilingual Nahuas who composed such works as the *Florentine Codex* under Sahagún's direction. Prominent even among this select group are don Antonio Valeriano (the most renowned Nahua Latinist of colonial Mexico), Alonso Vegerano, Martín Jacobita, Pedro de San Buenaventura, and Andrés Leonardo. Also worthy of mention is their contemporary, Hernando de Ribas (who worked with Molina and the Franciscan nahuatlato fray Juan de Gaona). Coming a bit later but undoubtedly contributing his share is Agustín de la Fuente, who worked with Bautista and Mijangos.

A striking example of the more favorable view of pagan times that influenced Hispanic perspectives is contained in a series of language lessons for priests originally written around 1570–80. The full range of conventions of the huehuetlahtolli is illustrated in conversations and speeches covering everything from an orator lauding a dead ruler to a woman greeting her older sister while on the way to market. The anonymous Nahua author (of the caliber of the Nahuas mentioned above) includes a conversation between an older noblewoman and a younger one with two children. The older woman compliments the younger one on how well her children are turning out, contrasting the present sad (Christian) times with the well-ordered (pagan) past:

---

60. Fray Alonso de Molina, *Doctrina cristiana en lengua mexicana* (México: Pedro Ocharte, 1578), fol. 35v.

61. The claim that pre-conquest drunkenness was strictly controlled and punished, in contrast to lax colonial times, can be found in: fray Bartolomé de las Casas, *Los indios de México y Nueva España* (México: Porrúa, 1979 [1559]), 134–35; fray Diego Durán, *Historia de las indias de Nueva España e islas de la tierra firme*, Angel María Garibay K., ed. (México: Porrúa, 1967 [1570]), 201–203; fray Bernardino de Sahagún, *Historia general de las cosas de Nueva España*, Angel María Garibay K., ed. (México: Porrúa, 1982 [1576]), 578–79; fray Gerónimo de Mendieta, *Historia eclesiástica indiana* (México: Porrúa, 1980 [1595–96]), 139–40; Ruiz de Alarcón, *Treatise*, 39 and 121; and fray Agustín de Vetancurt, *Teatro Mexicano: Descripción de los sucesos ejemplares, históricos, y religiosos del Nuevo Mundo de las Indias*, photoreproduction of the 1698 edition (México: Porrúa, 1982), 95. Exemplary punishment of adultery is asserted in: Las Casas, *Los indios*, 131–32; Durán, *Historia*, 36 and 184; Mendieta, *Historia eclesiástica*, 136–37; Vetancurt, *Teatro*, 95; and Father Francisco Javier Clavijero, *Historia antigua de México* (México: Porrúa, 1982 [1780]), 218. This is only a sampling of the available literature.

62. See Barry D. Sell, "'The Good Government of the Ancients': Some Colonial Attitudes About Pre-contact Nahua Society," *UCLA Historical Journal*, 1992, 12:152–76, especially 160–72.

The ancients who left us behind . . . took very great care. But how we raise our children today is a very different thing; bad behavior is no longer feared, for they no longer fear adultery, theft, drunkenness, and other kinds of bad behavior, because it is no longer punished as it used to be punished long ago, when they forthwith hanged . . . and destroyed people.[63]

The context in which these dialogues and their point of view were produced is well expressed by the translators and editors of these lessons:

Looking back to a Golden Age when everything was done right and austerity and severity prevailed, in contrast to one's own sad days when no one obeys or has respect, is characteristic of the time two or three generations after the conquest more than other times, of high nobles more than commoners, and especially of the nobles of the former imperial centers more than those of other towns. . . . [It was they] who convinced Spaniards that before the conquest hardly anyone drank pulque and all adulterers were forthwith stoned to death.[64]

By the time the *Confessionario* appeared in 1634 the view that the pre-Hispanic past was in some respects superior to the colonial present was commonly accepted, at least among specialists in Nahuatl and Nahua culture. Hence the assertion in the *Confessionario* that the ancients were "prudent, wise, fearful, and honoring and respecting each other"[65] is nothing more than the accepted wisdom of that time and place. An added benefit of this stance was that it gave clerics like Alva another rhetorical cudgel with which to club the Nahuas of the seventeenth century. Priests could—and did—play on Nahua respect for tradition and ancestors by insisting that their flocks live up to some of the idealized moral standards of their own forebears.

The picture Alva draws of the early seventeenth-century Nahua world rings true in many respects. The Nahua altepetl was the center of his parishioners' world, an impression confirmed in other publications and most importantly in the Nahuatl notarial record. The altepetl was the largest pre-Hispanic sociopolitical structure to survive Spanish conquest and colonization and was the basis of the colonial Hispanic-style municipality. This key indigenous term is rendered in the facing Spanish text as *pueblo*, which the unwary twentieth-century reader is better served by the translation "town, settlement, people" or even (with some reservations) "nation" than "[tiny Indian] village."[66]

Alva twice refers to the Nahua inhabitants of the altepetl as *macehualtin* (sing., *macehualli*), traditionally understood as "subjects, commoners," or sometimes "people" although in the facing Spanish text he uses *naturales* "natives" as its equivalent.[67] By Alva's time "macehualtin" had begun to shift in meaning and was well on its way to becoming the main Nahuatl term used to approximate the European word and concept "Indian," i.e., a person of the "New World" as opposed to someone from the "Old World."[68] Usage was still in transition, however, as a glance at contemporary publications will confirm.

A fellow cleric, the Dominican fray Francisco de Lorra Baquio, brought out his *Manual*

---

63. Frances Karttunen and James Lockhart, eds., *The Art of Nahuatl Speech: The Bancroft Dialogues.*, Nahuatl Studies Series (Los Angeles: UCLA Latin American Center, 1987), 155.

64. Ibid., 10. Brackets mine.

65. Alva, *Confessionario*, fol. 17r.

66. See "altepetl" = "pueblos" and "amaltepeuh" = "vuestros Pueblos" (ibid., 13r, 42r, respectively). Note that elsewhere Alva considers "çemaltepetl" as being "toda vna ciudad" (ibid., fol. 31r).

67. Ibid., 1r, 36r.

68. On the changing meaning of macehualli in Nahuatl manuscripts see Lockhart, *The Nahuas After the Conquest*, 114–16. Although I have not carefully checked all printed sources, my strong impression is that toward the end of the colonial period authors often used this term as a direct equivalent for "Indian" (e.g., "INDIOS" = "Macehualtin" in Paredes, *Promptuario*, 1).

mexicano de la administración de los santos sacramentos in 1634. Like the *Confessionario* of the same year it was cast mainly in a Nahuatl/Spanish format. Lorra Baquio goes all over the terminological map in trying to describe the indigenous people who comprised the altepetl. In one case the Nahuatl term "maçehualtin" is only "Naturales" (natives) as Alva has it, in another "timaçehualli" (you are a macehualli) serves double duty as "tu Natural, e Indio" (you, a native and an Indian), and in yet a third instance "maçehualtin" is borrowed in a Hispanicized form directly into the Spanish text: "los maceguales."[69] Sometimes the troublesome problem of finding the right expression for the Nahuatl text is resolved by directly resorting to the Spanish loanword *Indio* "Indian."[70] At other times the Nahuatl phrase *nican tlaca* (here-people, locals) is understood as "Naturales."[71] Pairs of what Lorra Baquio evidently considered synonyms are occasionally used: "in nican tlaca Indiostin" (the local people, [i.e.,] Indians), which is "los Naturales" in the Spanish.[72] The following three other Nahuatl terms are summed up tersely as "los Indios" (the Indians) in the Spanish text: "in anMexica, in annahuatlaca, yn anNueuaEspañatlaca" (you Mexica, you Nahua peoples, you [original?] peoples of New Spain).[73]

Usage continued to fluctuate widely during the next 10 years. A Dominican manual for priests took no chances, combining a native expression and a loanword: "in amèhuantin in nican antlaca naturales" (you who are local people, [i.e.,] natives), in the accompanying Spanish text translated as "vosotros los naturales" (you natives).[74] An Augustinian grammar leans on the traditional meaning of macehualli: "niquimitta in maceùaltin, yo miro a los pleueyos. . . . niquimùalleua in maçeùaltin, que quiere dezir, ayudo a leuantar a los pleueyos, ò a los trabajadores" ([Nah.] I see the macehualtin, [Sp.] I look at the plebeians. . . . [Nah.] I raise the macehualtin, which means, [Sp.] I help raise the plebeians or the workers).[75] The celebrated Jesuit grammar which Alva examined and approved contains various definitions of macehualli. Twice the more traditional meanings of *vasallo,* "vassal, subject," and once *gente,* "people," are used as equivalents, but in accordance with changing times it also is rendered three times as *Indio,* "Indian," and once in agreement with Alva as *natural,* "native."[76] Alva's use of macehualli is well within the broad and shifting conventions of his day.

The different people and objects of the Nahua world of the early seventeenth century are also present in Alva's *Confessionario.* There is a notably unselfconscious mix of what were originally indigenous and intrusive elements. From the Nahuatl vocabulary come the *tetlan nenqui,* "lowly household dependents;"[77] *tlacuilo,* "painter;" *quauhxinqui,* "carpenter;" *tetzotzonqui,* "stonemason;" and others who presumably own *caxitl,* "bowls;" use *copalli,* "copal incense;" wear

69. Francisco de Lorra Baquio, *Manual mexicano de la administración de los santos sacramentos* (México: Diego Gutiérrez, 1634), fols. 66v, 54v, 67r, respectively. See also fol. 1v: "in imaçehualhuan Dios" = "los Indios y naturales de Dios."

70. For "Indiome" (Spanish [sing.] "Indio" + the Nahuatl plural marking suffix *-me*), see: ibid., fols. 54v and 55v; for "Indiostin" (Spanish [pl.] "Indio" + the Nahuatl plural marking suffix *-tin*), see: ibid., fols. 55v, 60r, 61v.

71. Ibid., fol. 62r–v.

72. Ibid., fol. 60r and again on fol. 61v.

73. Ibid., fol. 56r. The Mexica were the specific Nahua grouping to which "Montezuma" belonged.

74. Fray Pedro de Contreras Gallardo, *Manual de administrar los santos sacramentos* (México: Juan Ruiz, 1638), fol. 143r.

75. Fray Diego de Galdo Guzmán, *Arte mexicano* (México: por la viuda de Bernardo Calderón, 1642), fol. 118r–v.

76. Carochi, *Arte,* fols. 69v, 118v; 84v; 84v, 89v, 110r; 113v, respectively. Much of Carochi's grammar is taken directly from an earlier one published by his teacher and fellow Jesuit, the nahuatlato Father Antonio del Rincón. Rincón's *Arte mexicano* of 1595 (México: Pedro Balli) contains a traditional definition of this term on fol. 75v: ". . . hombre, vil y plebeyo" (*Macehualli . . .* a base and common man).

77. Note that *tetlan nenque* (the plural form) is defined in the *Guide to Confession* as "those who serve and are with Spaniards" (Alva, *Confessionario,* fol. 19r). This specific association with Spaniards is found only in Alva's work, for in the Berlitz-style practical language guide mentioned above is the same general meaning found in other Nahuatl texts: "tetlan nenque—*siruientes*"; see Pedro de Arenas, *Vocabulario manual en las lenguas castellana y mexicana* (México: Henrico Martínez, 1611), 146, and see p. 49 for the same definition in reverse.

cactli, "sandals;" eat *elotl*, "corn on the cob;" and raise *totoltin*, "domestic fowls."[78] From the Spanish side and represented directly by loanwords are the high-ranking members of the community who serve as the *governador*, "governor," and *alcaldes*, "councilmen/judges" of the alte-petl.[79] Within their jurisdiction people might own *candelas*, "candles;" take *juramentos*, "oaths," when they are *testigos*, "witnesses;" count time by the *semana*, "week," and its subunits like *viernes*, "Friday," and *domingo*, "Sunday;" raise *caballos*, "horses," and spend their hard-earned *tomines* (coins worth one-eighth of a peso) in the place where *vino*, "wine," is sold.[80] Also of European origin but expressed as a Nahuatl circumlocution is *quaquauhe* (head-stick-owner), "cattle." More roundabout and by way of synecdoche[81] is the case of Nahuatl *ichcatl* "cotton" which first became extended in meaning to include the introduced product "wool" and then was applied to the animal from which it came, hence *ichcame*, "[pl.] sheep."[82]

Alva paints an incomplete picture, however, for he is relatively stingy in the range of people and things he lists for the altepetl. His entire book contains far fewer references to professions, for example, than does Molina in his much earlier confesional manual of 1569. In just six folios out of almost 120 of Nahuatl/Spanish text the famed Franciscan discusses in some detail merchants, sellers of cacao, avocados, cotton, and tamales, dealers in Spanish-style goods, makers of reed baskets, adobe bricks, and sandals, dyers and tanners, painters and weavers, operators of sweat baths, tutors of children, and still others.[83] Tax records from the mid-sixteenth century also give a far fuller picture of the trades in an altepetl.[84]

Looking beyond Alva's text, we see that the relationship between native and introduced elements was more than just a mosaic of independent pieces which had been tightly joined together. While a *tlacuilo* could be a "painter" he also could be an "(Hispanic-style) notary" writing documents in alphabetical Nahuatl; a *tomín* was an introduced unit of money and value to which Nahuas then added the meaning not present in Spanish of "money or cash in general," and it is still used in that sense by some modern speakers of Nahuatl.[85] There was nothing unusual about these transformations. Ideas, beliefs, practices, and things Nahuas took from the Hispanic world (willingly or unwillingly) often changed as they became part of the Nahuatl-speaking world, as did native elements under Hispanic influence.

Eighty years after the conquest of Mexico Tenochtitlan (later Mexico City) in 1521 a priest could report that Nahuas had been drastically reinterpreting a standard Christian formula on the Trinity. Almost all of them had taken the Nahuatl version to mean that "God is Father, Son, and Holy Spirit, three persons, [but] only one of them is the true god."[86] Such a reformulation has led to interpretations of Nahua attitudes as ranging from "heroic resistance" to "stubborn stupidity" by scholars of varying ideological stances through the centuries. Whatever truth there may be to these points of view, the fact that the Christian *Dios*, "God," changed once in Nahua hands is no more surprising than that the Nahuatl *tlacuilo* gained a Hispanicized meaning while the Spanish

---

78. For examples of these items see Alva, *Confessionario*, fols. 19r, 6r, 11r, 12v, 36v, 25v.

79. Ibid., fols. 6r and 19v.

80. Representative examples of these items can be found on: ibid., fols. 11r, 15v, 16r, 30v, 27r, 17v, 25v, 12v.

81. Using the name of a part for a whole as in "wheels" for "car."

82. Alva, *Confessionario*, fol. 25v, for *quaquauhe* and *ichcatl*. On the evolution of both see Lockhart, *The Nahuas After the Conquest*, 279–80, 562 n. 47–49.

83. Molina, *Confessionario*, fols. 35v–40v.

84. Arthur J. O. Anderson, Frances Berdan, and James Lockhart, *Beyond the Codices: The Nahua View of Colonial Mexico* (Berkeley and Los Angeles: University of California Press, 1976), 138–49.

85. Jane H. Hill and Kenneth C. Hill, *Speaking Mexicano: Dynamics of Syncretic Language in Central Mexico* (Tucson: University of Arizona Press, 1986), 312, 324, and passim.

86. Bautista, *Advertencias*, vol. 1, fol. 52r.

tomín gained a native one. Nahuas were not passive spectators of their own lives. To outside observers they "fought back" or "failed to understand" but more to the point is that their lives centered on their own communities, language, and culture. The varying pegs and holes of those lives, round and square, intrusive and native, accommodated one another as far as possible in order to adjust Nahua sensibilities to the constantly changing circumstances of colonial rule. This makes neither heroes nor fools of the Nahuas, but it does make them recognizably human.[87]

Nahua ethnocentrism should not be automatically equated with either ignorant parochialism or the "isolated Indian villager" of the recent scholarly past. Nahuas living in or near the biggest concentrations of Spanish speakers had ample opportunities to learn about Nahuas from other areas, other indigenous peoples, Hispanics, and anyone else who came along. It is precisely in the largest such place—Mexico City—that Alva betrays where he produced his work (or at least mentally located his model questions and speeches) when he writes: "nican Mexico" (here in Mexico [City]).[88] It is no coincidence that it appears in one of two references to the Japanese, the Nahuas' "younger brothers in the faith."[89]

It may seem inexplicably exotic to mention the Japanese in a Nahuatl guide to confession but this impression is only a result of the predominantly Hispanocentric literature now existing on early modern Mexico. A group of Japanese on the way to Europe had passed through cosmopolitan Mexico City more than twenty years prior to Alva's *Confessionario*. Their presence was noted by Chimalpahin, the greatest Nahua annalist of the colonial period. Of particular relevance is his comment that some of those who arrived in 1610 had stayed until 1614:

> Today, Friday, the fourteenth of the month of October of the year 1614, is when some Japanese people who had spent four years here in Mexico [City] began to go to their homes in Japan. They had come here to Mexico [City] to live [for a brief while but] some still went on staying here. They provide for themselves [by] engaging in commerce, selling here the goods they brought from there in Japan.[90]

To judge by Chimalpahin's well-informed observations the Japanese made a place for themselves among colonial Nahuatl's rich vocabulary of cultural, ethnic, and racial designations as quickly as they became part of the incessant market activity of the capital. References to them in Alva's work (at least in the Mexico City area) would not have seemed in the least exotic.

Nahuas no more existed in total isolation than did the Nahuatl portion of the *Confessionario* of 1634. This mestizo cleric's book continued and extended an already vigorous tradition of writing Nahuatl in alphabetical characters, a tradition that was close to a hundred years old when his guide to confession left the presses. This work, and the unquestionably expert nahuatlato who wrote it, well represent the classical period of Nahuatl writings.

---

87. This powerful mix of pragmatic resourcefulness and creative adaptability is still characteristic of modern Nahuas. Especially illuminating and eloquent on this point is Alan R. Sandstrom's *Corn is Our Blood: Culture and Ethnic Identity in a Contemporary Aztec Indian Village* (Norman, Okla.: University of Oklahoma Press, 1991).

88. Alva, *Confessionario*, fol. 12r.

89. Ibid., fols. 11v, 16v.

90. "Axcan martes ynic 14 mani metztli octubre de 1614 años, yhcuac nican Mexico onpeuhque cequintin Jabun tlaca, oyahque in inchan Japon, onauhxiuhtico yn nican Mexico onemico, cequintin oc nican omocauhtiaque, motlaecoltia tiamiqui quinamaca nican yn intlatqui ompa quihualcuique Japon" (*Die Relationen*, 2:139). For informed commentary about his entries on the Japanese see Miguel León-Portilla, "La embajada de los japoneses en México, 1614. El testimonio en nahuatl del cronista Chimalpahin," *Estudios de Asia y Africa*, 1981, 16(2): 215–41.

THE LITERARY ANTECEDENTS
TO ALVA'S *CONFESSIONARIO*

BY LU ANN HOMZA

IT WOULD BE EASY to conclude that Don Bartolomé de Alva's *Confessionario* belongs to an exclusively Mexican context, given who he was and what he wrote about. After all, as a *mestizo*, Alva had sufficient familiarity with Nahua culture and its language to name its idols and its burial practices, not to mention the errors in previous translation efforts from Nahuatl. Yet Alva's treatise pertains to more than an indigenous Mexican environment. Just as the sacrament of penance came from a European Christianity that had evolved over time, so his tract stems from a genre of Latin and vernacular literature that developed on the other side of the Atlantic and dates from the late twelfth century. In fact, Alva constructed his work by fusing elements from European literature with ones from his own milieu: he engaged in a process of intellectual adaptation.

From the historian's point of view, recognizing the ancestry of Alva's *Confessionario* is fundamental to understanding it, since its genealogy not only illuminates its conventions but fosters a more complex interpretation of it as a product of clerical culture. The most distant relative of Alva's guide is the medieval tract known as the *summa de casibus* or *summa confessorum*, which made its first appearance in the late twelfth and thirteenth centuries; its Latin title meant either a "compendium of cases" or a "confessors' compendium."[1] These *summae*, or confessors' manuals as they commonly are called, existed within an historical matrix that can influence our descriptions of them. In order to grasp the context in which they were written, we first have to ask how the practice of penance changed over time.

In the broadest possible terms, the institutional expiation of sins by Christians underwent two mutations before approximately 1100 C. E.: it shifted from an absolutely public ritual to a predominantly private ritual, and from a longer to a shorter period of atonement. We possess no testimony from the epoch of the Church Fathers, 250–600 C. E., regarding any confidential

---

1. The formal title of *summa confessorum* did not appear in the literature until after 1280; for problems of anachronistic usage, see n. 21 below.

penitential transaction between layperson and priest; rather, sacramental penance in early Christianity hinged on an overtly collective rite.[2] Persons guilty of serious sin—defined, by the sixth century, as ones who violated the Ten Commandments, or again as the seven deadly sins of pride, avarice, lust, envy, gluttony, anger, and sloth—presented themselves to the bishop and begged to be enrolled in the order of penitents.[3] They subsequently appeared before an assembly of their fellow Christians, received the bishop's imposition of hands, and entered their new position. As penitents they would wear different clothing and stand in a different part of the Church; though forbidden to receive the Eucharist, they could obtain the other sacraments and interact with the community of the faithful. Once they had completed their self-mortification, they would be fully reconciled to the group. Significantly, confession was of no importance in this scheme. Instead, penance in the early Church entailed literally laborious acts that connoted an interior conversion on the part of sinner.[4]

Antique penance involved a number of inconveniences. For one thing, penitents could undertake it only once in their lives. For another, by the fourth century enrollment in the order of penitents carried lifetime obligations that sequestered even the reconciled from civil life, because such individuals were forbidden to marry or remarry, perform military service, or hold public office after they were reunited with the community. Finally, since the ecclesiastical estate was incompatible with the penitential one, sinful clerics were enjoined from the latter altogether and degraded instead. As a result, by the early sixth century sinners customarily avoided atonement until they were dying and priests actively endorsed this strategy. Historians believe that this postponement had deleterious effects on all Christians: it hindered the development of pastoral theology, since a pivotal interaction between clergy and laity had devolved into a single and necessarily brief encounter; it harmed the psychological well-being of the laity, which constantly had its "sins before its eyes;" and the rite in general lost its impact when it became a routine rather than an extraordinary spiritual remedy.[5]

Given its infelicities, antique penance faltered in the face of an alternative system, namely the one that Irish missionaries carried to the Continent between approximately 600 and 800 C.E. The Celtic church had existed in virtual isolation from its Roman counterpart and apparently had no form of public penance.[6] Instead, it had developed a "tariffed" variety, whereby each sin corresponded to a precise and explicit penalty. The performance of the penalty expiated the sin, penance could be repeated as many times as the culpable party had sins to repent, and, notably, the process was inherently private rather than public.[7] Clerics were just as liable to this sort of penance as anyone else. And the new procedure spread throughout Europe despite ecclesiastical

---

2. Bernhard Poschmann, *Penance and the Anointing of the Sick*, trans. F. Courtney (London: Herder and Herder 1968), 85–86; Cyrille Vogel, *Le pécheur et la pénitence dans l'eglise ancienne* (Paris: Les éditions du Cerf, 1966), 10–11. The expiation of lesser or venial sins depended upon the performance of good works.

3. Sins of thought or intention did not fall under canonical penance. See Vogel, *Le pécheur et la pénitence*, 28–34; Morton W. Bloomfield, *The Seven Deadly Sins* (East Lansing, MI: Michigan State University Press, 1967).

4. Vogel, *Le pécheur et la pénitence*, 15, and for an example of the penitential works, 37; also idem, "Réflexions de l'historien sur la discipline pénitentielle dans l'Église latine," *En Rémission des Péchés*, ed. Alexandre Faivre (Brookfield, Vt.: Variorum Reprints, 1994), 1:30–31.

5. Poschmann, *Penance*, 107, seems, in this instance, to treat canonical penance from a teleological rather than a historicist stance; Vogel, "Réflexions."

6. Poschmann, *Penance*, 124; Vogel, "Réflexions," 1:32.

7. Vogel, "Réflexions," 1:32–34; John T. McNeill, *The Celtic Churches, a History A.D. 200–1200* (Chicago: The University of Chicago Press, 1974), chap. 10; John T. McNeill and Helen Gadamer, *Medieval Handbooks of Penance*, Records of Civilization: Sources and Studies, 29 (New York: Columbia University Press, 1938), Introduction.

and secular attempts to stop it in the name of tradition. From the ninth to the thirteenth century, public faults still merited public penance, but confidential ones, which made up the majority of sins, warranted the tariffed sort of expiation.[8]

This new style of atonement eliminated its predecessor's disadvantages, since it made procrastination irrelevant and dispensed with clerical immunity. Yet it provoked other difficulties. If sinners were especially culpable, the penalties assigned them could exceed the years they had left to live. For instance, the *Poenitentiale Theodori*, c. 690, prescribed seven or ten years of penance for murder, fifteen years for sodomy (after the age of twenty), and eleven years for perjury in a church, while "he who has committed many evil deeds, that is, murder, adultery with a woman and with a beast, and theft, shall go into a monastery and do penance until his death."[9] The severity of the tariffs or the simple impossibility of fitting a long fast into a feudal career also prompted "redemptions" of the penalties, whereby a cash payment could expunge an interval on bread and water.[10] Scholars have identified such commutations as the start of ecclesiastical indulgences, but for our purposes the significance of tariffed penance lies elsewhere: because such penance was linked to an exact correspondence between sin and expiation, and hence the minute recitation of transgressions, it sharpened the role of confession in the sacramental process.[11]

The final variation of penance that emerged between 1100 and 1200 C. E., which Alva would have recognized as typical, and which continues in the Catholic Church today, elevated the consequence of confession even further. The evolution of the sacrament in the High Middle Ages was reinforced by the recovery of classical antiquity, through recopying antique texts, that scholars describe as the twelfth-century renaissance. Between approximately 1050 and 1200 C. E., more of the Aristotelian corpus was recovered, and in more reliable versions, than had previously been available. Aristotle argued that ends were predicated on beginnings, or that what was *last* in order of execution was *first* in order of conception. Such a coherent vision of cause and effect may have encouraged theologians to underscore intention and sorrow in the assessment of sin and the process of divine forgiveness.[12] Their newly prominent emphasis on motive and grief was reflected in their eventual stipulation of confession itself as a penance, since a proper one entailed personal humiliation and self-abnegation. The importance of personal disclosure was only reinforced by the emphases of Roman law; as a result of its resuscitation, medieval intellectuals labelled confession the "queen of proofs," or *regina probationum*.[13] The Church Fathers had acknowledged misdeeds in thought as well as action, and deathbed statements must have implied that remorse carried some expiatory force, since works at that point were moot. Still,

---

8. One reason for the popularity of tariffed penance was that it harmonized with the German system of compensation for wrongs, known as the *wergeld*. For the continued existence of public penance, see Vogel, "Réflexions," 1:33; and especially Mary C. Mansfield, *The Humiliation of Sinners: Public Penance in Thirteenth-Century France* (Ithaca and London: Cornell University Press, 1995).

9. McNeill and Gamer, *Medieval Handbooks*, 187, 185, 190. James A. Brundage, *Law, Sex and Christian Society in Medieval Europe* (Chicago: The University of Chicago Press, 1987), 152–168, has suggested that the penitentials targeted sexual sin over any other.

10. Jean Delumeau, *Sin and Fear: The Emergence of a Western Guilt Culture, 13th–18th Centuries* (New York: St. Martin's Press, 1990), 196–97, presents a succinct overview of the tariffed system, including the practice of commutation.

11. Vogel, "Réflexions," 1:33.

12. Pierre Michaud-Quantin, *Sommes de casuistique et manuels de confession au moyen âge (XII–XVI siècles)*. Analecta Mediaevalia Namurcensia 13 (Louvain: Éditions Nauwelaerts, 1962), 109.

13. Edward Peters, *Torture* (New York: Basil Blackwell, 1985), 44, 46–47.

modern historians fix the twelfth and thirteenth centuries as the epoch in which the concept of penance became much more "interiorized."[14] In the High Middle Ages the contrite confession replaced the "laborious act," confession and absolution occurred in succession and in a single interview, and priests began to act as judges who had to know the mental, emotional, and circumstantial landscape of the penitent's transgression.[15]

Thus by the thirteenth century, the sacrament of penance entailed a private confession of sins by laypersons to priests. The latter evaluated the intensity of grief evinced by the former, as well as the magnitude of the sin they confessed; the priests then prescribed penitential acts to be performed, which might or might not entail a literal compensation to a victim. Ecclesiastics finally absolved their penitents by virtue of Jesus' merits, the scriptural example of Peter and the keys, and the formal pronunciation of the sacramental words.[16] Priests now had to measure the details around and the motives behind a sin as well as the formal act itself; the new stress on interiority meant that they had to gauge sins of thought as well as action. The thoroughness of confession thus became increasingly important.

Significantly, the last and conclusive form of private penance radically augmented the clergy's responsibilities. The Fourth Lateran Council of 1215 expanded those duties even further when it reacted to the sacramental changes already underway and issued the canon *Omnis utriusque sexus*: henceforth annual confession would be obligatory for all men and women who had reached the age of reason. The potential body of penitents was consequently enlarged, and in 1221, Pope Honorius III commissioned the Dominican order to hear them. The question, though, was whether the secular or even the regular clergy were sufficiently prepared for their task: the *summae de casibus* and *summae confessorum*, from which Alva's *Confessionario* descends, were composed to remedy that situation.[17] Clerics such as Robert of Flamborough, Thomas of Chobham, and Raymund de Peñyafort wrote their *summae* for the intellectual improvement of their peers, who in turn might carry out the *cura animarum*, or the care of souls, with a surer awareness of ecclesiastical doctrine and law, and thereby fulfill their obligations to God and humankind.[18] The summae, then, were supposed to tell priests and monks what they had to know in order to administer the sacrament of penance properly; the scope of

---

14. Thomas N. Tentler, *Sin and Confession on the Eve of the Reformation* (Princeton: Princeton University Press, 1977), 18–19 on the presence of sorrow in tariffed penance, although he notes that the twelfth century moved from "shame and expiation" to "guilt and remorse," 52, and points to Peter Abelard's and then Peter Lombard's stress on contrition as the principal element in the sacrament, 18–22.

15. Obviously these developments occurred in a non-synchronous way. The joining of confession and absolution into a single act was already a given by the time of Burchard of Worms' *Decretum*, dated c.1000, Poschmann, *Penance*, 145. For other confirmations of the sacrament's increasingly internal trajectory, its newly personal nature, and the implications of such developments for confessors, see Amédée Teetaert, O. Cap., "La `Summa de poenitentia' de Saint Raymond de Penyafort," *Ephemerides theologicae lovanienses* 5 (1928):54; Pierre Michaud-Quantin, "A propos des premières *Summae confessorum*," *Recherches de theologia ancienne et moderne* 26 (1959):265–69; idem, *Sommes de casuistique*, 109–11; John Bossy, "The Social History of Confession in the Age of the Reformation," *Transactions of the Royal Historical Society*, 5th ser., 25 (1975):21–38; Jean Delumeau, *Sin and Fear*, 193–202, who insists that the confessor acted as a judge in tariffed penance too, but agrees that this variety of the sacrament stressed material offenses over intentions.

16. For the theological development of penance in the High Middle Ages, Poschmann, *Penance*, 146–83, and Tentler, *Sin and Confession*, chap. 5, though Tentler's insinuation that it became a fundamentally irrational sacrament calls for some circumspection on the part of the reader.

17. The term "regular" clergy (from the Latin *regula*, or "rule") refers to those ecclesiastics who lived under some form of monastic rule; secular clergy, in contrast, did not.

18. A pastoral angle strongly argued by Leonard E. Boyle against Tentler; see "The Summa for Confessors as a Genre, and Its Religious Intent," in *The Pursuit of Holiness in Late Medieval and Renaissance Religion*, ed. Charles Trinkaus, with Heiko Oberman. (Leiden: Brill, 1974), 126–130.

these guides varied according to their authors' sense of what was essential for carrying out their work.[19]

Still, though nearly everyone recognizes that guides to confession were produced to remedy a specific predicament within the Christian Church, scholars disagree over when they first appeared as well as whether they arose from primarily legal or pastoral impulses. For instance, Raymund de Peñyafort, General of the Dominican Order, devoted his *Summa casuum* in 1225 to particularly problematic cases of sins against God, sins against neighbors, and impediments to ordination, among other topics.[20] Scholars cite his text as evidence that the summae developed out of canon law.[21] Then again, Thomas of Chobham, a thirteenth-century subdeacon at Salisbury cathedral, clarified the instruments of baptism and the Eucharist under a heading entitled "what the priest should necessarily know" in his *Summa confessorum*, which began to circulate around 1216. Historians use his example as proof that the summae ensued from moral considerations about the ministry.[22]

In fact, the summae usually blended the canonical and the pastoral so thoroughly that it is nearly impossible to arrange them according to distinct categories of legal or pastoral concerns: Raymund's text, after all, shared the same didactic objective as Thomas's, though it related legal cases instead of prayers; at the same time, Thomas pondered impediments to marriage within his discourse on the sacraments.[23] If historians try to trace a shift in the summae from legal to moral emphases, they run into similar difficulties. For example, Thomas preceded Raymund in history, but the latter's work was copied much more frequently than the former's. Yet what circulated as Raymund's *summa* after 1280 differed from its original incarnation, for John of Freiburg glossed it according to the moral insights of Thomas Aquinas' *Summa theologica*, and thereby altered its character.[24] The critical point is that guides to the sacrament of penance had to grapple with the assessment of sin, which in turn involved calculations about greater and lesser faults and larger and smaller expiations. Such appraisals typically accompanied moral teachings about right and wrong thoughts and actions. Modern scholars often have difficulty grasping the presence of such apparently contradictory elements in a single work. Some respond by slanting the pedagogical axis of the summae toward intrigue, whereby they accent

---

19. Michaud-Quantin, "A propos," 291.

20. "Distinguitur ergo per tres particulas, in quarum prima agitur de criminibus, quae principaliter et directe committuntur in Deum; in secunda de his, quae in proximum; in tertia de ministris irregularibus et irregularitatibus, et impedimentis ordinandorum, dispensationibus, purgationibus, sententiis, poenitentiis et remissionibus." Cited in Amédée Teetaert, O. Cap., "La 'Summa de Poenitentia' de S. Raymond de Penyafort," 60.

21. Notably Leonard Boyle, "The *Summa confessorum* of John of Freiburg and the Popularization of the Moral Teaching of St. Thomas and Some of His Contemporaries," in *Pastoral Care, Clerical Education and Canon Law, 1200–1400* (London: Variorum Reprints, 1981), 3:247, who calls Raymund's text the "standard work of confessional practice" but recognizes that John of Freiburg inserted moral theology from Thomas Aquinas into it; see below. Boyle labels the treatises of Robert Flamborough and Thomas of Chobham as "pastoral manuals" that popularized the teachings of IV Lateran rather than as "confessors' manuals;" he finds the latter term anachronistic when applied to texts before 1300. See "Robert Grosseteste and the Pastoral Care," ibid., 1:9; and "The *Summa confessorum* of John of Freiburg," ibid., 3:248, n. 18.

22. Though his comments initially might seem theological rather than moral in intent, Thomas was more concerned with practical difficulties that could arise in the administration of the sacraments, such as what to do about infants baptized by laypersons and whether mass could be celebrated by a heretic. Thomas of Chobham, *Thomae de Chobham summae confessorum*, ed. F. Broomfield, Analecta Mediaevalia Namurcensia 25 (Louvain: Éditions Nauwelaerts, 1968), 91–111. In his introduction, Broomfield argues that *summae confessarum* are defined far too narrowly (xvii) if that definition turns on canon law. The original title of Thomas' work is *Summa Cum miserationes domini*.

23. Michaud-Quantin, "A propos," 275, 295, argues that instead of two categories, moral theology and canon law, the texts evince a "morale juridisée."

24. Boyle, "The *Summa confessorum*."

their judicial focus, their elevation of the priest as intermediary, and their stress on contrition, and conclude that these texts were an attempt to secure ecclesiastical tyranny over a guilt-ridden laity.[25] Such an interpretation tends to overlook the obstacles to gauging emotional states in epochs far removed from our own, as well as the fact that clerics too received the sacrament of penance and hence fell under the same admonitions as their secular counterparts. Finally, the rendition of penance-as-oppression implies a homogeneous, conspiratorial clergy and absolutely passive laymen and women; it seems to reveal more about modern perceptions of the Catholic Church than past religiosity.[26]

If the initial summae contained what their authors conceived as most pertinent to the sacrament of penance, their later incarnations went in the opposite direction and embraced everything that was in any way relevant. By the late thirteenth century, authors had alphabetized their material; by the fifteenth and sixteenth they were citing ever-larger numbers of authorities and could dedicate as many as thirty folios to varieties of excommunication.[27] Though a *summa* was explicitly intended to be practical, later clerics' concern for completeness diminished the utility of their works in one basic respect: their inclusivity meant that as their content grew more extensive the size of their volumes increased; it thus became more difficult physically to carry the manuscripts or books from place to place. One solution was to supplement the Latin works with scaled-down manuals in the vernacular. Such vernacular manuals had other advantages besides their portability: they facilitated the dissemination of crucial information to clerics whose Latin was flawed, and they routed their messages from the bottom up as well as the top down, at least to some extent.[28]

French, Spanish, Italian and German confessors' manuals appeared as early as 1280 and became increasingly widespread over the next three hundred years.[29] They are the closest analogues to Alva's *Confessionario*; they unequivocally relied upon their Latin counterparts as authorities. They followed their structures and their interpretations. For instance, in the thirteenth century Thomas of Chobham noted that because the Ten Commandments prohibited every evil, they encompassed the seven deadly sins as well:

> Next, the Holy Fathers say that all sins are forbidden through the Decalogue, therefore the seven capital sins are forbidden in the Decalogue. And it is clear that anger is forbidden when it is said,

---

25. Such can be the case even for scholars who recognize that clerics themselves were subject to penance, who dislike ahistorical judgments, and who attempt to ascribe some positive aspects to the sacrament. Contrast Tentler, *Sin and Confession*, 345–49, 359, 362, with idem, 363–67; and Delumeau, *Sin and Fear*, 198–205, vs. idem, *L'aveu et le pardon* (Paris: Fayard, 1990), 41, 172–74. A more directly negative assessment can be found in Steven Ozment, *The Reformation in the Cities* (New Haven, Conn.: Yale University Press, 1975), 22–32, 47–56, who treats Reformation polemics as descriptions of practice and accordingly concludes that the sacrament of penance was enormously burdensome for laymen and women. For a corrective to this point of view, Lawrence G. Duggan, "Fear and Confession on the Eve of the Reformation," *Archiv für Reformationsgeschichte* 75 (1984):153–75.

26. Lawrence G. Duggan, "Fear and Confession."

27. For alphabetization, Tentler, *Sin and Confession*, 33, 49. Sylvester Prieras' *Summa summarum quae Sylvestrina dicitur*, Strausburg, 1518, devoted fols. 163v–194v to problems of excommunication. Delumeau, *Sin and Fear*, 200, states that Prieras "used the works of forty-eight theologians, 113 jurists, and eighteen other 'Summaists'."

28. Given the theses of Tentler and Delumeau, we might suppose the vernacular manuals advanced the cause of clerical hegemony more thoroughly and efficiently than their Latin counterparts, if only because of their greater accessibility. However, they contain elements that subvert any such enterprise, simply conceived.

29. Delumeau, *Sin and Fear*, 200–205, offers a quick survey of this literature; for some Italian components of it, Roberto Rusconi, "Manuali milanesi di confessione editi tra il 1474 et il 1523," *Archivum Franciscanum Historicum* 6 (1972):107–156, and Miriam Turrini, *La coscienza e le leggi: morale e diritto nei testi per la confessione della prima Età moderna*. Annali dell'Istituto storico italo-germanico, monografia 13. (Bologna: Società editrice il Mulino, 1991).

"do not kill," and that lust is forbidden when it is said, "do not commit adultery," and that avarice is forbidden when it is said, "do not covet your neighbor's belonging."[30]

Thomas extrapolated the fourth commandment to include allegorical as well as literal parents: "By father and mother are understood all those to whom we owe honor or favor."[31] He enumerated those professions that were especially vulnerable to sin and then supplied particular questions for their practitioners. He also suggested that the confessor inquire into the penitents' knowledge of the Our Father, pay close attention to the circumstances of their misdeeds, and admit his own sinful state in order to assuage any embarrassment or fear on the part of the laity.[32]

Thomas's points became standard elements in both Latin and vernacular works on confession; they recur in Spanish manuals from the late fifteenth and sixteenth centuries.[33] Hernando de Talavera, the first archbishop of newly conquered Granada, thoroughly entangled the Decalogue and the seven deadly sins in his *Breve forma de confesar* when he noted that the sin of pride dominated transgressions against the first commandment.[34] In his 1514 tract, *Arte de bien confesar*, Pedro Ciruelo, a professor of thomistic theology at the University of Alcalá, remarked that the fourth commandment consisted of sins against carnal, spiritual, and temporal fathers.[35] Pedro Covarrubias, a Dominican whose sermons were published in Paris, spent some thirty-four folios on sins that could afflict certain professions in his *Memorial de pecados*; he also depicted the confessor as a sinner.[36] And an anonymous monk from the Order of St. Jerome entitled the fourth chapter of his *Arte para bien confesar* "how we are obliged to confess the circumstances of sins, and of what sort and which they are."[37]

Sixteenth-century Spanish authors recited the same catalogues of sin as their Latin counterparts: they too detailed transgressions according to the Decalogue, the seven deadly sins, the five senses, the fourteen works of mercy, and the seven sacraments, among other schemes.[38] They underscored the importance of self-examination in preparation for the sacrament and noted that

---

30. "Item, dicunt sancti quod per decalogum prohibentur omnia mala, ergo prohibentur in decalogo septem criminalia vitia. Et patet quod ira prohibetur cum dicitur: *non occides*, et quod luxuria prohibetur cum dicitur: *non mechaberis*, et quod avaritia prohibetur cum dicitur: *non concupisces rem proximi tui*." Thomas of Chobaum, *Summa confessorum*, 32.

31. "Per patrem et matrem intelliguntur omnes illi quibus debemus honorem vel beneficium . . ." Ibid., 29.

32. On professions, ibid., 290–309; on the importance of being able to recite the *Pater Noster*, 289; on the pivotal role of circumstances, without which "cannot be known the quantity of the sin, and unless the quantity of the sin is known, it cannot be known how much penance should be imposed for some sin" ["... sine quibus [circumstantiis] non potest sciri quantitas peccati, et nisi sciatur quantitas peccati, non potest sciri quanta penitentia alicui peccato sit injungenda."], 45. On the confessor's attempts to soothe the penitent, 326.

33. Chobham's structures and points also are amply demonstrated in Latin and French works by Jean Gerson (1369–1429), chancellor of the University of Paris, conciliarist at the Council of Constance, and prolific devotional author. For instance, in his *Examen de conscience selon les péchés capitaux* Gerson placed the sins of idolatry and blasphemy beneath pride and envy and explicitly coupled the Decalogue with the seven sins; *Opera omnia*, ed. Msgr. Pierre Glorieux (Paris: Desclée, 1960), 7:394–95, 398. His *Le miroir de l'âme* addresses metaphorical as well as natural parents under the fourth commandment and again mingles the two dominant paradigms of sin; ibid., 7:193–206. His *De arte audiendi confessiones* directs the confessor to attenuate any modesty or shame on the part of the penitent that could interfere with a complete confession; ibid., 8:11–12.

34. "Contra este primero mandamiento es por la mayor parte el pecado de la sobervia . . ." Hernando de Talavera, *Breve forma de confesar*, n.d. [after 1492], ed. Miguel Mir, Nueva Biblioteca de Autores Españoles 1 (Madrid: Casa Editorial Bailly, 1911), 7; also 8–9.

35. I have used the Valladolid 1534 edition of the *Arte*; see fols. 28r–29v on the fourth commandment, fol. 6v on the *Pater Noster*.

36. *Memorial de pecados y aviso de la vida Christiania copiosa . . . provechoso assi para los confessores como para los penitentes*, Sevilla, 1521, fol. A4v.

37. "como somos obligados a confessar las circunstancias de los peccados, y de que manera y quales son." Toledo, 1524, chap. 4.

38. For instance, Talavera, Covarrubias, and Ciruelo included all or most of these categories, while the Hieronymite went further and expounded the theological virtues of faith, hope, and charity; sins against the Holy Spirit; the seven gifts of the Holy Spirit, and the twelve articles of the faith.

sins could occur in thought as well as deed. Many of them also reiterated one variation or another of the queries that would elicit all the requisite details of penitents' transgressions, which Raymund de Peñyafort set down as "who, what, where, by whom, how many times, why, in what manner, and when," and which the Hieronymite monk duplicated verbatim.[39]

Nonetheless, Spanish authors of vernacular texts did not produce mirror images of the Latin summae, and there is no reason to think their European counterparts did either. Instead, Talavera, Covarrubias, and their peers retained or discarded a range of discursive and topical elements from what by now were veritable encyclopedias on confession and penance, and their preferences could be startling. Perhaps the most important difference between their own writings and their Latin models was their deliberate inclusion of the laity as part of the audience, something no *summa* ever indicated. Some Spanish authors switched voices within their treatises as they addressed what penitent and confessor would say respectively. Covarrubias, for instance, reproduced the first-person voice for the penitent and invoked the second-person for the confessor.[40] The Hieronymite modeled the general confession as if he were the penitent:

> I, a sinner, very unworthy and guilty and full of sins, have erred against God and against His saints and against my soul and my neighbors, violating His holy commandments and the arrangements of the holy mother church . . .[41]

When he exhorted his audience to "look, look with enormous diligence and with all your power into your heart," he not only emphasized the importance of interiority, but implied the potential connection between confessors' manuals and preaching which one modern scholar has posited for Italian sources from the fifteenth century.[42]

It is difficult to imagine that Spanish authors would have attempted such rhetorical effects had they not expected laymen and women to read their works; they also could express that objective frankly, as when Ciruelo noted that his tract would be of greater use to a larger number of people because he had written it in Spanish.[43] Furthermore, there is no doubt that his manual and those of his peers found a secular as well as an ecclesiastical audience in light of recent scholarship on literacy and the book market in sixteenth-century Spain. Not only could more men and women read than most of us ever expected, but what they read consisted, to a great extent, of works on morality and piety composed in the vernacular. For example, a 1556 inventory from a bookseller and printer in Toledo contained an enormous quantity of devotional titles in Spanish, including 2,020 copies of confessors' manuals out of a total of 33,324

---

39. "quis, quid, ubi, per quos, quoties, cur, quomodo, quando." Raymundus de Peñaforte, *Summa, textu sacrorum canorum*, Paris, 1720, 431–32; *Arte para bien confessar*, fol. B3r. Thomas of Chobham related it in nearly the same terms, except that he omitted "quoties" and substituted "quibus auxiliis" ["by whose help"] for "per quos;" see his *Summa confessorum*, 48–49. The formula was attributed to Cicero.

40. *Memorial de pecados*, fols. A2r, A4r–v.

41. "Yo, peccador, muy indigno y culpado y lleno de peccados, he errado contra dios y contra sus santos y contra mi ánima y mis próximos, traspassando sus sanctos mandamientos y las ordenaciones de la sancta madre yglesia. . ." *Arte para bien confesar*, fol. B7r.

42. "Mira pues con muy gran diligencia y con todas tus fuercas pon [sic] tu corazon . . ." Ibid., fol. A4r. Roberto Rusconi, "Manuali milanesi," 111–12.

43. "The present work . . . in our common language of Spain will be useful not only for the confessors who have to examine the consciences of their penitents, but also for prudent laypersons who, with this doctrine, will be able to complete fully the apostle's counsel, who says `Let a man pronounce judgment on himself' etc." ["el presente tratado . . . qual en nuestra comun lengua de España provechará no solamente para los confesores que han de examinar las conciencias de sus penitentes: mas también para los discretos seglares que con esta doctrina podrán bien cumplir el consejo del apostol: que dize, `Probet autem seipsum homo,' etc."] *Arte de bien confesar*, fol. 2r.

items.[44] Given such data, not to mention the sheer number of times certain manuals were reprinted—in the sixteenth century Ciruelo's went through twenty-two editions and the Hieronymite's eighteen—clearly vernacular guides to penance were routine elements of Spanish intellectual and religious culture.[45]

As to whether the Spanish authors modified their Latin models' didactic material to suit their audience, the evidence is equivocal. On the whole, references to authorities decreased, probably in the interest of curtailing the length of the vernacular manuals. Many authors reduced the number of speculative queries that had delighted their predecessors, such as "Next, one day another danger occurs: a spider or a poisonous fly falls into the chalice. What should the priest do then?"[46] Some emended a summa technique by siding with narrative over a series of specific examples in which each point usually began with "whether" or "if."[47] They also could advance highly theoretical statements such as Ciruelo's on the Decalogue, or Domingo de Valtanás's on the difference between attrition and contrition.[48] But others omitted an overarching argument to tie their points together and offered a sequence of lists instead. Talavera remarked that blasphemy involved "those who blaspheme Our Lord or His saints, saying injurious words, as in 'damn so-and-so,' or 'so-and-so has no power,' or 'I don't believe in so-and-so, damn that saint,' or 'I deny that saint,' and similar things."[49] Covarrubias' didactic efforts amounted to the barest mandates, such as "To our principal intercessor, the blessed mother of God, salute her, saying the Ave Maria. Pray the rosary or some other devotion."[50] Still, even a reduction in the number of references or an augmented exposition was no guarantee of coherence: Juan de Pedraza and Valtanás attempted both, but still managed to insert dialectical statements that they neglected to reconcile.[51]

Nevertheless, in one way every vernacular manual transmitted an explosive educational message. Whether writing in Spanish, French, or Italian, authors of such works deliberately conveyed the proper administration of penance to laymen and women: they told priests what

---

44. Sara T. Nalle, "Literacy and Culture in Early Modern Castile," *Past and Present* 125 (1989):65–96. The Spanish phenomenon was not unique; Rusconi believes that a proportion of his Italian materials so involved the laity that it nearly constitutes a variety of devotional literature. "Manuali milanesi," 116–19. Blanco Sánchez Antonio, "Inventario de Juan de Ayala, gran impresor toledano (1556)," *Boletín de la Real Academia Española* 67 (1987):207–51. Ciruelo's manual represented 314 copies, or between 15 and 16 percent of the total number of confessional works in Ayala's shop.

45. Undoubtedly because of their similar titles, five editions of Ciruelo's and the Hieronymite's manuals are cross-referenced to each other: Zaragoza 1500/1501; Zaragoza 1509; Burgos 1527; Toledo 1536 and 1543. Only Martín de Azpilcueta's *Manuale*, written originally in Latin and then translated into Spanish, went through more printings than Ciruelo's in the sixteenth century. Antonio Palau y Dulcet, *Manual del librero hispano-americano*, (Barcelona: J. M. Viador, 1948), 1:609–11, lists fifty-four editions of Azpilcueta's *summa* in Latin and eighteen printings in Spanish.

46. "Item, quandoque accidit aliud periculum quod incidit aranea vel musca venenosa in calicem. Quid faciet tunc sacerdos?" Thomas of Chobham, *Summa confessorum*, 138.

47. These authors could utilize exposition for only part of their texts. For instance, in the *Arte de bien confessar*, Ciruelo handled the first commandment in a highly expository, if dialectical, manner, but then presented the second as an enumeration of transgressions.

48. Valtanás, a member of the Dominican order, became a zealous supporter of the Society of Jesus and eventually was prosecuted by the Inquisition. For his distinction between attrition and contrition, *Confessionario muy cumplido: con un tratado de materias de excomunicaciones*, Sevilla 1555, fol. A5r. For his biography and bibliography, see the introduction to his *Apologia sobre ciertas materias morales en que hay opinión* and *Apologia de la comunión frequente*, eds. Alvaro Huerga and Pedro Saínz Rodriguez (Barcelona: Juan Flors, 1963).

49. "... los que blasfeman de Nuestro Señor o de sus santos, diciendo palabras injuriosas, como pese a tal o no ha poder en tal, o descreo de tal, pese a tal santo, o reniego de tal santo, o semejantes cosas." *Breve forma de confesar*, 5.

50. "A nuestra principal abogada bendita madre de Dios: saludays la, diciendo Ave Maria. Rezays el Rosario o otra devoción." *Memorial de pecados*, fol. B1r.

51. Namely, Pedraza on the whether conversation with demons was a sin, *Summa de casos de conciencia*, Alcala 1568, fol. 11r; and Valtanás on the potential dissolubility of marriage, probably with an eye to Henry VIII's difficulties, *Confessionario*, fol. 33v.

questions a diligent confessor should ask, in what order he should proceed, what sins he should reserve to the bishop, what queries or issues a given occupation could legitimately prompt, and so forth. These authors thereby allowed their lay audience the power of knowing when penance was administered correctly and when it was not; moreover, in their writings they detailed *clerical* as well as lay sins. As a result, a text like Ciruelo's *Arte de bien confesar* not only promoted the self-examination that allowed a "prudent layperson" to prepare for the sacrament, but furnished the flock with the ability to gauge the performance of its shepherd. Ciruelo observed that parish priests, regular clerics, and preachers were very often guilty of concealed theft; he rebuked the chastity of ecclesiastics in particular.[52] Talavera's treatise contains example after example of ecclesiastical misdeeds, from joking during a baptism to refusing to bury the dead.[53] Every vernacular manual I've surveyed addresses the possibility that the confessor could be an imbecile, and instructs the penitent accordingly.[54] In fact, I would suggest that these texts gave the laity the chance to scold the clergy rather than simply the reverse, a possibility that one Italian cleric betrayed when he enjoined penitents from arguing with the confessor so long as that confessor was relatively educated; implicitly, at least, he allowed for contention if the confessor was ignorant.[55] Though the Spanish texts probably enumerated no more clerical sins than their Latin counterparts in terms of quantity, they made that repertory available to a greatly enlarged readership, if only by virtue of presenting it in the vernacular.

Not surprisingly, Bartolomé de Alva's *Confessionario* raises the same issues of constituency and authority as do the Spanish and Latin manuals that precede it, for the latter contained the paradigms from which he drew his material. Alva delineated sin according to the Ten Commandments, the five rules of the Church, the fourteen works of mercy, the five senses, and the seven deadly sins, as did his Spanish peers. He handled the Decalogue first, concentrating the body of his exposition on the first commandment, as did Ciruelo. He too read the first commandment in its New Testament rather than Old Testament version.[56] When he described the seven deadly sins, he cast them through a standard mnemonic device, *saligia*, that appeared in Latin and Spanish texts, and whose letters were the initials of Latin words for pride, avarice, lust, anger, gluttony, envy, and sloth.[57] By treating gluttony as the "principal cause for committing all

---

52. *Arte de bien confesar*, fol. 41v, 52r.

53. *Breve forma de confesar*, 10–11, 13.

54. Tentler, *Sin and Confession*, 124–27, finally rejects the possibility that the manuals empowered laymen and women by allowing them to gauge the intellectual qualifications of their confessors. He believes such instructions only enhanced ecclesiastical authority. Delumeau construes the significance of a dual audience in a similar direction: by helping laypersons to cooperate in their own "internalization and enlargement" of guilt, the manuals' authors, and by extension the Church, expanded their control over them. *Sin and Fear*, 200–205, 213–44.

55. Francesco da Mozzanica, O.F.M., noted in his *Breve introductione*, Milan 1510, "the confessor being learned and intelligent as he ought," the penitent "should avoid arguing or disputing with him during the act of confession." ["E fuge dal vento de contendere ne disputare cum il confessore in lo acto de la confessione siando luy docto e intelligente come debbe essere."] Cited in Rusconi, "Manuali milanesi," 120, n. 2.

56. "Have you loved God above all things, and His Divine Majesty above all of them, with all your heart, mind and will?" *Confessionario*, 16. Like nearly all his Spanish predecessors, Alva cited Jesus' encapsulation of the commandments in Matthew 22:37–39; unlike them, however, he may not have realized he was following Thomas Aquinas. Acting on Aristotelian metaphysics—whereby the last in order of execution was the first in order of conception—and Paul's statement in Romans 10:4 that Jesus was the *end* of the Law, Aquinas considered the two precepts of Matthew as the principles from which the Law in Exodus 20 flowed. The former had to take precedence over the latter. See the *Summa theologica* Ia–IIae, qu. 100, art. 8.

57. *Confessionario*, 58; in Latin, *superbia, avaritia, luxuria, ira, gula, invidia,* and *accidia.* The first letter of every word spells "saligia," a term Alva did not formally use, probably because of the impossibility of rendering it into Nahuatl. Compare Ciruelo, *Arte de bien confesar*, fol. 49r.; anonymous Hieronymite, *Arte para bien confesar*, chap. 21. The formula was the last important codification of the sins, and was popularized in the thirteenth century. Bloomfield, *The Seven Deadly Sins*, 88–87.

the types and kinds of sins" against the Decalogue, Alva invoked the idea of a "head" [*caput*] or "capital" sin popularized by Gregory I (d. 604), and followed by Talavera and Valtanás.[58] When he described the confessor as a doctor of sins, he invoked another of Gregory's concepts and an even more consistent element in Spanish sources than the notion of caput.[59] Finally, like his Iberian counterparts, Alva retained a section on particular questions for specific occupations.

As for the importance of preparation and sorrow, Alva maintained the structures and emphases of his Spanish prototypes. He followed a standard arrangement when he devoted the first part of his manual to preparation for the sacrament. He counseled his readers to ponder their past in order to recall their sins, and urged them to memorize their faults:

> You who have the will and desire to cleanse and wash the wounds and blemishes of your soul, first you must turn your eyes to a reflection on your past, remembering and reconsidering the faults and sins with which you have offended your God and Lord . . . that you have them all prepared and ready in your memory . . .[60]

He offered the Decalogue as an aid to the process: ". . . go through the Ten Commandments in the order set down here, and with this you will remember in what you have sinned, and what you've incurred, concerning the first, the second, etc."[61] In the midst of his queries on preparation, he admonished forgetful penitents to go home, ponder their faults, and return the following day.[62] None of his counsel was even slightly unusual. Valtanás suggested that penitents devote three days to the recollection of their sins. Pedraza urged readers to investigate their consciences according to the commandments and the seven sins. In cases of insufficient preparation, the Hieronymite advised confessors to send penitents home for further reflection.[63] All these authors worried about a possibly incomplete confession and a consequently invalid sacrament; the same consideration lay behind their preoccupation with codified systems of inquiry. Asking about sins through patterns diminished the chance that penitents might fail to disclose a transgression. It was this possibility of omission that drove Alva's concern with order and the clarity of language.[64]

---

58. *Confessionario mayor*, 58–59; Bloomfield, *The Seven Deadly Sins*, 72–73, 87–88. Talavera, *Breve forma de confesar*, 8–9, noted that pride has twenty-one daughters or branches, while Valtanás explained that we derive the term "capital" sins from their position as the heads of others; *Confessionario*, fol. 72v.

59. Alva, *Confessionario*, 73. The metaphor is such a cliché that it would be unusual to find a confessors' manual without it. To wit, Ciruelo described the confessor as a "medico spiritual," *Arte de bien confesar*, fol. 59r, and the Hieronymite, Valtanás, and Pedraza portrayed him in the same way: *Arte para bien confesar*, chap. 1; *Confessionario*, fol. 17v; *Summa de casos de conciencia*, fol. 5v.

60. "Tu que tienes voluntad, y desseo de limpiar, y lavar las llagas y maculas de tu alma: Primeramente debes volver los ojos de la consideracion a la vida passada, trayendo a la memoria, y recapacitando las culpas, y pecados, con que as offendido a tu Dios, y tu Señor . . . que todos los tienes apercevidos, y promptos en tu memoria . . ." *Confessionario*, 3–4.

61. ". . . discuriendo por los diez Mandamientos, por el orden que aqui va puesto, y con esso te acordarás en que as pecado, y incurrido, acerca del primero, acerca del segundo, etc." Ibid., 6.

62. *Confessionario*, 13–14. Alva presented the situation in dialogue form, with the penitent rejoining, "Si Padre, yo volveré mañana, y te agradesco mucho el bien que me hazes."

63. Valtanás, *Confessionario*, fol. 42r, whose counsel undoubtedly owed much to the number symbolism of both the Trinity and the *triduum*, the latter being the seventy-two hour period from Good Friday to Easter Sunday. Pedraza, *Summa de casos de conciencia*; Hieronymite, *Arte para bien confesar*, chap. 8.

64. Consider, for instance, his injunctions against "a multitude and imposing structure of words" that could render the confession incomprehensible, *Confessionario mayor*, 4–5; or his example of a faulty confession in the *Confessionario menor*, 71–73, wherein the confessor declares that the penitent has recounted his sins in such a confusing way that he cannot understand them. Still, there is one exception to this concern with system, namely Pedro Covarrubias, who quipped that since there was little order in the way sins were committed, there wasn't much need for it in the confession of them. ["Especialmente pues en hazer los pecados no hay orden: tampoco en dezirlos es necessaria tan artificiosa orden: en tal que se diga todo lo que es menester."] He did recognize the importance of a complete account. *Memorial de pecados*, fols. A2v–A3r.

Like his Spanish counterparts, Alva expected penitents to reveal their sins with great pain and contrition. He attempted to move his audience with emotional language:

> O you poor wretch whom the devil brings blind and lost in that dark night of superstitious ignorance! How will you appear before the reverence of God, Who knows all and perceives all?[65]

Alva's rhetoric was directly comparable to the Hieronymite's:

> You, sinner, where will you appear? Over there the saved will hear the sweet voice of our redeemer . . . but the wicked and the sinners will hear the sad and bitter voice that will condemn them to the eternal fire.[66]

Alva's shift in persona again implies a potential link between confession and preaching; indeed, his expositions on the sacraments of extreme unction and matrimony in the *Confessionario menor* are so hortatory and so thoroughly cast in the second person that they might be sermons.[67] As for pedagogy, Alva deleted all theory from his interrogatory and instead presented a series of questions, which made his writing resemble Talavera's. But since he also interpolated a series of lengthy "pláticas," or conversations, throughout both the larger and smaller guides to confession—in which he explained the sacraments, idolatry, and gluttony—he did not exclude doctrine from his manual. Finally, lest we attempt to discriminate too much between pláticas for priests and those for laypersons, we must remember that the two guides were bound together, and whoever could read one of them could read the other, as Alva implied when he noted in the *Confessionario menor* that "we [already] have said in other places all that pertains" to penance. His remark amounted to an invitation to turn to the front of the volume.[68]

Of course, Alva did not simply reproduce the content of works by his analogues, despite his reflection of precedent. Just as theologians in Spain emended their treatises vis-à-vis their Latin models, so he altered the content of his treatise according to his perception of his audience's needs.[69] For example, whereas Valtanás had reveled in the difference between imperfect and perfect sorrow, or the distinction between attrition and contrition, Alva explained transubstantiation, or how the Host changed into the body of Jesus during the Mass; he went on to reassure his readers that consuming only a part of the wafer did not signify receiving only a fragment of God. Whereas Ciruelo illustrated the type of reverence owed to God on the one hand and saints on the other, or *latria* and *dulia*, Alva clarified why the external appearance of the Eucharist—in formal theological terms, its "accidents"—remained the same after its substance had been altered.

If Alva offered more basic expositions of theology than his Spanish peers, he also could curtail his definitions and categories—in certain instances by invoking the most straightforward meaning of his terms. He depicted the seventh deadly sin as general laziness, although the Latin term, *accidia*, connoted spiritual sloth, or an unwillingness to carry out one's religious

---

65. "O pobre de ti, a quien el Demonio trae ciega [sic], y perdido, en aquella tenebrosa noche de ignorancias supersticiosas? Con que cara pareces ante el Acatamiento de Dios, que todo lo sabe, y alcanca?" *Confessionario*, 18.

66. "Tu peccador donde pareceràs? Allí oyràn los justos la dulce voz de nuestro redemptor . . . mas los malos y peccadores oyràn la triste y amarga voz que los condenarà al fuego sin fin . . ." *Arte para bien confessar*, fol. A4r.

67. For instance, "Now children, our mother the Church gathers you here and marries you now, for as long as you might live you have to be together. . . . And thus now take some time to consider what you are doing, and the yoke you are assuming as a responsibility." ["Aora hijos os junta nuestra madre la Iglesia, y os desposa ya para mientras vivieredes aveys de estar juntos. . . . Y assi ahora con tiempo mirad lo que hazeis, y el yugo que os echais a cargo . . ."], *Confessionario menor*, 93.

68. Ibid., 84.

69. Though Alva's objective of writing a useful tract does not diminish the question of reportage versus literary imitation; see n. 74 below.

obligations. He blended the meaning of the second and eighth commandments to such a degree that they ultimately signified the same thing, namely a prohibition of false testimony in a judicial setting.[70] More importantly, he also would abandon conventional theological terms, such as "contrition," when they did not translate easily into Nahuatl.[71] The same sensitivity to environment is equally apparent in Alva's injunctions to count sins with corn kernels and his description of hell as a burning place without a smoke vent or chimney.[72] Such awareness of place could have prompted his exhortations against drunkenness, which appear extraordinarily vehement when juxtaposed against Spanish sentiments. Spaniards would link gluttony to luxury, just as Alva did, but they were much more likely to indict violations of fasts than the consumption of alcohol. When they isolated one of the seven sins as especially deleterious, they usually followed Gregory I and fixed on pride rather than overindulgence in food and drink.[73]

In each of these instances, Alva took a paradigm or an element from the Latin and vernacular summae and deployed it differently than his predecessors. Perhaps the most significant example of his simultaneous appropriation and adjustment occurs in his treatment of idolatry, in which he recounted ceremonies whose end was the acquisition of some material benefit.[74] He belittled the "little idols of chalchihuite" that were supposed to bring riches and earthly goods in return for being warmed by the sun, wrapped in cotton, and treated with veneration and respect.[75] He disparaged sacrifices made to the ahuaques, the gods who resided on the mountain of Tlaloc and produced rain.[76] He indicted any belief in dreams, herbs, and peyote, all of which probably were used for divinatory purposes.[77]

Alva's repertory of idolatry looks very different from Spanish ones. The latter never addressed ahuaques, but focused on necromancy; conversation with demoniacs; divination through signs in nature, such as birdcalls; and the composition of spoken and written spells, called respectively *ensalmos* and *nóminas*.[78] The dissimilarity between the two catalogues was rooted in the very premises of the texts. On the one hand, Alva was contrasting pre- with post-Christianization, which led him to place his admonitions in a historical framework and focus on

---

70. As a result, when he reached the eighth commandment he had almost nothing to say; compare 30–32 to 51.

71. Ibid., 84.

72. Ibid., 46, 27.

73. Talavera offers a good example of the connection between gluttony and luxury in a Spanish source, but with a different slant on the former transgression; *Breve forma de confesar*, 28.

74. There remains the question of whether Alva grounded his exposition on rituals he actually had observed. Although he remarked in two footnotes that he had witnessed or heard of certain idolatrous practices, there always remains the possibility that he drew his material from clichés in Latin American sources as well as from experience, a possibility that an expert in the field would have to determine. The point is that his *Confessionario* is a piece of literature as much as an ethnographic transcription of reality. Certainly imitation was so common among Spanish authors—who very often drew their material from Aquinas or from each other—that we have to treat the connection between their descriptions and practice cautiously. For a consideration of diabolism in the colonial period based on the intellectual links between Europe and New Spain, see Fernando Cervantes, *The Devil in the New World* (New Haven, Conn.: Yale University Press, 1994).

75. *Confessionario*, 17.

76. Ibid., 21.

77. Ibid., 16, 30.

78. When compared to his peers, Ciruelo provided by far the most extensive exposition on the first commandment and idolatry: *Arte de bien confesar*, fols. 4r–22r. He expanded his treatment even further in his *Reprobación de supersticiones y hechicerías*, Alcalá, 1530, which became the most frequently reprinted treatise on sorcery in sixteenth-century Spain. The numerous scholars who invoke the latter never have recognized its explicit antecedant in the confessors' manual. For the connection between the two, see my doctoral dissertation, "Religious Humanism, Pastoral Reform and the Pentateuch in Early Modern Spain: Pedro Ciruelo's Journey from Grace to Law" (The University of Chicago, 1992), chaps. 2–3.

the transmission of rituals and beliefs from ancestors to contemporaries. His outlook on idolatry was highly dichotomous and his illustrations hardly subtle: to him, idolatrous practices smacked of paganism and were immediately identifiable. In contrast, Iberian writers imagined Christians directing their devotion to inappropriate ends or manipulating the rites of their religion in illegitimate ways. Such authors did not treat the issue of generational difference; they worked with a smaller range of deviation from an already fundamentally Catholic axis. They consequently indicted more delicate forms of misbehavior. For example, they routinely classified the improper veneration of saints as idolatry; Ciruelo told the confessor to ask "if the penitent, praying before church statues, has known not to address his prayer to speak with the statues themselves, but with the holy things that they represent in the other world."[79] These Spanish clerics distinguished between spells that employed sanctioned language and ones that did not; Talavera implicitly exempted *nóminas* drawn from the Gospels.[80] They also censured anomalous behavior imbedded in a proper activity, such as special postures or particular hours for prayers.[81] Alva never entertained such issues because he expected more basic and blunter sorts of transgression.

Yet Alva's approach to idolatry was not utterly disparate from that of his Spanish peers. He too placed this sin in the domain of the first commandment and understood it as a failure to love God above all other things.[82] More importantly, when he referred to the chalchihuites as ""demonic figurines," or to sacrifices as "diabolical works," or to certain burial rites as "diabolical customs," his language revealed a notion that informed all Continental treatments of witchcraft and sorcery, namely the theory of the implicit demonic pact. In the course of attacking ancient magicians, Augustine had outlined the concept when he contended that demons acted as the agents of all magic, since they either had invented the rituals in question or intervened in their performance. He also thought demons could intercede on the basis of pre-established signs that were invisible to observers.[83] His successors systematized and expanded the concept to the point that by the fifteenth century, Jean Gerson could write:

> A ritual for the working of some effect, which cannot be rationally expected either from the miraculous workings of God or from natural causes, must be held among Christians as superstitious and suspect of a secret pact, implicit or explicit, with demons.[84]

The Devil's objective was to diminish God's rightful preeminence. Superstition directed the practitioner's attention away from God. Furthermore, the Devil and his demons were consummate liars, who actively sought ways to corrupt weak individuals.[85] As a result of this chain of reasoning, a superstitious act such as praying while standing on one foot, which had no recog-

---

79. "Si haziendo su oracion delante las ymagines de la yglesia a sabido enderezar su oracion a hablar no con las ymagines: sino con las cosas sanctas a quien representan del otro mundo." *Arte de bien confesar*, fol. 15r.

80. "Item, los que hacen y traen nóminas en las cuales hay palabras que no son del santo evangelio." *Breve forma de confesar*, 22.

81. Ciruelo, *Arte de bien confesar*, fol. 20r–v.

82. See n. 56 above.

83. *City of God* (Middlesex, U.K.: Penguin, 1972), book 7, chap. 35; book 8, chap. 19; book 10, chaps. 8–9. Also see idem, *On Christian Doctrine* (Indianapolis: The Liberal Arts Press, Inc., 1958), 59–60.

84. "Observatio ad faciendum aliquem effectum qui rationabiliter exspectari non potest a Deo miraculose operante nec a causis naturalibus, debet apud christianos haberi superstitiosa et suspecta de secreta pacto implicito vel explicito cum daemonibus." *De erroribus circa artem magicam, Opera omnia*, 10:79.

85. The idea of demons as active inventors and tantalizers comes from various interpretations of 1 Peter 5:8, "Be sober and watch: because your adversary the devil, as a roaring lion, goeth about seeking whom he may devour."

nized claims to supernatural or natural efficacy, could be defined as diabolical and ensuing from the secret operation of demons, whether the practitioner realized it or not.[86] The same rationale allowed Alva to label offerings to the ahuaques as diabolical, since he viewed those rites as possessing neither supernatural nor natural power.

If Alva and his Spanish predecessors shared high theological concepts, they also revealed a similar concern for a decidedly popular audience. There is no doubt that Alva intended his *Confessionario* for laypersons as well as ecclesiastics, and for both Nahuatl and Spanish speakers. He implied that extensive readership by his use of the second- rather than the third-person voice to duplicate the penitent's responses and to reiterate the Pater Noster, the Ave Maria, and the Salve Regina at the end of his text. Since historians have shown that Nahua literacy was established well before 1634, I think we can presume that Alva found his audience.[87]

Nevertheless, the matter of audience provokes in turn the question of power in Alva's vision of the clergy and the laity. His treatise presents a more complex and less sanguine picture of that relationship than treatises of his Iberian counterparts. Alva stripped away negative reflections on priests, which routinely appeared in Spanish sources. He omitted the typical instructions to confessors about avoiding unnecessary queries.[88] Unlike his Spanish peers, he evinced no anxiety about scrupulosity, that is, the penitents' inappropriate fixation on their own culpability. Conversely, his admonitions about fear—whether he intended to hinder or encourage it—were more plentiful than in the analogues from Spain, and he spent more time adjuring the confessor to be calm.

Yet other evidence in Alva's work blurs to some extent a line of authority that moved only from priest to penitent. Alva made the description of proper sacramental practice accessible to secular individuals; in his rite, clerics expressed themselves kindly, took the secrecy of confession seriously, and identified themselves explicitly as sinners.[89] Despite the fact that these admonitions occurred in the *Confessionario mayor* rather than the *Confessionario menor*, they were equally available because of the one treatise being fastened to the other. Even though Alva refrained from explicitly condemning clerical misbehavior in both texts, his audience could use his descriptions to measure the distance between the actual and the ideal. Certainly he assumed his readers were sufficiently rational to engage in comparable calculations on other topics; otherwise he would not have expected them to see the absurdity of Nahuatl speakers praying in

---

86. If the superstitious act worked, its demonic origin was even clearer. See Ciruelo, *Arte de bien confesar*, fols. 20r–21r. For examples of praying in odd postures, including the one that Talavera classified as idolatrous, see the *Breve forma de confesar*, 23.

87. Frances Karttunen, "Nahuatl Literacy," *The Inca and Aztec States, 1400–1800: Anthropology and History*, eds. George A. Collier, Renato I. Rosaldo, and John D. Worth (New York: Academic Press, 1982), 395–417; Barry D. Sell, "Friars, Nahuas, and Books: Language and Expression in Colonial Nahuatl Publications" (Ph.D. diss. UCLA, 1993), 63–68.

88. Although Alva failed to include such counsel, he certainly would have known about it. It was a commonplace in both Latin and vernacular *summae* to caution the confessor against posing irrelevant or superfluous queries; see, for instance, Tommaso de Vio (known as Cajetan), *Summula Caietani*, Lyon, 1581, 66; Ciruelo, *Arte de bien confesar*, fols. 40v, 49r; Hieronymite, *Arte para bien confesar*, chap. 3. Tentler and others have pointed to the sheer number of inquiries in the average manual as evidence of manipulation and the inculcation of guilt, especially when those questions pertained to sexual practice: see *Sin and Confession*, xix, 35. What many scholars fail to realize is that no cleric ever pitched all the questions in a *summa*, but used his discretion instead to gauge which were appropriate and which were not, something determined by the penitent's age, status, and circumstances.

89. *Confessionario*, 7–10; his attack on priests who violated the principle of secrecy was his only explicit censure of a clerical sin. Alva admonished the confessor to reiterate the rule of confidentiality in order to secure a complete confession, so his motives were quite complex. Nevertheless, the laity could use his illustration of clerical misbehavior for its own purposes.

Latin.[90] Thus if the *Confessionario* coerced from one side—with its condescending language, shaming mechanisms, and attempts to reshape endemic customs according to European Christianity—it empowered from another.[91] Like its Spanish and Latin counterparts, Alva's text preserved the confessor as judge. But it also presumed and encouraged a shared, if hierarchical, pastoral enterprise.

---

90. Ibid., 97.

91. As Alva himself implied when he wrote that confessors engaged in as much teaching as warning; ibid., 6. For further consideration of power and the vernacular manuals, see chap. 5 of my *Religious Authority in the Spanish Renaissance* (Baltimore: The Johns Hopkins University Press, forthcoming).

THE
CONFESSIONARIO

CONFESSIONARIO MAYOR, Y MENOR EN LENGVA MEXICANA.

Y platicas contra las Supresticiones de idolatria, que el dia de oy an quedado a los Naturales desta Nueua Espana, é instrucion de los Santos Sacramentos &c.

AL ILLVSTRISSIMO SEÑOR DON
Francisco Manso y Zuñiga, Arçobispo de Mexico, del Consejo de su Magestad, y del Real de las Indias &c. Mi señor.

NVEVAMENTE COMPVESTO POR
el Bachiller don Bartholome de Alua, Beneficiado del Partido de Chiapa de Mota.

Año de 1634.

¶ *CON LICENCIA*

Impresso en *MEXICO*, Por Francisco Salbago, impressor del Secreto del Santo Officio. Por Pedro de Quiñones.

GUIDE TO CONFESSION, LARGE AND SMALL, IN THE MEXICAN LANGUAGE.

And speeches against the superstitions of idolatry that nowadays remain with the natives of this New Spain, and instruction in the holy Sacraments, etc.

TO THE MOST ILLUSTRIOUS LORD DON
Francisco Manso y Zúñiga, Archbishop of Mexico, of the Council of His Majesty, and of the Royal Council of the Indies, etc. My lord.

NEWLY COMPOSED BY
Bachiller Don Bartolomé de Alva, Holder of the Benefice of the parish of Chiapa de Mota.

Year of 1634.

¶ *WITH OFFICIAL PERMISSION*

Printed in *MEXICO* by Francisco Sálbago, printer of the Office of Cases of Faith of the Holy Office. By Pedro de Quiñones.

DON RODRIGO PACHECO OSSORIO
Marques de Zerraluo, del Consejo de Guerra,
Virrey lugarTeniente del Rey nuestro señor,
Gouernador, y Capitan General de esta Nueua
España,
y Presidente de la Audiencia, y Chancilleria Real,
que en ella reside, &c.

POR Quanto, el Bachiller don Bartholome de
Alua, Beneficiado de Chiapa de Mota, me a hecho
relacion, que atendiendo al bien, y
aprouechamiento de los Naturales desta Nueua
España, àcerca de la Dotrina Christiana, y buena
in[s]truccion en las cosas de nuestra santa Fè
Catolica, y para el mayor, y mas facil exercicio de
sus Curas, y Ministros, tiene compuesta vna obra,
que se intitula *Confessionario mayor,* y platicas
contra las supresticiones de idolatria, que el dia de
oy an quedado a los dichos Naturales, la qual
tiene con las aprouaciones y pareceres de las
personas doctas à quienes el señor Arçobispo la
remitio, en cuya conformidad le fue despachada
licencia, para poderla imprimir, y para poderlo
hazer, me pidio le mandase dar licencia, y
Priuilegio, para que co[n] ella se pueda imprimir
el dicho libro, y por mi se mando lo biese el Padre
Antonio de Caruajal de la Compañia de Iesus, y
me informase, en cuyo cumplimiento lo hizo. Y
por mi visto, por la presente doy licencia al
dich[o] Bachiller don Bartholome de Alua, para
que por tiempo de diez años primeros
siguientes pueda imprimir el dicho libro, intitu-
lado *Confessionario mayor,* y platicas contra las
supresticiones de idolatrias, en la forma que la
pide. Y mando que distante el dicho tiempo
ninguna persona lo pueda imprimir, sin su per-
misso, pena de ducientos pessos de oro comun, y
de perder los moldes, y aderentes que se hallaren,
con mas los cuerpos impressos que tuviere del
dicho libro, aplicado todo para la Camara de su
Magestad, Iuez, y denunciador por iguales partes,
fecho en Mexico, a diezinueve de Agosto de mil y
seiscientos y treinta y quatro años.

El Marques de Zerraluo.

Por mandado de su Excelencia.

Luis de Touar Godinez.

DON RODRIGO PACHECO OSSORIO,
Marquis of Cerralbo, of the Council of War,
Viceroy and deputy of the King our lord,
governor and captain-general of this New Spain,
and president of the Royal Audiencia and
Chancellery,
which resides in it, etc.

INASMUCH as the Bachiller Don Bartolomé de
Alva, holder of the benefice of Chiapa de Mota, has
reported to me that, attentive to the well-being and
development of the natives of this New Spain concerning the Christian doctrine and good instruction in matters of our holy Catholic faith, and for
the greater and easier exercise of the responsibilities of their priests and ministers, he has composed
a work entitled *Confesionario mayor* and speeches
against the superstitions of idolatry that nowadays
have remained among the said natives, which he
has along with the approvals and opinions of
learned people to whom the archbishop remitted
it, in conformity with which he sent him official
permission to be able to print it. In order to do this
he asked me to order that official permission and
privilege be given, so that with it the said book
could be printed. I ordered that Father Antonio de
Carvajal of the Society of Jesus see it and report to
me, in compliance with which he did. And seen by
me, I hereby give official permission to the said
Bachiller Don Bartolomé de Alva, so that
for the period of the next ten years
he could print the said book entitled *Confesionario
mayor* and speeches against the superstitions of
idolatry, in the manner in which he requests. And
I order that until that time no one [else] can print
it without his permission, under penalty of 200
pesos of common gold and of losing the molds
and accessories that may be found, along with the
volumes printed of the said book, all applied in
equal parts to the chest of His Majesty, the judge,
and the person who denounces the wrongdoer.
Dated in Mexico, nineteenth of August of the
year 1634.

The Marquis of Cerralbo.

By order of his Excellency.

Luís de Tovar Godínes.

NOS DON FRANCISCO MANSO Y ZVñiga,
por la diuina gracia, y de la santa Sede Apostolica,

Arçobispo de Mexico, del Consejo del Rey nuestro
señor, y del Real de las Indias &c.

POR Quanto el Bachiller don Bartholome de Alua,
Beneficiado del Partido de Chiapa de Mota de
nuestro Arçobispado, presentò ante nos vn tratado
Confessionario mayor, *que a compuesto en lengua*
Mexicana, para la administracion de los santos
Sacramentos, a los Naturales, y nos pidio y suplicò
le mandasemos por la vtilidad que se les sigue a los
Ministros, y indios Naturales, nuestra licencia para
poderlo imprimir. Y visto por nos, acordamos de lo
remitir al Doctor Iacinto de la Serna nuestro
Visitador general y al Padre Iuan de Ledesma lector
de Theologia, de la Compañia de Iesus, para que
hauiendolo visto, y examinado con su parecer,
proueyesemos lo que conuiniese, y porque de su
aprobacion nos consta que el dicho tratado es
importante, vtil, y prouechoso para la dicha
administracion, y de grande aliuio para los dichos
Naturales, por no auer en el dicho tratado cosa que
contradiga a nuestra santa Fè Catolica y buena
enseñança de los feligreses, antes facilidad para los
dichos Ministros, tubimos por bien de mandar
despachar la presente, por la qual le damos licencia,
para que por qualquiera impressor de los desta
Ciudad imprima el dicho tratado como el dicho don
Bartholome de Alua pretende. Dada en Mexico, à
ocho dias del mes de Iunio de mil y seiscientos y
treinta y quatro años.

Francisco Arçobispo de Mexico.
Por mandado del Arçobispo mi señor.
Pedro Aluarez de Saa.

WE, DON FRANCISCO MANSO Y ZÚÑIGA,
by divine grace and the holy Apostolic See,
Archbishop of Mexico,
of the Council of the King our lord, and of the
Royal Council of the Indies, etc.

INASMUCH as the Bachiller Don Bartolomé de
Alva, holder of the benefice of the parish of Chiapa
de Mota of our archbishopric, has presented before
us a treatise—Confesionario mayor—which he
has composed in the Mexican language for the
administration of the holy Sacraments to the
natives, and asked and beseeched of us our official
permission in order to be able to print it, we agreed
to send it to our inspector general Doctor Jacinto de
la Serna and to Father Juan de Ledesma, reader of
theology of the Society of Jesus, so that having seen
and examined it, with their opinion we might
decree what is suitable. And because by their
approval it is clear to us that the said treatise is
important, useful, and beneficial for the said
administration [of the Sacraments], and of better-
ment for the said natives, on account of there not
being in the said treatise something which might
contradict our holy Catholic faith and good instruc-
tion of the faithful, rather facility for the said minis-
ters, we consider it proper to order the present
license expedited, by means of which we give him
official permission so that as the said Don
Bartolomé de Alva has requested, any printer of this
city might print the said treatise. Given in Mexico,
the eighth day of the month of June of the year
1634.

Francisco, Archbishop of Mexico.
By order of the archbishop my lord.
Pedro Álvarez de Saa.

APROVACION DEL PADRE IOAN DE LEdesma
Lector de Theologia en la Compañia de Iesus.

EL Confessionario en lengua Mexicana, que de nueuo á compuesto el Bachiller don Bartholome de Alua, y Vuestra Illustrissima me remitio, para que diesse mi parecer, he visto, y es muy digno su Autor, que Vuestra Illustrissima le haga merced de darle licencia para que se imprima, porque demas de no auer cosa que lo impida, sera muy vtil a los Ministros de indios, a quienes el Autor con la eminencia que tiene en la lengua Mexicana, pretende ayudar, y facilitar, para el exercicio de su ministerio, en este Collegio de la Compañia de Iesus de Mexico, 7. de Iulio de 1634. Años.

Ioan de Ledesma.

*APROVACION DEL PADRE ANTONIO
DE CARVAJAL*
de la Compañia de Iesus.

EXcelentissimo señor, el Confessionario Mexicano, ordenado por el Bachiller don Bartholome de Alua Beneficiado de Chiapa, que Vuestra Excellencia me mandò viesse he visto, y jusgo ser obra pia, y prouechossa para los curas y Ministros de indios, por estar fielmente traducidos los misterios de nuestra santa Fee con puridad y propiedad de su original, idioma que ayuda mucho a que den facil credito a los Ministros Euangelicos que les instruyen en mas altas verdades, y assi se podra seruir Vuestra Excellencia de darle al Autor grata licencia para que lo estampe, de nuestra casa Professa de la Compañia de Iesus de Mexico, quinze de Agosto de 1634.

Antonio de Caruajal.

APPROVAL OF FATHER JUAN DE LEDESMA,
reader of theology in the Society of Jesus.

THE Confesionario in the Mexican language that the Bachiller Don Bartolomé de Alva has recently composed and that Your Grace sent to me, that I might give my opinion, I have seen; and its author is very worthy of Your Grace's doing him the favor of giving him official permission so that it be printed, because besides having nothing that would impede it, it will be very useful to the ministers of the Indians, whom the author (with the superiority he has in the Mexican language) is attempting to help and facilitate, for the exercise of their ministry. In this College of the Society of Jesus of Mexico, seventh of July of the year 1634.
Juan de Ledesma.

*APPROVAL OF FATHER ANTONIO
DE CARVAJAL*
of the Society of Jesus.

MOST excellent lord, the Mexican Confesionario, arranged by the Bachiller Don Bartolomé de Alva, holder of the benefice of Chiapa, that Your Excellency ordered me to see, I saw. And I judge it to be a pious work, beneficial for the priests and ministers of Indians, because the mysteries of our holy faith are faithfully translated with purity and propriety from their original language which greatly helps to give easy credence to the ministers of the gospel who instruct them in the loftiest truths. And thus Your Excellency would be well-served giving him free license so that he can print it. From our Casa Profesa of the Society of Jesus, fifteenth of August of 1634.

Antonio de Carvajal.

APROVACION DEL DOCTOR IACINTO DE LA SERNA,

Visitador general, y Examinador sinodal de suficiencia y lengua Mexicana deste nuestro Arçobispado.

ILLustrissimo señor, el *Confessionario* en lengua Mexicana, que compuso el Bachiller don Bartholome de Alua, Beneficiado de Chiapa, he visto por mandado de Vuestra Señoria Illustrissima y en el no ay cosa que contradiga a nuestra santa Fé Catolica, y buena enseñança: antes por la erudicion, y prouechosa Doctrina que contiene para los indios, es muy digno que Vuestra Señoria Illustrissima de licencia para imprimirse, y muy digno su Autor que Vuestra Señoria Illustrissima le honre, para que se anime a sacar a luz otras obras, que assi por la eminencia en la lengua, como por experiencia de ministro con que escriue seran muy de el seruicio de Nuestro Señor importantes a los ministros, y prouechosas a los indios. Xalatlaco 20. de Iulio de 1634.

Doctor Iacinto de la Serna.
AL ILLustrissimo Señor Don Francisco Manso y Zuñiga, Arçobispo de Mexico, del Consejo del Rey nuestro Señor, y del Real de las Indias &c. Mi señor.

[COAT OF ARMS]

APPROVAL OF DOCTOR JACINTO DE LA SERNA

inspector general and synodal examiner of competency and Mexican language of this our archbishropic.

MOST excellent lord, I have seen by order of Your Lordship and Grace the *Confesionario* in the Mexican language that the Bachiller Don Bartolomé de Alva, holder of the benefice of Chiapa, has composed, and there is nothing in it that contradicts our holy Catholic faith and good instruction. Rather, because of the erudition and useful doctrine that it contains for the Indians it is very worthy of Your Lordship and Grace's giving official permission for it to be printed, and its author very worthy of Your Lordship and Grace's honoring him so that he may be moved to publish other works. As much for the superiority in the language as for experience as a minister with which he writes, they would be of great service to our Lord, of importance to the ministers, and of use to the Indians. Xalatlaco, twentieth of July of 1634.

Doctor Jacinto de la Serna.
TO THE most illustrious lord Don Francisco Manso y Zúñiga, Archbishop of Mexico, of the Council of the King our lord and of the Royal Council of the Indies, etc. My lord.

[COAT OF ARMS]

CVYDADOS, y temores affligian al Santo Patriarcha Iacob en el Capitulo 31. del Genesis, fundados en la enemistad de su hermano Esau, que ni por la sangre convencido, nor por las cortesias obligado, Tirano le perseguia, quando à braço partido le desafia vn Angel, y sin attender la desigualdad de las fuerças lucha con el toda vna noche. Vencedor el Angel pide á Iacob, que le suelte: *Dimitte me,* porque apuntaua el Alua: *Iam enim ascendit Aurora.* Y aunque para vn rendido era la peticion de comodidad: la pretendio mayor no dexandole ir sin que primero le bendixiesse: *Non dimittam te nisi benedixe[r]is mihi.* Mostrose en esto mas prudente que presumido; porque no era justo perdiessen por el Alua las vigilias, y trauajos de la noche su premio, y bendicion. Alcançola venturoso, y en ella pronosticos de vencedores sucessos: contra homines prœualebis. Exemplo tuve en esto Illustrissimo Señor, para que, ni los cuydados del beneficio, ni los temores de mi cortedad me desanimassen á no valerme de Vuestra Señoria que fue luchar con vn Angel, de quien me confiesso vencido con las honras, y rendido con los fauores, á quien offresco humilmente trauajos, y desuelos en la noche de Mexicanas ignorancias, pidiendo no pierdan la bendicion de Vuestra Illustrissima, porque llega el Alua, si no que como Angel, Principe en el ministerio, y dignidad los bendiga, para que cobren fuerzas à maiores empressas, que yo las fio benditas de tales manos: las quales veso, diziendo siempre lo que Iacob: *Non dimittam te nisi benedixeris mihi.*

Illustrissimo Señor.
Humilde Capellan de Vuestra Señoria Illustrissima.
Bachiller don Bartholome de Alua.

CARES and fears afflicted the holy patriarch Jacob in chapter 31 of Genesis, founded in the enmity of his brother Esau, who neither persuaded by family ties nor obliged by courtesies was hunting him down like a tyrant. When an angel challenged him to hand-to-hand combat (and without paying attention to the difference in strength) he struggled with him an entire night. Jacob being victorious, the angel asked him to let go of him: *Let me go,* because dawn [Alva] was beginning to break: *For now the dawn is breaking.* And although for one who had conceded defeat it was a request of convenience, [Jacob] attempted it mainly in order to not let him go before he blessed him: *I will not let you go until you bless me.* He showed himself in this more prudent than presumptuous, because it was not fair that one lose by the dawn [i.e., the Alva] the rewards and blessings of the vigils and labors of the night. He attained them [i.e., blessings/the Alva] a fortunate man, and with them [i.e., blessings/the Alva] promise of victorious events: *you will prevail against men.* I took an example from this, most illustrious lord, so that neither the cares of the benefice nor fears of my shortcomings might dishearten me from availing myself of Your Lordship. That was [like] struggling with an angel, with regard to whom I confess myself conquered with honors and defeated with favors, and to whom I humbly offer the labors and vigils in a night of Mexican ignorance, pleading that they do not lose the blessing of Your Grace, because the dawn [i.e., the Alva] comes, if not like an angel, [then like] a prince in the ministry. And may dignity bless them so that they gather strength for greater enterprises that I entrust to them, blessed by such hands which I kiss, always saying what Jacob did: *I will not let you go until you bless me.*

Most Illustrious Lord.
Humble Chaplain of Your Lordship and Grace.
Bachiller Don Bartolomé de Alva.

CONFESSIONARIO MAYOR

En lengua Mexicana, y Castellana.

CON TODAS LAS PLATICAS PARA
reprehender los vicios de los Naturales,
y mouerlos a la virtud.
Necessarias para todos los Ministros.

PLATICA, QVE en commun, y general se deue
hazer á los naturales, del Sacramento de la
Penitencia, quando sus Ministros los juntan en las
Yglesias las Quaresmas.

§§

DIos Soberano, y todopoderoso, que es á cuya
voluntad viuimos, os dè, y comunique su Diuina
luz a todos los que aqui

LARGE GUIDE TO CONFESSION

in the Mexican and Spanish Languages.

WITH ALL THE SPEECHES FOR
reproving the vices of the natives
and moving them to virtue.
Necessary for all the ministers.

SPEECH THAT in common and in general
should be made to the natives about the
Sacrament of penance, when their ministers
gather them together in the churches during Lent.

§§

MAY God sovereign and all-powerful, by Whose
will we live, give and communicate His divine
light to all of you who here

[1 RECTO]

CONFESSIONARIO MAYOR
En lengua Mexicana, y Castellana.

CON TODAS LAS PLATICAS PARA
reprehender los vicios de los Naturales,
y mouerlos a la virtud.
Necessarias para todos los Ministros.

*TENONOTZALIZ*tli inic moçennonotzazque
maçehualtin in itechcopa monemachtizque in
inneyolcuitiliz, in yquac Teopan quinçentlalia,
quincenquixtia in inTeopixcahuan Quaresmatica.
§§
MA Yehuatzin in çemanahuac ipalnemoaloni
Dios, amechmomaquili in ilhuicac iteotlanetzin:
in nican axcan oàhuallaque oàçenquiza-

[1 RECTO]

LARGE GUIDE TO CONFESSION
in the Mexican and Spanish Languages.

WITH ALL THE SPEECHES FOR
reproving the vices of the natives
and moving them to virtue.
Necessary for all the ministers.

ADMONITORY speech with which all the natives
are counseled about preparing themselves for their
confessions when their priests congregate and
gather them together in the church during Lent.
§§
MAY God, the Giver of life in the world, give His
divine and heavenly radiance to you who today
have come and gathered together here

[1 VERSO]

en su San[1 verso]to Templo os aveis juntado, y
concurrido; para que en aqueste tiempo sanctissimo de la Passion, y muerte de nuestro Señor
Iesu Christo, os vañeys, y laueys de vuestras
culpas, y pecados: pues á sido seruido de abrir por
nosotros aquella Diuina, y Celestial fuente del
santo Sacramento de la Penitencia, de donde
manan, salen, y proceden aquellas clarissimas, y
cristalinas aguas, con que se laua, limpia, y
purifica toda llaga, y macula del alma. Agora pues
es muy necessario, y conuiene aduertiros de
muchas cosas, con que todavia proseguis, y andais
en vna muy obscura, y tenebrosa noche de ignorancias, de que los demas Christianos vuestros
proximos los Españoles se admiran, marauillan, y
espantan: viendo particularmente quan [2 recto]
flaca, miserable, y desuenturada sea vuestra Fee, y
obras, que parece que hasta agora no á echado
rayzes, en vuestros corazones:

[2 RECTO]

pues que siendo tan dulce, tan suaue, y sabrosa la
ley de Dios, vosotros si no es á pura fuerza, y
temor de vuestro coraçon, y voluntad, no hazeys
actos de fee. Pues aduertid que no es esso lo que
Dios quiere; sino que con muy entrañable amor la
aueis de receuir, y exercitar, particularmente lo
que agora os propongo acerca del Santo
Sacramento de la Penitencia, que á de ser de la
manera siguiente.

Tu que tienes voluntad, y desseo de limpiar, y
labar las llagas y maculas de tu alma:
Primeramente debes voluer los ojos de la consideracion á la vida passada, trayendo a la memoria,
y re[2 verso]capacitando las culpas, y pecados,
con que as offendido a tu Dios, y tu Señor, y dexado de amar, y querer a aquel que infinitamente
debe ser amado, y querido.

[1 VERSO]

have gathered together and assembled in His holy
temple, so that in this most holy time of the
Passion and death of our Lord Jesus Christ you
wash and cleanse yourselves of your faults and
sins. He has been pleased to open for us that
divine and celestial fountain of the holy
Sacrament of penance, [and] from which there
flow, come out and proceed those exceedingly
clean and crystalline waters with which all the
wounds and blemishes of the soul are cleansed,
cleaned, and purified. Now then it is very necessary and it behooves you to pay attention to many
things which you still carry on and are engaged in,
in a very dark and gloomy night of ignorance,
about which the rest of the Christians your neighbors the Spaniards are astonished, amazed, and
appalled, particularly seeing how weak, miserable,
and ill-fated are your faith and works, that it seems
that until now it has not taken root in your hearts.

[2 RECTO]

Now then, the law of God being so sweet, so
gentle and pleasant, if it is not purely by force and
fear in your heart and will, you do not make acts
of faith. Well, notice that is not what God wants!
Rather, that with very deep love you are to receive
and exercise it [i.e., the faith], particularly what I
propose to you now concerning the holy
Sacrament of penance, which is to be in the
following way.

You who have the will and desire to cleanse
and wash the wounds and blemishes of your soul:
first you must turn your eyes to a reflection on
your past life, remembering and reconsidering the
faults and sins with which you have offended your
God and Lord, and ceased loving and wanting
Him Who must be infinitely loved and wanted.

[1 VERSO]

co, in iteopanchantzinco inic anmaáltizque anmopapacazque in axcan ipan itlaçomahuiztlahiyohuilizcahuitzin in totlazotemaquixticatzin Iesu Christo: canel topampa quimonequiltia, quimotlapolhuiz in ilhuicac teoalhuaztli Santo Sacramento neyolcuitiliztli, in ye oncan quiza meya, molloni, in yectli, in chipahuac, in tlazotehuiltic, Atl, in iehuatl ic mopapaca ic mochipahua in itliliuhca in icatzahuaca in toyolia. Auh huel zenca monequi, in acachtopa axcan, tamechizcalizque, tamechixtlapozque in itechcopa in cantlehuatl [sic] in za ie noma tlai[o]huayan mextecomac, annemi, in huel ic anquintetzahuia in oc zequintin, amohuampohuan christianostin caxtilteca, auh ca yehuatl inic amechytta in àmo, antlaneltoquiliztlapaltique, in za ye noma axcan ayamo monelhuayotia ayamo motlaaquilotia in itech in amoyolo in teotlanelto-

[2 RECTO]

quiliztli; ipampa in itlaneltoquilitzin Dios, ihuan in itlayecoltilocatzin zenquizcatzopelic zenquizcahuiac; auh in amehuantin intlacamo tecuicuitlahuiliztica temamauhtiliztica, ámo anquiyolocacopahuia in teotlaneltoquiliztlachihualli auh ca, ámo yehuatl in quimonequiltia in Dios ca mozenyolocacopahuiz oc zenca qualca in tlen ic axcan namechnonotza neyolcuitiliztli Sacramento, ca iuhqui in in mochihuaz moneltiliz.

In ac tehuatl in ticnequi in ticelehuia, ticchipahuaz in icatzahuaca, in itliliuhca in moyolia: ca nican ca in ticchihuaz in ticneltiliz, acachtopa micampa motepotzco timocuepaz ticytaz ticilnamiquiz in monemiliz: auh ticpoaz, ticzentocaz, in ixquich motlatlacol, inic i[x]tzinco icpactzinco otinen in moteotzin motlatocatzin Dios inic oticmoteopohuili in ámo teopoalloni inic ámo ticmotlazotili in çen-

[1 VERSO]

in His temple in order to bathe and wash yourselves now in the precious honored time of suffering of our beloved Savior Jesus Christ, for on our account He wants to open the heavenly and divine fountain of the holy Sacrament of confession where bubbles and effervesces the good, pure and preciously transparent water with which our soul is washed and purified of its sinful blackness and dirtiness. Now first it is very necessary that we teach you, opening your eyes concerning what is the dark and obscure night in which you still live and with which you greatly frighten and scandalize the other Christians who are your neighbors, the Spaniards. For they see that you are not strong in the faith, that still today the holy faith has not yet taken root and borne fruit in your heart.

[2 RECTO]

Wherefore God's faith and service to Him is perfectly sweet and fragrant—and as for you, if it is not by force and fear, you do not willingly make acts of faith. But this is not what God wants for it is to be completely willingly, especially what I inform you of now concerning the Sacrament of confession; it is to be done and realized in the [following] way.

You who want and desire to purify your soul of its sinful dirtiness and blackness: here is what you will do and carry out. First you will turn to look behind you at your past life, counting and going after all the sins with which you offended God, your Deity and Ruler, with which you offended Him who does not merit offense, with which you did not love Him Who is entirely worthy of being honored and loved.

[2 VERSO]

Y estando ya muy satisfecho, y enterado, que todos los tienes aperceuidos, y promptos en tu memoria, sin que nada te quede que remnerda¹ tu conciencia, y dè pena a tu coraçon: con summo dolor, y contricion, los descubrirás y confessarás al Confessor, començando los pecados graues y mortales, dexando para la postre los leues y veniales, que son con los que vosotros siempre començays, diziendo, murmurè, reî, &c. No trayendo en vuestra confession multitud, y maquina de palabras con que la confundis, y no la days a entender a vuestros confeßores, enfadandolos con tantos cir[3 recto]cunloquios, modos, y rodeos de hablar que tiene vuestra lengua. Pensays, que todos la mamaron en la leche, y se criaron con ella? Sino que de la manera que sucedio, è incurristes en el pecado; assi mismo lo aueis de descubrir, y manifestar al Confessor, no achacandolo a otros

[3 RECTO]

disculpandoos con ellos. Ni tampoco dexando de confessar pecado alguno, tragandolo para esconderlo en vuestro coraçon, por graue, è inorme que sea, como algunos de vosotros torpes, y necios lo suelen hazer; porque con esso hazeis nulla, y de ningun prouecho vuestra confession, de tal manera que sera necessario voluer a confessar de nueuo quantos pecados auiades confessado, por el tiempo que ocultasteis el tal pecado, aunque los ayais confessado muchas vezes, y os ayan absuelto por [3 verso] ellos por auer mentido ante el Diuino Acatamiento de Dios que todo lo está mirando, y no se le esconde cosa alguna, todo está patente a su divina Magestad, hasta los mas escondidos rincones de nuestros coraçones. Y por esto cometen vn grauissimo sacrilegio, los que tal hazen por querer engañar a quien no puede ser engañado. Y para cumplir con tu obligacion, y hazer vna verdadera, y entera confession:

[2 VERSO]

And now, being very satisfied and informed that you have them all prepared and ready in your memory, with nothing remaining to gnaw at your conscience and pain your heart: with great distress and contrition you will reveal and confess them to your confessor, beginning with the grave and mortal ones, and leaving for the last the lesser and venial ones, which are those with which you always begin, saying "I gossiped," "I laughed," etc., not bringing into your confession a multitude and imposing structure of words with which you confuse it and do not make it understandable to your confessors, annoying them with so many circumlocutions, ways and roundabout manners of speaking that your language has. Do you think that everyone suckled it in their mother's milk and grew up with it? Rather, in the way the sin happened and you fell into it, likewise you are to reveal and manifest it to the confessor, not attributing it to others,

[3 RECTO]

excusing yourselves with them. Nor failing to confess some sin, swallowing it in order to hide it in your heart, however grave and enormous it might be, as some of you who are dense and stupid are accustomed to do. Because with this you make null and void your confession, such that it will be necessary to return to again confess as many sins as you had confessed during the time you hid the said sin, even though you have confessed them many times and they have absolved you of them, on account of having lied before the Divine Reverence of God Who sees everything and from Whom nothing is hidden, everything is patent to His Divine Majesty, even the most hidden corners of our hearts. And for this reason those who do such a thing commit a great sacrilege, wanting to deceive Him Who cannot be deceived. In order to comply with your obligation and make a true and complete confession,

---

1. remnerda: read *remuerda.*

[2 VERSO]

mahuiztlazotlaloni. Auh intla ye iuhqui intla moch oticzentlali in motlatlacol, intla àoctle quitequipachoa in moyolo, niman yca tichocaz, yca telçizihuiz titlaocoyaz, in oticmoteopohuili in mahuizTeotzintli Dios auh niman tipehuaz in ticpohuiliz ticpantlaxiliz in moteyolcuiticauh yca tipehuaz in huehuei in temictiani tlatlacoli, zatepan tictenehuaz in tepiton, in azo teca otimononotz otihuetzcac oticamanalo &c. Auh ámo titlatolzaçacaz ámo tlatoltica tictlatiz ticquimiloz in motlatlacol, ca ic ticohuetiliz in moneyolcuitiliz, auh ca àmo melahuac mitzcaquiz in moteyolcuiticauh ca zan ic ticxiuhtlatiz, canel oc zentlamantli in amotlatol; cuix mochi tlacatl ipan omohuapauh omozcalti? Ca cenca ohue. Zan in quenin omochiuh in quenin ipan otihuetz tlatlacoli zan ye no huel iuhqui in ticmocuitiz in ticytaz ámo no tetech tictla-

[3 RECTO]

miz, teca timoquixtiz. Auh niman àmo ze ticpinahuizcahuaz nozo ticmauhcacahuaz in manel ye zenca tetzauhtlotlacoli[1] in yuhqui oc zequintin xolopitin quichihuani ypampa intla yuhqui ticchihuaz ca ic ticnenquixtia ticnenpoloa, in moneyolcuitiliz, ca àcan onpohui ca oc zepa monequi in ixquixihuitl otictlatitinenca tlatlacoli ticmocuitiz yancuican in izquixiue[2] tlatlacoli tlapilchihuali yeica ca in oquic otiztlacatinenca ca àtle onpouh in moneyolcuitiliz in manel ye zaço quezquipa otiteochihualoc, canel oticmotlatililizquia in Dios in tlatlacoli in moch quimotztilitica in moch ixpantzinco panhuetztica in ixquich toyolo itec tictlatiznequi, auh yeica in in çenca huei tlatlacoli quichihua in aquique quimoztlacahuiliznequi in áic huel iztlacahuiloni. Auh in huel ic tictzonquixtiz ticneltiliz in melahuac in mahuiztic neyolcuitiliztli ti-

[2 VERSO]

And if it is in this manner, if you gathered together all your sins, if there is nothing eating away at your heart, then weep, sigh and be sad because you offended the honored deity God. Then begin talking to your confessor revealing your sins to him, beginning with the great and mortal sins, afterwards mentioning the small ones (perhaps you spoke ill of another or laughed at him or made jokes about him, etc.). Do not speak nonsense, do not hide and wrap up your sins with [a multitude of obscure?] words, for thus you will put your confession in danger and the confessor will not rightly understand you, he will become impatient with it since your language is another thing altogether. Has everyone been reared and raised in it? For it is very difficult. Just how it happened, how you fell into the sin; in the very same fashion you will confess what you saw, not shifting the blame to others

[3 RECTO]

to excuse yourself. Do not omit even one because of shame or fear even though it is a very great and abominable sin as other fools are accustomed to doing, because if you do so you uselessly waste and lose your confession, for it is insufficient and lacking. It will again be necessary for all the years you hid the sin that you confess anew all your big sins and failings because while you lied your confession was insufficient and lacking even though you were given absolution many times, since you would have hidden the sin from God Who sees all and before Whom all that we want to hide in our hearts is patent. And because of this, those who want to deceive Him Who is never worthy of being deceived commit a very great sin. To bring properly to a conclusion and realize the true and honorable confession you

---

1. tetzauhtlotlacoli: read *tetzauhtlatlacoli*.
2. izquixiue: perhaps to be read *ixquich in huei*.

[3 VERSO]

aduierte, y mira si tienes a tu cargo alguna cosa, que satisfacer, ora sea de honra, ora sea de hazienda: y vueluela luego, y restituyela, sin que quede a tu cargo cosa alguna. Y si estuuieres muy pobre: pon el cuydado debido para vuscarla, porque si no es desta manera: no cumples con tu obligacion, y con tu confession. Y mucho mas si no vuelues luego la [4 recto] honra que eres a cargo, desdiciendote ante quien la quitaste. Y para que en el discurso de tu confession no te perturbes, y confundas tu memoria: ve discuriendo por los diez Mandamientos, por el orden que aqui va puesto, y con esso te acordarás en que as pecado, y incurrido, acerca del primero, acerca del segundo, &c. Que tambien tu Confessor te yra preguntando por ellos aduirtiendote, y enseñandote en todas faltas que as cometido, en cada vno dellos conforme se fuere offreciendo, y no por esto a de auer castigo, ni açotes, sino que el te dará piadosamente

[4 RECTO]

la penitencia que conuenga, y tu la reciuirás con toda humildad, y reuerencia, y la cumpliras luego.

COMIENZA EL Confessionario Mayor.

[4 VERSO]

PLATICA, con la qual se le da á entender a el Penitente, el secreto que está obligado á tener el Confessor de los pecados que se les confiessan, por tener los Naturales muy entendido lo contrario, con que siempre niegan los pecados mas enormes.

HIjo mio, pues á sido Dios Nuestro Señor seruido de darte vida hasta esta tiempo, en que vienes

[3 VERSO]

Notice and pay close attention to whether you are responsible for providing satisfaction in something, whether it might be of honor or property, and return it right away and give it back, without you remaining responsible for anything [else]. And if you are very poor: put the appropriate care into looking for it, because if it is not [done] in this way, you do not comply with your obligation and fulfill your confession. And much more so if you do not then restore the honor for which you are responsible, retracting what you said before the one from whom you took it. And so that in the course of your confession you do not disturb yourself and confound your memory: go through the Ten Commandments in the order set here, and with this you will remember in what you have sinned and incurred concerning the first, concerning the second, etc. Your confessor will also go along advising and teaching you about all the mistakes you have made, in each one of them in accordance with what may present itself, and not on this account does there have to be punishment nor lashes, rather that he will kindly give you

[4 RECTO]

the appropriate penance, and you will receive it with all humility and reverence and carry it out right away.

THE Large Guide to Confession begins.

[4 VERSO]

SPEECH with which the penitent is given to understand the secrecy that the confessor is obliged to have concerning the sins confessed to him, on account of the natives having understood the opposite, whereupon they always deny [committing] the biggest sins.

MY child, God our Lord has been good enough to give you life until this moment in which you come

cytaz intla itla momamal mochiuhtica in aço
teaxca tetlatqui nozo temahuizo, auh niman
mitzcahuaz tictecuepiliz, ahue[3] intla zenca
ticnotlacatl timotolinia mitztequipochoz[4] inic
tictemoz tictecuepiliz yeica intlacamo mitzcahua
in tlen momamal mochihua ca amo ticaxiltiz in
melahuac neyolcuitiliztli oc zenca qualca[5] in
temahuizo, ca teixpan timotlatolcuepaz inic
tictecuepiliz. Auh inic amo cana timotzotzonatiuh
timotlalnamiquiliztlapaloltiz[6] in ipan
moneyolcuitiliz, Zan xictepotztocatiuh in nican
micuiloa in tetlatlaniliztli in itechcopa matlactli
teotenahuatili ca oncan moyolo maçiz in tlen
ticytlaco in itechcopa ze in itechcopa ome &c.
Auh ca zan ye no ipan mitztlatlanitiaz in
moteyolcuiticauh; auh in canin imonecyan ca ic
mitznonotzaz ca ic mitzyzcaliz in tlein moyolo
quimati oticchiuh, auh àmo mecatica zan paca
yocox-

ca mitzmacaz in tlen motlamazehualiz Penitencia,
auh in tehuatl mozéyolocacopa ticzeliz ihuan
ticneltiliz inic ticaxiltiz in tlein quimonequiltia in
Dios.

§§

*NICAN, OMPE*hua in huei neyolcuitiliz, Amatl.[7]

¶ Tenonotzaliztli ic momelauhacacaquiltiz[8] in
moyolcuitia, in quenin, huel ynahuatil in teyolcuitiani in huel qnipiaz,[9] huel quitlatiz in tetlatlacol, ypampa in maçehualtin ca niman àmo yuh
quimati, ypampa in mochipa, quitlatia in huehuei
tlatlacoli.

*NO*tlaçopiltzine, in nican axcan, otihualmo-
huicac, in oquimonequilti in Dios oc no tehuan
otaçico in ipan inin cahuitl

are to see if perhaps someone else's goods and
property or honor have become your responsibility. Then you are to be relieved [of obligation];
you will make restitution. If you are a very poor
and needy person you will anxiously search for
the restitution you will make because if you are
not relieved of what has become your responsibility you will not comply with your obligation to
make up for what is lacking [to make your] confession true, especially [as concerns] honor—you
will make restitution by publicly retracting your
statements. And so that nowhere in your confession will you be doubtful and remember things in
a confused manner, just go along following the
questions written here about the Ten Commandments of God, for there you will remember with
certainty concerning the first sin you committed,
concerning the second, etc. Likewise your confessor will question you on it, and where it is necessary he will admonish and instruct you
concerning what your heart knows you did, and
not with whips but peacefully and calmly

he will give you your penance, and you will
receive it with all your heart and carry it out so
that you comply with what God wants.

§§

HERE BEGINS the large book of Confession.

¶ Admonitory speech with which he who is confessing is correctly given to understand how the
confessor is very obligated to guard and hide well
other people's sins, because the natives do not
regard it as that way at all, wherefore they always
hide the big sins.

MY beloved child, you have come here today, and
in addition God has willed that we have [lived to]
reach this time

---

3. ahue: perhaps to be read *auh ye.*

4. mitztequipochoz: read *mitztequipachoz.*

5. oc zenca qualca: here and elsewhere, perhaps to be
read *oc zenca ca hualca.*

6. timotlalnamiquiliztlapaloltiz: read *timotlalnamiquil-
iztlapololtiz.*

7. neyolcuitiliz, Amatl: read *neyolcuitilizAmatl.*

8. momelauhacacaquiltiz: read *momelahuacacaquiltiz*
(see Molina 1977, 55r).

9. qnipiaz: read *quipiaz.*

[4 VERSO]

a labar las llagas, y maculas de tu alma, que á sido
vna merced, y vn fauor del Cielo, muy graude;[2]
porque quantos, y quantos tuvieron por muy
cierto de llegar a merecer los que agora alcanças, y
no les dio lugar la muerte? Aora pues hijo no te
turbes, ni tengas verguença de mi; porque aunque
estoy en lugar de Dios y soy su Ministro, soy
hombre como tu, y si me dexa [5 recto] de su
mano, puede ser que cayga y me enlode en mayores pecados, que tu. Y assi hijo mio, dî, y confiessa tus culpas, que avnque sean las que se
fueren, no me han de espantar pues estamos en el
mundo, y no te ponga por delante el demonio,

[5 RECTO]

que sea posible, que yo pueda reuelar tus pecados;
porque el mesmo Dios nos á mandado guardemos
secreto en la confession, y si por desgracia algun
Confessor se descuydasse en alguna cosa, acerca
desto, le yria muy mal, castigandole
rigurosissimamente nuestra madre la santa
Iglesia, privandole de su officio, para siempre, y
dandole otra mayor pena y castigo, y assi hijo
mio, di tus pecados sin ningun rezelo, pues saues
que en nada me è de enfadar sino oyrte de muy
buena gana, que á Dios confiessas tus [5 verso]
culpas cuya misericordia es infinita, pues quiso
por el amor que nos tiene morir en vna Cruz:
agora pues no tengas miedo,

[4 VERSO]

to wash the sores and blemishes from your soul.
That has been a great mercy and favor of Heaven,
because how many were certain of reaching the
point of deserving what you now have reached,
and death gave them no chance? Now then, child,
do not be disturbed, do not be ashamed [before]
me, because although I am in the place of God
and am His minister I am a man like you, and if
He releases me from his grasp it could happen
that I would fall and dirty myself in greater sins
than you. And thus, my child, say and confess
your offenses that, be they what they may, they
cannot frighten me since we are [together] in
[this sinful] world, and let the devil not put
before you

[5 RECTO]

the possibility that I might reveal your sins,
because the same God has ordered us to guard the
confidentiality of confession, and if unfortunately
some confessor is careless in something concerning this it will go very badly with him, our mother
the holy Church punishing him most rigorously,
depriving him forever of his office and giving him
other greater penalties and punishments. And
thus, my son, speak your sins without any mis-
giving, since you know that I will be angered by
nothing but rather very willingly hear you; it is to
God whose mercy is infinite that you confess your
faults, since He died on a cross on account of the
love He has for us. Now then, have no fear

---

2. graude: read *grande*.

[4 VERSO]

inic axcan ticpapacaz, ticchipahuaz in moyolia
maniman anca nele axcan çenca huei in
omolhuiltic omomaçehualtic, in ilhuicac
tetlauhtilli, quexquichtin in oc no tehuan,
omomatia oquimomacehuizquia in ye axcan
ticmomaçehuia, auh áocmo quimomaçehuique.
Auh inin macamo quen xicmochihuili in mix in
moyollo, macamo xinechpinahua macamo
xinechmamati, ca in maçihui in i, yeyantzinco[10]
nica in Dios, yhuan nixiptlatzin, ca nitlalticpac
tlacatl yuhqui tehuatl, ca no huelitiz in ninalahuaz
ninoçoquipetzcoz yhuan oc qualca ninoçoquine-
loz in ámo tehuatl; intlacamo nechmopalehuilli in
Dios in ihuicpa ninomaquixtiz in tlatlacolli; auh
in axcan xicmitalhui xicpoa, in tlen motlapil-
chihual, in manel çenca temamauhti teyçahui, ca
àmo ic nimitznotetzahuiz canel tlalticpac in
ticate, yhuan macamo no mitzilnamicti in tla

[5 RECTO]

catecolotl, in aço aca huel nicilhuiz nicnextiliz, ca
niman amo huel mochihuaz, yeyca in titeyol-
cuitia, ca otechmoçennahuatilli in Dios inic ytec
in toyollo ticcentzatzaquazque ticpiazque in
tetlatlacol, auh intla çe teyolcuitiani, quenmanian,
ytla, quicama, macahuani,[11] ca çenca huei in ipan
mochihuazquia, ca çenca huey inic quimotlatza-
cuiltilizquia, in santa Iglesia; ca ycenmayan
quicahualtizquia, in itequiuh, in teyolcuitiliztli,
yhuan ytla oc çentlamantli, oc qualca huei,
tetlatzacuitiliztli, ypan mochihuazquia. Auh in
axcan xicmitalhui, xicmopohuilli, in motlatlacol,
ca amo ic ninotequipachoz, ca huel noçenyolo-
cacopa, in nimitzcaquiz, canel yehuatzin in Dios
in ticmolhuilia, in ixpantzinco timoyolcuitia, auh
ca çenca icnoancatzintli,[12] canel çenca huei,
tetlaçotlaliztica, mopampa Cruztitech
omomiquilli, auh in axcan amo ximotequi-

[4 VERSO]

so that now you bathe and purity your soul, such
that truly indeed today you have been fortunate
and enjoyed a very great heavenly favor. How very
many others thought they deserved what you now
enjoy and did not attain what they deserved? Now
then, do not disturb your spirits, do not be
ashamed [or] embarrassed before me, for even
though I am taking God's place and am substitut-
ing for Him I am a person of the earth like you. It
is also possible for me to slip and slide in the mud
[of sin] and get myself more mixed up in the
muck [of sin] than you, if God had not helped me
save myself from my sins. Now speak up and
recount what are your sins; even though they are
very frightening and scandalous I will not be
scandalized by them since we are in a world [of
sins], and also do not let the devil make you think

[5 RECTO]

that I might say and reveal them to another. It can
in no way occur because God has ordered all of us
confessors to completely shut up and guard in
our hearts other people's sins. And if a confessor
sometime lets something slip from his mouth it
will go very badly with him, for the holy Church
will punish him severely, prohibit him forever
from [exercising] his job as a confessor, and other
especially great punishments would happen to
him. Now speak up and recount your sins. I will
not be uneasy with them for most willingly I will
hear them from you since you are speaking to and
confessing before God Himself. He is very compassionate since with very great love and charity
He died for you on the cross. And now, do not
trouble yourself

---

10. i, yeyantzinco: read *iyeyantzinco*.
11. quicama, macahuani: read *quicamamacahuani*.
12. icnoancatzintli: read *icnouacatzintli*.

[5 VERSO]
sino muy gran dolor de hauer offendido a quien jamas debe ser ofendido, y el que te a de perdonar. Persignate di la Confession.

Per signum Crucis de inimicis nostris libera nos Deo[3] noster, in nomine Patris, & Fili, & spiritus Sancti &c.

Confiteor Deo omnipotenti, Beatœ Mariœ semper Virgini, beato Michaeli Archangelo, beato Ioanni Baptistœ, sanctis Apostolis Petro & Paulo, Nomine omnibus Sanctis, & tibi Pater, quia peccaui nimis cogitatione, verbo, & opere mea culpa, mea culpa, mea maxima culpa: ideo precor

[6 RECTO]
beatam Mariam semper Virginem, beatum Michaelem [6 recto] Archangelum, beatum Ioannem Baptistam, sanctos Apostolos Petrum, & Paulum Nomine omnes Sanctos, & te Pater orare pro me ad Dominum Deum nostrum.

PREGVNTAS, y *Respuesta*s vniuersales, para antes de la Confession.

Pregunta. Quanto tiempo á que te confessaste. *Respuesta*. Ha vn año, dos, tres, &c.

En que entiendes? Qual es tu oficio, en que ganas de comer? *Respuesta*. Soy Gouernador Alcalde, &c. l. soy Pintor Carpintero, Albañi[l], labrador, &c.

[5 VERSO]
but rather greater sorrow at having offended Him who must never be offended and Him Who is to pardon you. Cross yourself; say the confession.

Through the sign of the cross from our enemies deliver us our God. In the name of the Father and of the Son and of the Holy Spirit. etc. [sic]

I confess to Almighty God, to blessed Mary ever virgin, blessed Michael the Archangel, blessed John the Baptist, the holy apostles Peter and Paul, all the saints, and you Father that I have sinned exceedingly in thought, word and deed, through my fault, through my fault, through my most grievous fault. Therefore I beseech

[6 RECTO]
blessed Mary ever virgin, blessed Michael the Archangel, blessed John the Baptist, the holy apostles Peter and Paul, all the saints, and you, Father, to pray for me to the Lord our God.

UNIVERSAL questions and *Answer*s for before confession.

Question. How long since you confessed? *Answer*. It has been one year, two, three, etc.

What do you do? In what occupation do you make a living? *Answer*. I am a governor, alcalde, etc. / I am a painter, carpenter, bricklayer, farm laborer, etc.

---

3. Deo: read *Deus.*

[5 VERSO]

pacho, çan huel xictonehua in moyolo, inic oticmoteopohuilli, in amo teopoaloni, ca mitzmopalehuiliz, mitzmocnoytiliz Ximixicuilo, xicyto in Confession.

Ica in imachio in Cruz ninomachiotia, ma xitechmomaquixtili, toTeotzine, in inhuicpa in toyaohuan, yca in itocatzin teTatzin, Tepiltzin, spiritu Sancto, ma yuh mochihua.

Ninoyolcuitia ixpantzinco in çenhuelitini, teotl Dios, yhuan in mochipa moçemaçitzinotica çenquizcachipahuac ichpochtli Santa Maria yhuan in San Miguel Archangel, San Iuan Baptista Santotin Apostoles San Pedro San Pablo in mochintin Sanctome yhuan tehuatzin tinoteyolcuiticatzin, canel çenca onitlatlaco, tlalnamiquiliztica, tlatoltica tlachihualiztica, ica in notlatlacol in notlatlacol, ica in nohueytlatlacol. Auh ypampa in cenca nicnotlatlauh-

[6 RECTO]

tilia in çemicac moçemacitzinotica, çenquizcachipahuac ichpochtli, Santa Maria, yhuan in San Miguel Archangel, San Iuan Baptista, Sanctotin Apostoles San Pedro San Pablo, yhuan in tehuatzin tinoteyolcuiticatzin ma nopampa xicmotlatlauhtilican in notlatocatzin Dios, ma yuh mochihua.

¶ *TETLATLANILIZ*tli ic moçentlatlanizque in ixquichtin moyolcuitiznequi, in ayamo quipehualtia in inneyolcuitiliz.

YE quexquich cahuitl in otimoyolcuiti *Respuesta.* ca ye ze xihuitl ye òxihuitl &c.

Tlen motequiuh, tlen moficio? Tlen ic timotla-yecoltia, *Respuesta.* Ca niGouernador Nalcalde &c. l. nitlacuilo niquauhxinqui nitetzotzonqui, nitlalchiuhqui &c.

[5 VERSO]

but make your heart really burn with the pain of having offended Him Who does not merit offense, for He will help you and have mercy on you. Cross yourself; say the confession.

I make the sign of the cross on myself. O our God, save us from our enemies. In the name of the Father, Son and Holy Spirit. Amen.

I confess before the all-powerful deity God, and the ever perfectly and completely virgin Saint Mary, and Saint Michael Archangel, and Saint John the Baptist, and the holy apostles Saint Peter and Saint Paul, and all the saints, and you my confessor, for I have sinned with thought and word and deed, with my sins, my sins, with my great sins. Because of this I greatly implore

[6 RECTO]

the eternally perfect and completely pure virgin Saint Mary, and Saint Michael Archangel, and Saint John the Baptist, and the holy apostles Saint Peter and Saint Paul, and you my confessor: pray to our Ruler God for me. Amen.

¶ *QUESTIONS* which all who want to confess will be asked before they begin their confession.

HOW long has it been since you confessed? *Answer.* One year, two years, etc.

What is your job? How do you make a living? *Answer.* I am a governor, I am an alcalde, etc. / I am a painter, a carpenter, a stonemason, I work the land, etc.

[6 VERSO]

Que estado tienes? Eres casado, viudo, ò soltero. Y si fueren mugeres les preguntará desta manera.

Eres casada, viuda, ò soltera, o doncella. [6 verso]

Respuesta. Soy casada, l. soy viuda, l. soy soltera, l. soy doncella.

Sabes la Dotrina Christiana? Las quatro Oraciones, y los Articulos. *Respuesta.* Si se, l. no.

As examinado tu conciencia, y hecho memoria de tus pecados para que me los confiesses? *Respuesta.* Si Padre, todos los tengo recorridos, y en la memoria. Por ventura quieres esconder, y dexar de confessar algun pecado, de miedo o de verguença? O lo as dexado de confessar y lo ocultaste en alguna confession passada? *Respuesta.* Si l. vn pecado dexè de confessar, por miedo, y verguença que tuve en las confessiones passadas, sin quererlo manifestar ni descrubrir,

[7 RECTO]

remitiendolo para la hora de mi muerte, y entonces confessarlo, y dezirlo.

No, sino que luego lo con[7 recto]fiesses, y me digas que pecado es, y no tengas miedo, ni verguença, pues saues que me tiene Dios en este lugar para labar tu alma de todas tus llagas, y podres, que no me marauillare de ti; pues todos somos pecadores *Respuesta.* Si Padre muy bien dizes que pues estás para vañar, y limpiar nuestras almas donde nos as de echar, ò embiar? Digo pues que hize, y cometi como flaco, y mal que soy, vn grauissimo pecado de Sodomia, y es que estando borracho tube acto carnal con otro hombre, &c.

Y quantas vezes, te as confessado despues que niegas esse pecado? *Respuesta.* Quatro, l. cinco vezes, &c. Hijo lo que te importa es, que aora de nueuo tornes a examinar todos los pecados que as cometido en esse tiempo, que á que niegas esse pecado. Por[7 verso]que avnque te confessauas; por razon de dexar de confessar esse pecado, hazias las confessiones nullas, è invalidas, avnque v[e]ias que te absoluian por los demas pecados. Aora pues ve a tu casa,

[6 VERSO]

What is your marital status? Are you married, a widower, or single? And if they are women they will be questioned in this way.

Are you married, a widow, or a maiden? *Answer.* I am married / I am a widow / I am single / I am a maiden.

Do you know Christian doctrine? The four prayers and the articles of the faith? *Answer.* Yes, I know / no.

Have you examined your conscience and tried to remember your sins in order to confess them to me? *Answer.* Yes, Father, I have gone over them and have them in mind.

Perhaps you want to hide and leave off confessing some sin from fear or shame? Or did you fail to confess it and you hid it in some past confession? *Answer.* Yes / I failed to confess a sin on account of the fear and shame I had in past confessions, not wanting to show and reveal it,

[7 RECTO]

putting it off until the hour of death, and then confessing and saying it.

No, rather that you confess it right away and tell me what sin it is, and do not be afraid nor ashamed, since you know that God has me in this place in order to cleanse your soul of all your sores and pus; I will not be amazed at you, for we are all sinners. *Answer.* Yes, Father, you are very right to say that you are for washing and cleansing our souls; where will you cast or send us? So I say I did and committed, like the weak and bad [person] that I am, a very grave sin of sodomy, and that is being drunk I had a carnal act with another man, etc.

And how many times did you confess after denying that sin? *Answer.* Four / five times, etc. Child, what is important to you now is to reexamine again all the sins you have committed in that time [while] you denied that sin. Because [7 verso] although you went to confession, by reason of failing to confess that sin you made your confessions null and void, even though you saw that they absolved you for your other sins. Now then go to your home,

[6 VERSO]

Cuix tinamique? Cuix ticnooquichtli? Cuix zan iuh tinemi? Titelpochtli? Auh intla çihuatzitzintin motlatlanizque.

Cuix tinamique cuix ticnoçihuatl, cuix nozo zan iuh tinemi, cuix nozo huel oc timaçitica t, ichpochtli?[13] *Respuesta.* Ca ninamique ca nicnoçihuatl ca çan iuh ninemi ca huel oc ninazitica nichpochtli.

Cuix ticmati, in teoyotl? In nauhtlamantli, yhuan in neltoconi? *Respuesta,* ca quemaca ca nicmati, l. àmotzin.

Cuix o moch tic, ilnamic[14] in motlatlacol? Cuix o moch ticnechico, inic axcan nixpan, ticmocuitiz. *Respuesta.* Ca quemacatzin, ca o moch nicçentlali?

Azo çe ticmauhcacahuaznequi, ticpinauhcacahuaznequi anozo o çe ticpinahuizcauh oticpinahuiztlatih in yquac oc cepa otimoyolcuiti. *Respuesta.* Ca quemaca ca o çe nictlatica nicpinahuizcauhca, nicmauhcacauhca, in notlatlacol ámo nicnocuitica ca

[7 RECTO]

nicytoa, ca quin iquac in nomiquiliztepan nicnextitehuaz nicpantlaztehuaz.

Xicyto, xictenehua catle, huatl[15] ámo ximo-mauhti ámo xipinahua, ca ic nican nechmo-tlalillia, in Dios in nicpapacaz in miyaca in mopalanca, ca àmo nimitznotetzahuiz canel titla[tla]coonime.[16] *Respuesta* Ca melahuac in ticmitalhuia ca timoteàaltilia ca timotepapaquilia timoteçencahuilia, campa nel nozo tinechmo-tlaxiliz? Auh ca onicchiuh ca onicnotequiuhti in áchihualoni tetzauhtlatlacolli, ca in iquac nitlahuanqui çe tlacatl oquichtli itech onacic &c.

Auh quezquipa, in ye ipan timoyolcuitia, inon tlatlacolli? *Respuesta.* Ca ye nauhpa, macuilpa, &c. In axcan monequi oc çepa iancuican tictepotztocaz oc çepa, in izquixiuhtlatlacoli, in oquic otictlatica oticteneuh axcan, yeica ca àtle, ompouh in izqui oticchiuh neyolcuitiliztli. Auh in axcan xiauh in mo-

[6 VERSO]

Are you married? Are you a widower? Are you single? A young unmarried man? And if they are women they will be asked:

Are you married? Are you a widow? Or are you single? Or perhaps you are still a maiden? *Answer.* I am married, I am a widow, I am single, I am still a maiden.

Do you know spiritual things? The four [prayers] and the [14] articles of the faith? *Answer.* Yes, I know them / no.

Have you remembered all your sins? Have you gathered them all together to confess them now before me? *Answer.* Yes, I have gathered them all together.

Do you want to leave one out because of fear and shame or perhaps you left one out and hid it because of shame when you confessed on another occasion? *Answer.* Yes, I hid my sin, I left it out because of shame and fear. I did not confess it, for

[7 RECTO]

I say that then at the time of my death I will quickly reveal and manifest it.

Say and declare what it is. Do not be afraid [or] ashamed for God has placed me here to wash away your sinful stink and rottenness; I will not be scandalized by you for we are [all] sinners. *Answer.* What you say is true, for you bathe and wash people, preparing them. What else would you do with me? And I have committed and been responsible for what is unworthy of doing, the abominable sin [of sodomy], for when I was drunk I committed a carnal act with [another] man.

And how many times have you confessed since [you committed] that sin? *Answer.* It is already four times, five times, etc. Now again it is neces-sary to newly pursue this matter for the years of sin while you had hidden the one you mentioned today, because all the confessions you made [dur-ing that time] are insufficient and count as noth-ing. Now go to your

---

13. t, ichpochtli: read *tichpochtli.*
14. tic, ilnamic: read *ticilnamic.*
15. catle, huatl: read *catlehuatl.*
16. titla[tla]coonime: read *titla[tla]coanime.*

y examina, y quenta quantos pecados as hecho,
desde que ocultas esse pecado, para que todos
juntos me los bueluas a confessar aqui donde, de
muy buena gana quedo aguardandote, para aiu-
darte, que para esso me puso Dios aqui, y me lo
manda. *Respuesta.* Si Padre, yo voluere mañana, y
te agradesco mucho el bien que me hazes.

Traes proposito firme de no pecar, ò tienes en
tu casa alguna mala ocasion, que presumes, que es
proxima a que peques con ella. *Respuesta.* Si
Padre, vna muger tengo en mi casa, y á mucho
tiempo que no quiero dexar su [8 recto] amistad.

Pues hijo ve aora luego y embiala a su casa, y
quitate della; porque de otra manera no valdra
nada la confeßion que hizieres: porque estás en
peligro de yr a pecar otra vez con ella. *Respuesta.*
Si Padre, yo hago firme proposito de apartarme
della.

Quantas vezes as reiterado este pecado, y
quantas te á mandado el Confessor,

que lo dexes, y te apartes della? *Respuesta.* Quatro,
ò cinco vezes.

Diote alguna penitencia el Confessor?
Respuesta. Si Padre. Cumpliste la Penitencia.
Respuesta. No Padre. Porque no la cumpliste?
estuviste impedido? *Respuesta.* No Padre, sino que
la dexè de cumplir, por pereça. Aora pues te
mando, cumplas luego la penitencia, que te doy
pues saues que con ella has de satisfacer a Dios
por tus pecados. [8 verso]

PREGVNTAS, y *Respuesta*s particulares, sobre los
diez Mandamientos de la ley de Dios, y los cinco
de la Yglesia, Siete obras de Misericordia, Sentidos
Corporales, Potencias del Alma,

and examine and count how many sins you have
committed since you hid that sin, so that when we
are together you confess them again here where
very willingly I remain awaiting you in order to
help you, since for that purpose God put me here
and commands me to it. *Answer.* Yes, Father, I will
return tomorrow, and I thank you very much for
the good you have done me.

Do you bring a firm resolve to not sin, or do
you have in your house some evil occasion that
you surmise is the proximate occasion that you
will sin with her? *Answer.* Yes, Father, I have a
woman in my house, and for some time I have
not wanted to break off our relationship.

Then, son, go right now and send her to her
[own] home and get rid of her, because otherwise
the confession you make will be worthless, [and]
because you are in danger of going to sin again
with her. *Answer.* Yes, Father, I firmly resolve to
keep away from her.

How many times have you repeated this sin,
and how many times

has the confessor ordered you to leave her and
keep away from her? *Answer.* Four or five times.

Did the confessor give you some penance?
Answer. Yes, Father. Did you perform the
penance? *Answer.* No, Father. Why did you not
perform it? Were you impeded [in some way]?
Answer. No, Father, rather I failed to perform it
on account of laziness. Now then I order you to
perform the penance that I [now] give you since
you understand that with it you are to satisfy God
for your sins. [8 verso]

SPECIFIC questions and *Answer*s about the ten
commandments of the law of God and the five of
the Church, the seven works of mercy, corporal
senses, the faculties of the soul,

[7 VERSO]

chan moch xictepotztoca xictlaolpoa, in
izquixiuhtlatlacolli quin moztla nozo huiptla,
tihualaz, timoyolcuitiquiuh, ca nican nimitzc-
hixtica, ca nozenyolocacopa, nimitzpalehuiz,
nimitzçencahuaz, canel notequiuh, canel
nonahuatil. *Respuesta.* Ca ye qualitzin
otinechmocnelilli ca moztla oc çepa nihualaz.

    Cuix oticçemixnahuati? Cuix otictelchiuh in
tlatlacolli, cuix noço àca mochan ticpia, in axcan
in mitztlatlacolcuititica. *Respuesta.* Ca quemaca ca
çe çihuatzintli nochan nicpixtica auh ca ye
ixquich, cahuitl in àmo niccahuaznequi.

    Xiauh niman axcan xicquixti, xicyhua
xictlalcahui, zatepan timozencahuaquiuh, yeica
intlacamo ca àtle onpohuiz in moneyolcuitiliz, ca
oc çepa, ynahuac titlatlacotiuh. *Respuesta,* Ca
quemaca ca tel axcan niccentelchihuaz.

    Auh xihualauh ye quezquipa in mitzcahualtia
in teyolcuitiani in tlatlacoli,

[8 RECTO]

in mitztlacahualtia, in amo ticcahuaznequi.
Respuesta. Ca ye nauhpa macuilpa, &c.

    Cuix omitztlamaçehualizmacac? *Respuesta.* Ca
quemaca. Auh cuix, oticneltili, in tlen ic, omitztla-
macehualmacca [sic]? *Respuesta.* Ca àmotzin.
Tleyca? Tle ypampa cuix àmo tihuelit? *Respuesta.*
Ca àmotzin ca çan onitlatziuh, ca ipampa in
oniccauh. Axcan niman xicneltilitihuetzi, in tlen
nimitznahuatia tlamazehualiztli, àmo xiccahua,
canel ic ticmoyolpachihuitilia in Dios in ipampa,
otitlatlaco.

    ¶ *TETLA[TLA]NILIZ*tli in ytechcopa in matlactetl,
yteotenahuatiltzin in Dios, yhuan ytechcopa in
macuiltetl inahuatiltzin Santa Iglesia, yhuan
ytechpa in izqui teicnoytaliztlachihualli, yhuan in
inematiliz in tonacayo, yhuan in ihuelitiliz in toyolia, yhuan no ytechcopa in

[7 VERSO]

home, pursue all of them, count with dried kernels of maize the sins of all the years. Then
tomorrow or the day after return to confess for I
am waiting for you; with all my heart I will help
and prepare you for that is my job and obligation.
Answer. That is good, thank you. Tomorrow I will
come again.

    Have you firmly resolved to despise sin or do
you now have in your home some person who
makes you sin? *Answer.* Yes, I am keeping a
woman in my house and for some time I have not
wanted to leave her.

    Go then, make her leave today, send her away,
make her relinquish her place, and later come to
confess, because if not your confession will be
insufficient and count as nothing for you will go
to sin with her again. *Answer.* Yes, [you are right],
but now I will scorn her.

    But come: how many times has the confessor
restrained you from sin,

[8 RECTO]

impeded you, and you did not want to relinquish
it? *Answer.* Four times, five times, etc.

    Did he give you some penance? *Answer.* Yes.
And did you carry out what he gave you as
penance? *Answer.* No. Why? For what reason? You
couldn't do it? *Answer.* No. I abandoned it just
because I was lazy. Now then, promptly carry out
the penance he ordered for you. Do not abandon
it, since with it you will give God satisfaction for
your sins.

    ¶ *QUESTIONS* concerning the ten divine com-
mandments of God, and concerning the five regulations of the holy Church, and about all the
works of mercy, and the senses of the body, and
the faculties of our souls, and also concerning

[8 VERSO]

y siete Pecados mortales, &c. Con las Platicas, y reprehensiones que son a proposito para cada lugar.

AS amado a Dios, sobre todas las cosas, y adorado, a su Diuina Magestad, sobre todas ellas, con todo tu coraçon, entendimiento, y voluntad? O as puesto el amor en otra criatura suya, adorandola, y teniendola por diuina, y venera[n]dola como a tal. *Respuesta.* Si è amado con todo mi coraçon, pero algunas vezes è creido en sueños, en yerbas, en el ololiuqui, y peyote, y otras cosas.

Creistelas con todo tu co[9 recto]raçon? *Respuesta.* No Padre, sino que por hauerlo oydo assi, de algunos, vna vez que otra lo he creydo.

As dudado

[9 RECTO]

en algun misterio de la Fe. *Respuesta.* No Padre.

As creydo, y tenido por muy cierta alguna supresticion, o seta,[4] de las que dexaron dichas tus Mayores, los viejos? *Respuesta.* Si, l, no.

Tienes hasta oy algunos idolillos de Chalchihuite? *Respuesta.* Si, l, no.

Los sacas al Sol a calentar, emboluiendolos en blandos algodones, con mucha veneracion, y respeto? *Respuesta.* Si, l. no.

Crees, y tienes por muy cierto, que los tales Chalchiguites te dan el sustento, como erradamente lo creyan los viejos tus mayores, que murieron en el gran pecado de la idolatria. Y crees, que te dan las riquezas, y bienes [9 verso] temporales, y todo lo que posees, y alcanças? Porque sauemos, y tenemos por muy cierto, que ay hasta el dia de oy muchos de vosotros,

[8 VERSO]

and the seven mortal sins, etc. With speeches and reprimands that are appropriate for each place.

Have you loved God above all things, and His Divine Majesty above all of them, with all your heart, mind and will? Or have you placed your love in another creature of His, worshipping it, taking it for divine, and venerating it as such? *Answer.* Yes, I have loved with all my heart, but sometimes I have believed in dreams, in [hallucinogenic] herbs, in ololiuhqui and peyote and other things.

Did you believe in them with all your heart? *Answer.* No, Father, rather on account of having heard it [was] so, one or another time I have believed it.

Have you doubted

[9 RECTO]

some mystery of the faith? *Answer.* No, Father.

Have you thought and believed to be very true some superstition or sect of those that your elders the ancients said? *Answer.* Yes / no.

Do you have even up to today little idols of chalchihuite? *Answer.* Yes / no.

Do you put them out in the sun to warm, wrapping them up in soft cotton with great veneration and respect? *Answer.* Yes / no.

Do you think and believe to be very true that the said chalchihuites give you sustenance, as the ancients your elders (who died in the great sin of idolatry) mistakenly used to believe? And do you believe that they give you riches and earthly goods and all that you possess and attain? Because we know and believe to be very true that there are up until today many of you

---

4. seta: read *secta.*

[8 VERSO]

in [sic] chicontetl, temichiani[17] tlatlacolli, auh no nican motlallia in izquitetl tenonotzaliztli in huel iyeyeyan.

CVix oticmotlaçotilli oticmoçenteomachiti, in çan huel yçeltzin in Dios, ipalnemoani, in huel mochi yca in moyolo in motlalnamiquiliz? Cuix noço, ytla, oc, zentlamantli in zan, ytlachihualtzin o itech, otimotlapololti in oticneltoca[c] oticteotlapiqui oticteoma. *Respuesta.* Ca quemaca onicnozentlaçotili mochi yca in noyolo, yeçe ca quenmanian, onicneltocac in temictli, in xiuhtzintli in peyotl in ololiuhqui? Yhuan in oc cequi tlamantli.

Cuix mochi yca in moyolo, oticilnamic oticneltocac, *Respuesta.* Ca àmotzin ca zan ipampa in que[n]mania[n] yuh niquinca[qui]lia in zequintin nohuanpohuan, &c.

Cuix itla teo, tlanelto-[18]

[9 RECTO]

quiliztlamahuiçolli o ytech timotlapololti? *Respuesta.* Ca ámotzin.

Cuix ytla, tlateotoquiliznecauhcayotl, in quiteneuhtihui huehuentoton, mocolhuan tlateotocanime oticneltocac, oticnelticama? *Respuesta.* Ca quemacatzin.

Cuix tiquinpixtica in mochan in chalchiuhcoconeme, chalchiuhtamaçoltin? *Respuesta.* Ca quemacatzin.

Cuix tonayan tiquinquixtia cuix, tiquintotonia? Cuix tiquimiychcaquimiloa tiquinmahuiztillia? *Respuesta.* Ca quemaca.

Cuix ticneltoca in ca yehuantin mitzmaca, in mocochca in moneuhca in yuh moztlacahuitihui huehuentoton mocolhuan in ipan omique in huey tlatlacolli tlateotoquiliztli? Auh cuix yuh timomati inca inpal tipactica, in ca yehuantin quitotonilia in moquiahuac in mothual in ca mitzmaca in axcaitl in necuiltonolli netlamachtilli? Ypampa ca ticmaticate ca amoncate anmiaquintin in amech

[8 VERSO]

the seven deadly sins. Also set down here are all the admonitory speeches, [each] in its separate place.

Have you loved and completely worshipped the only God, Giver of life, with all your heart and thoughts? Or have you become confused by something else, just a creature of His, believing in it, creating a false god, regarding it as divine? *Answer.* Yes, I have loved Him with all my heart, but at times I have believed in dreams, [hallucenogenic] herbs, peyote and ololiuhqui and other things.

Have you remembered them, believed in them with all your heart? *Answer.* No, it was just because at times I have heard such [and such a thing] from my neighbors, etc.

Have

[9 RECTO]

you become confused about some divine miracle? *Answer.* No.

Have you believed in and judged to be verified some remaining idolatries proclaimed by the little old men, your grandfathers and idolaters? *Answer.* Yes.

Are you guarding in your home [idols called] "turquoise children" and "turquoise toads"? *Answer.* Yes.

Do you bring them out into the sun to warm them? Do you wrap them up in cotton, honoring them? *Answer.* Yes.

Do you believe they give you your daily sustenance as the little old men your grandfathers (who died in great sin and idolatry) went along deceiving themselves? And do you think that by their grace and through them you are well off, that they enrich your household and give you property, wealth, and prosperity? Because we know that still today the devil goes about confusing many of you.

---

17. temichiani: read *temictiani.*
18. teo, tlanelto-: read *teotlanelto-.*

[9 VERSO]

que todavia lo hazen? *Respuesta.* Si Padre, es verdad lo que dizes, que no te lo tengo de negar pues estás en lugar de Dios, en mi casa tengo las cosas que me has dicho.

O pobre de ti, a quien el Demonio trae ciega [sic], y perdido, en aquella tenebrosa noche de ignorancias supersticiosas? Con que cara pareces ante el Acatamiento de Dios, que todo lo saue, y alcança? Que te importa el ser Christiano, y ser del rebaño del vnico, y verdadero Dios es posible que aun no acabas de estar enterado, y firme en el Credo, y Articulos de la Fè, que enseñan claramente, que solo Dios es el todopoderoso, y que solamente su [10 recto] diuina Magestad, es el que dá y aumenta todos los bienes, assi corporales, como espirituales? Pues que poder tienen essas pedresuelas? Por ventura tienen entendimiento, ò discurso? No por cierto, porque son vnas gomas de los riscos y peñascos. Agora

[10 RECTO]

vuestros proximos los Españoles buenos Christianos, que os exceden de manera en bienes espirituales, y temporales, que ninguno de vosotros les iguala, andan calentando al Sol, y emboluiendo en delicados algodones, Idolos, muñecas, y çapos de Chalchiguietes [sic] como hazeis vosotros? En solo Dios todopoderoso tienen puesta su fee, y esperança, á quien siempre estan rogando, y pidiendo lo que an menester, y venerando tan solamente la Imagen Sanctissima de Nuestro Señor Iesu Christo, y de su Madre [10 verso] bendita, y de todos sus Santos, á quien[es] occurren en sus trauajos, a pedir fauor, y ayuda, para sus necesidades? Que poder tiene el Demonio, que aun hasta el dia de oy no sabeis que es condenado, y aborrecido de Dios?

Aora pues, te mando, que no quieras hazerte ciego: pues claramente echas de ver que con esso quebrantas la Fè Catolica,

[9 VERSO]

who still do it. *Answer.* Yes, Father, you speak the truth, I cannot deny it to you since you represent God; in my house I have the things you spoke about.

O you poor wretch whom the devil brings blind and lost in that dark night of superstitious ignorance! How will you appear before the reverence of God, Who knows all and perceives all? What does it matter being Christian and of the flock of the only true God? Is it possible that you still do not comprehend and are firm in the Credo and articles of the faith that clearly point out that only God is the All-powerful, and that only His Divine Majesty is what gives and increases all goods, those of the body as much as those of the spirit? What power do little rocks have? Do they have understanding or speech? Certainly not, for they are excretions of cliffs and boulders. Now

[10 RECTO]

your neighbors the Spaniards (good Christians), who greatly exceed you in spiritual and earthly goods, whom none of you equal—do they walk around warming idols, dolls and little creatures of chalchihuite in the sun, and wrapping them up in delicate cottons as you do? They place their faith and hope only in Almighty God, to Whom they are always praying and asking for what they need, and venerating only the most holy image of our Lord Jesus Christ and of His blessed mother and of all His saints, to whom they turn in their hardships to ask for kindness and help with their pressing needs. What power has the devil, that even up to today you do not know that he is condemned and abhorred by God?

Now then, I order you to not want to make yourself blind, since you are beginning to clearly perceive that with this you undermine the Catholic faith

[9 VERSO]

tlapololtitinemi in tlacatecolotl in ça ye noma axcan? *Respuesta.* Ca quemaca ca melahuac in ticmitalhuia cuix nimitznotlatililiz? Canel tixiptlatzin in Dios, ca nochan niquinpixtica in otiquinmotenehuilli.

Tla[19] xihualauh nopiltze, timotolinia, in oc noma ça ye axcan tlayohuayan mextecomac mitznemitia in tlacatecolotl; auh quen moxayac ticchiuhti[ne]mi in ixpantzinco in Dios, in moch quimoçemmachiltitica; auh cátlehuatl inic timotenehua tiChristiano, inic, itetzinco tipouhqui in zan çe huel nelli teotl Dios ámo ye yuh ca in moyolo in ipan in huel nelli neltoconi Credo ihuan Articulos in ca zan huel yceltzin in Dios in zenhuelitilicecatzintli ca zan iceltzin quimotemaquilia in axcaitl in tlatquitl necuiltonolli netlamachtili. Tlen in hueli in tetotontin? Cuix tlacaqui? Cuix yolizmati? Amo zan tetl texcali ycocopalo, yocotzoyo in axcan

[10 RECTO]

àmohuampohuan Caxtilteca qualtin Christianos, in tlapanahuia ic mocuiltonoa motlamachtia in ámo anquimacizque cuix Chalchiuhcoconeme Chalchiuhtamazoltin quitotonitinemi? Quimiychcaquimilotinemi? Amo zan quimoçenmachiltitinemi in çan huel, yçeltzin neli teotl Dios, quimoçentlatlauhtilitinemi yhuan in imahuizixiptlatzin in totlaçotemaquixticatzin IESV Christo, yhuan in imahuizixiptlatzin in totlaçomahuiznantzin Santa Maria yhuan in intlaçoSanctotzitzihuan in quimoçenmachiltia, quinmotlatlauhtilia quinmotlaytlanililia, cuix itla ic quineneloa, in iuhqui amehuantin in tlaneltoquiliztlachihualli, auh tlen yhueli in tlacatecalotl?[22] Cuix ámo no motolinitinemi? Amo ytlatelchihualtzin in Dios?

Axcan nimitzçennahuatia nopiltze áocmo çepa tixpopoyotiz ca ic ticitlacoa in motlaneltoquiliz in

[9 VERSO]

Answer. Yes, what you are saying is true. Since you are God's representative: [how] can I hide it from you? In my home I have that which you have mentioned.

Come,[20] my wretched child, whom the devil still today maintains in the darkness of sin and the gloom [of ignorance]. With what countenance will you appear before All-knowing God? What of it that you call yourself a Christian and belong to the only true deity, God: are you not sure and firm in what is worthy of belief, the Credo and the articles of the faith, that absolutely only God is the Almighty and that only He gives people goods and property, wealth and riches? What power do miserable little rocks have? Do they have understanding? Are they prudent, wise and creative? No—just the excretions[21] of rocks and volcanic outcroppings. Now

[10 RECTO]

your neighbors the Spaniards (good Christians), surpassing [you] and you not reaching [i.e., equaling] them in wealth and riches: do they go around warming up little idols called "turquoise children" and "turquoise toads"? Do they go around wrapping them up in cotton? No, they just go around putting their faith and hope in the only true deity, God, praying as one to Him, and praying to and making petitions to the honored image of our beloved Savior Jesus Christ and to the honored image of our precious esteemed mother Saint Mary and to their beloved saints. Do they mix up works of faith with something [else] like you [do]? What power does the devil have? Is he not miserable, is he not condemned by God?

Now I firmly order you, my child, do not be blind again, for thus you damage your faith and

---

19. Beginning with this line and in the left margin is the following: *Platica primera, en la qual se les refuta, con proprios, y naturales terminos la falsa opinion, que a los Naturales, les ha quedado, el dia de oy, en creer, que los Chalchihuites, é Idolos de piedra de ijada, les dan los bienes temporales.*

22. tlacatecalotl: read *tlacatecolotl.*

20. Beginning with this line and in the left margin is the following: *First speech, in which with suitable and native terminology is refuted the false opinion that has remained nowadays with the natives in believing that the chalchihuites or idols of jade give them earthly goods.*

21. excretions: tentative translation here and in the facing passage.

que professas. Traeme luego essas figuras del
demonio, para echarlas por ay, que con esso te
darè la penitencia que conuenga para salud de tu
alma: porque el Demonio tiene muy aßido vuestro coraçon, y andays muy ciegos y herrados, y os
anda perturbando, y equiuocando en la Fé: para
que no acaueys de entender, y creer, que solo Dios
Nuestro Señor es el todopoderoso, y que de sola
su Diuina Magestad viene, y procede todo lo [11
recto] que aquesta maquina del mundo, á menester para su sustento, y conseruacion: el es el vni-
uersal dueño, y Señor de todo. No ay criatura por
bella, y hermosa que sea como lo son el Sol, Luna,
y Estrellas, que tenga algun poder de dar alguna
cosa: porque todas dependen de su diuina voluntad, y prouidencia: de tal manera, que si su diuina
Magestad no quisiera, ninguna se mouiera;

todas estan debaxo de su poder, y mano.

Crees hasta aora, que ay Ahuaquez?[5] *Respuesta.*
Si Padre.

Y crees, que estos tales, salen, y vienen del
serro Tlaloc, y de otros altos, y encumbrados
montes, quando al entrar de las aguas, se cubren,
y tocan de nuves, por quanto por el calor del Sol
vaporiçan las humedades de la tierra, y se con-
dençan en nuves, y [11 verso] agua? &c. Y tu estás
muy persuadido, que esto no sucede sino, por
medio de los Ahuaquez, y que ellos producen los
aguaceros. *Respuesta.* Si.

Y tienes muy creydo, que por ellos se dan los
frutos de la tierra, y vaisles a ofrecer hasta el dia
de oy, candelas, vasos copal? *Respuesta.* Si Padre,
lo que me preguntas es mucha verdad.

Y quantas vezes has hecho este pecado?
Respuesta. Tres,

that you profess. Bring me right away those
demonic figurines so that they can be tossed away,
that with this I will give you the penance appropriate for the health of your soul; because the
devil has firmly grasped hold of your heart, and
you go about very blind and mistaken, and he
makes you upset and mistaken in the faith, so that
you do not come to understand and believe that
only God our Lord is the All-powerful, and that
only from His Divine Majesty comes and pro-
ceeds all that imposing structure of the world
[and what] is necessary for its sustenance and
conservation: He is the universal Master and Lord
of everything. There is no creature, however
beautiful and lovely (as are the sun, the moon,
and the stars) that has any power to grant something, because all depend on His will and providence, such that if His Divine Majesty were not
willing, nothing would move,

all are under His power and hand.

Do you believe until now that there are
Ahuaques?[6] *Answer.* Yes, Father.

And do you believe that they come and go
from the mountain Tlaloc and from other high
and lofty mountains; [that] when the rainy season
begins they become overcast and touch the
clouds, and so by the heat of the sun the moisture
of the earth vaporizes and condenses into clouds
and water, etc.? And are you very convinced that
this does not happen except through the
Ahuaques, and that they produce the rainstorms.
Answer. Yes.

And do you strongly believe that by means of
them the fruits of the earth grow, and that up
until today you go to offer them candles, vessels,
and incense? *Answer.* Yes, Father, what you ask me
about is very true.

And how many times have you committed this
sin? *Answer.* Three,

---

5. To the right in the margin: *Ahuaquez, O Tlaloquez.*
Dioses que en la gentilidad eran de las lluvias.

---

6. To the right in the margin: *Ahuaques, or Tlaloques:*
Gods of rain in heathen times.

[10 VERSO]

tlen ticmotequitia, nican nixpan xiquinhualhuica in tlacatecolotl ixiptlahuan inic motepehuazque mocenmanazque. Auh in tehuatl, monemiliz, in tlen motlamazehualiz timacoz: ca huel oc noma quitzitzquitinemi in tlacatecolotl in ámoyolo huel oc noma amixpopoyome: zan ye ihui in amech-tlaneltoquilizitlacotinemi inic ámo, anquimozen-machiltizque in çan huel içeltzin in nelli teotl Dios in mochi, yhuelitzin;[23] auh ca zan yehuatzin iceltzin in itechcopatzinco, hualehua in ixquich in quexquich in itech monequi in zemanahuactli, ca çan içeltzin in centlatquihuacatzintli; ca atle onca ytla oc çentlamantli in manel huel mahuiztic tlachihuali in iuhqui ilhuicatl, tonalli metztli çiçitlaltin, in ma ó ye ihueli inic itla quitemacaz, ca mochin quimoçentemachiliticate in Dios, auh intlacamo quimonequilti, ca ayac moliniz ca

[11 RECTO]

ayac mocuecuetzoz, ca àtle inhuelli ca çemicac icxitlantzinco molinitinemi momalacachotinemi.

Cuix oc noma za ye axcan ticneltoca, timomati in oncate ahuaque? *Respuesta.* Ca quemacatzin.

Auh cuix ticneltoca in ca itech, hualquiza, hualehua in tepetl tlaloc, ihuan in oc zequi, huehuecapan tepetl, in iquac iancuican momexotia, in yquac ica, y, totonillo[24] in tonalli quipotoc, quixtia[25] in tlalli ca yauh cuepa in atl, auh in tehuatl, cuix yuh timomati in acame oncate Ahuaque in iuh quichihua, in yancuican quiyolitia in mixtli, in quiahuitl? *Respuesta.* Ca quemaca.

Cuix ticneltoca in huel yehuantin inpampa tlamochihua, in tlalticpac, auh cuix çan ye ihui in anquintlamamaca in, candela, caxitl, copalli, &c? *Respuesta.* Ca quemaca ca melahuac in ticmitalhuia.

Auh quezquipa in oticmotequiuhti? *Respuesta.* Ca yexpa

[10 VERSO]

what you have undertaken. Now bring before me the images of the devil so that they can be thrown to and scattered on the ground. As for your life and what penance you will be given: the devil still goes about with a grip on your heart, you are still blind. Likewise you go about damaging the faith so that you do not entirely put your hope in the only true deity, God the Almighty, and that from Him alone comes all and how[ever] much the world needs—He alone is the complete Master of the owner[s] of property. Even though there are really marvelous works like the heavens, the sun, the moon and the stars—there is nothing else that has the power to give people things, it is God who completely gives everything to people. And if He does not will it, no one will move,

[11 RECTO]

no one will stir, for they have no power [of their own]: they eternally go about moving and turning at His feet.

Do you still now believe and think there are Ahuaques? *Answer.* Yes.

And do you believe they emerge and come from the mountain Tlaloc and other lofty mountains when clouds newly form, when with the heat of the sun it makes the humidity of the earth come out and go changing into water? And as for you: do you think that there are some Ahuaques who do thus, who first give life to the clouds and rainstorms? *Answer.* Yes.

Do you believe that because of them things abound on earth? And is it such that you serve them [up offerings]: candles, bowls, copal incense, etc.? *Answer.* Yes, what you are saying is true.

And how many times have you been responsible for this sin? *Answer.* Three times,

---

23. mochi, yhuelitzin: read *mochi yhuelitzin* (and see remarks on 48r–50r).
24. y, totonillo: read *ytotonillo*.
25. quipotoc, quixtia: read *quipotocquixtia*.

quatro, cinco, &c.

Lo hiziste con todo tu coraçon? *Respuesta.* Si Padre, l. no.

O ciegos, y perdidos, que hauiendoos amanecido el claro, y resplandeciente Sol de nuestra Santa Fè: querays andar, y proseguir en perpetuas tinieblas! Volued los ojos atras (que mejor diria adelante) y mirad á la Nacion de los Iapones[es], y otras que siendo vuestros herma[12recto]nos menores en la Fé, y muy modernos, y nuevos en ella, os an dexado muy atras, con actos, y demonstraciones que an hecho, siendo muy firmes y constantes: no tienen vuestras supersticiones, y reçabios; porque de vna vez dieron de mano, y desterraron de sus coraçones la idolatria en que andaban siegos (como vosotros) quando tubieron conocimiento

de la diuina luz, y Fè, la que aora vosotros dexais de fixar en vuestros coraçones; por lo qual aora, á hecho firmissimos fundamentos en sus coraçones, de tal manera, que no ay cosa que les mude: por la Fè mueren regando la tierra con su sangre en testimonio de su heroyca firmeza, haziendose grandes Martyres è insignes Santos, como vosotros los visteis los dias passados, en las fiestas, que les celebrò nuestra [12 verso] Madre la Iglesia, por hauerlos Canoniçado, y declarado por Santos, el Summo Pontifice Vicario de Christo acá en la tierra, escrito, y numerado en el numero de los demas bienauenturados, que estan gozando de Dios.

Y vosotros, que soys mas antiguos en la Fè, y que

four, five, etc.

Did you do it with all your heart? *Answer.* Yes, Father / no.

O blind and lost ones, the clear and resplendent sun of our holy faith has dawned on you, [yet] you want to go along and continue in perpetual darkness! Turn your eyes back (better I should say forward) and look at the nation of the Japanese and others who, being your younger brothers in the faith and very modern and new in it, have left you far behind, being very firm and constant with the acts and demonstrations they have made. They do not have your superstitions and bad habits, because straight off when they had knowledge of the divine light and faith (which you now fail to fix in your hearts) they laid hands on and banished from their hearts the idolatry in which they blindly (like you) used to go along.

Therefore now [knowledge of divine faith] has made very firm foundations in their hearts, such that there is nothing that makes them change. They die for the faith watering the earth with their blood in testimony to their heroic steadfastness, making themselves great martyrs and notable saints, as you saw them days past in the feast days that our mother the Church celebrated, on account of His Holiness the Pope having canonized them and declared them saints, written down and numbered among the rest of the blessed who are enjoying God.

And you who are more ancient in the faith, and who

[11 VERSO]

nauhpa macuilpa &c.

Cuix huel mochi yca in moyolo in oticchiuh [Respuesta.] ca quemaca. l. amotzin.

Iho[26] xolopitine in axcan ye o àmopan tonac ye o [a]mopan tlathuic auh oc noma anquinequi in tlayohuayan mixticomac a[n]nemizque amicampa àmotepotzco ximocuepacan, (noço, oc achi quali nicytoz amixpampa) auh xiquimitican, xiquinmahuiçocan, in tlaneltoquiliztica amote-[ic]cahuan Iapon tlaca, yhuan in oc zequintin in quin axcan oquizelique in tlaneltoquiliztli, ca ye, tlaneltoquiliztlachihualtica, óamechpanahuique, óamechtlaztiquizque canel àtle ic quitzotzona quitlacoa in tlaneltoquiliztli ca àmo tlateoto-quilizxolopiyotl, ic quineneloa in yuhqui amehuantin ca ye içenmayan oquizentelchiuhque oquiçemixnahuatique in tlateotoquiliztli ipan onenca (in yuhqui amehuantin) in, yquac oquitaque oquimahuiço-

[12 RECTO]

que in ilhuicac tlanextli, tlaneltoquiliztli, in axcan amehuantin anquimixcahualtia. Auh, in axcan ca ye huel ytech in inyolo, omonelhuayoti, ca aoc otle[28] huel quen quinchihua, ca ypampa in tlaneltoquiliztli, miqui, ca ypampa imezo in tlalli ic catequia, ic quinextia, ca çenca tlaneltoquiliz-tlapaltique. Auh huehueintin Martyres mochihua, tlaçoSanctotin mocuepa in yuhqui oanquima-huiçoque, in ye nechca nican Mexico oquinmo-hueiilhuichihuilili in tonantzin Santa Iglesia in ipampa in çemanahuac tlatocateopixqui Summo Pontifiçe in totecoyo [sic] IESV, Christo, ixiptlatzin nican tlalticpac oquinmoSanctotene-huili, oquinmoSanctomahuiçotili, inhuan oquinmopohuili inhuan oquinmicuilhui in oc zequintin Sanctotin ilhuicatl itec motlamachtiticate itlantzinco in Dios. Auh in teotlaneltoquiliztica antetiachcahuan in huel oanquin

[11 VERSO]

four times, five times, etc.

Did you do it with all your heart. [Answer.] Yes / no.

Ah,[27] O foolish ones, the sun [of the true faith] has come upon you, [the true faith] has dawned on you, and you still want to live in the darkness of sin and the gloom [of ignorance]! Turn around backward (or better I should say toward your front) and look and marvel at the people of Japan, your younger brothers in the faith, and others who have recently received the faith, for already they have surpassed you in works of faith, throwing you quickly [to one side]. For they do not doubt and damage the faith with anything, mixing it up with [other] things as you [are accustomed to do]. Once and for all they despised and firmly dismissed the idolatry in which they (like you) had lived when they saw and marveled at

[12 RECTO]

the heavenly light, the faith, that you now lose through sin and negligence. And now it has taken such root in their hearts that nothing disturbs them, for because of the faith they die and water the earth with their blood, thus manifesting that they are strong in the faith. And they become great martyrs, turn into beloved saints, as you observed here in Mexico a little while ago. Our mother the holy Church celebrated a great feast day for them because the ruler-priest, the High Pontiff, representative of our Lord Jesus Christ here on earth, declared them saints, honored them as saints, counted and wrote them among the other saints who are greatly enjoying them-selves in Heaven with God. And you, people's older brothers in the faith who should be able

---

26. Beginning with this line and in the margin to the left is the following: *Platica Seguuda* [sic], *en que se disuade á los Naturales, la creencia, que tienen el dia de oy, en que ay Ahuaquez, dueños de las lluvias, à quienes la siega gentilidad lla-maua, Tlaloquez, y el dia de oy, les van a ofrecer en los altos montes y en las lagunas candelas, y copal, y yiauhtli, [12r] como se halló en Pantitlan, el año de [16]31. Offrecidas, a los dos Idolos, que estan alli llamado el vno, Tlaloc, y el otro, Matlalcueye.*

28. otle: probably to be read either *atle* or *itla.*

---

27. Beginning with this line and in the margin to the left is the following: *Second speech, in which the natives are dis-suaded from the belief they have nowadays about there being Ahuaques, masters of the rains, whom blind heathendom used to call Tlaloques. And nowadays they go to offer them candles, copal incense and anise-like incense in the high mountains and the pools, as was found in Pantitlan, year of 1631, offerings to two idols that are there; the one is called Tlaloc, and the other, Matlalcueye.*

por esto les auiades de lleuar muchas ventajas, os
aueys quedado muy atras. Y esto prouiene de no
acabar de desterrar de si, y aborrecer los antiguos
reçauios, y supresticiones, y otras obras diabolicas
que se originan, y tienen su rayz de aquellos
viejos, vuestros passados, que siempre andubieron
en perpetuas tinieblas.

Por ventura quando murio alguno, o tu pariente, ò otro qualquiera enterrasteslo, echandole
en la sepultura manta de Nequen, piciete, mecapal, çapatos, dineros, [13 recto] comida, y veuida,
y todo á escusas de vuestro Ministro? *Respuesta.*
afirmatiue, Si Padre, assi lo è hecho, negatiue, no
Padre, no se nada desso.

Y esta diabolica costumbre, que vsays, es por
entender que lo preuenis de las cosas dichas;
porque pensays, que ha de boluer

for this reason should have an advantage over
them, have remained very much left behind. And
this stems from not completely banishing from
oneself and loathing the ancient bad habits and
superstitions and other diabolical works that
originate and have their root in those ancients,
your ancestors, who always walked in perpetual
darkness.

Perhaps when someone died, either a relative
of yours or anyone else, you buried him, casting
on him in the grave a blanket made of henequen,
[along with] tobacco, a tumpline, shoes, money,
food, and drink, and all without the [knowledge]
of your minister? *Answer* (affirmative) Yes, Father,
I have done so. (negative) No, Father, I do not
know anything about that.

And this diabolical custom that you use, is
because it is understood that you are preparing
the things that have been mentioned for him.
Because you believe that he has to return

[12 VERSO]

panahuizquia ye huel teycampa tetepotzco,
oanmocauhtiquizque auh huel yehuatl quichihua
inic oc noma ayamo anquiçentelchihua amo
anquiçemixnahuatia in tlateotoquiliznecauhcayotl, in tlateotoquiliztlachihualli, in intech
hualehuatica, hualnelhuayotica in cemicac
tlayohuayan onenque amocolhuan tlateotocanime.

    Cuix in, yquac aca omomiquili in àço
mohuayolqui in áço, oc çe tlacatl, cuix Ayatl,
piçietl, mecapalli, cactli, tomin, atl, tlaqualli,
oanquihuicaltique, in ipan oanquitocaque,
oanquiquimiloque in amo oquima in teopixqui?
Respuesta. afirmatiuè ca quemacatzin ca melahuac
ca oticchiuhque *negatiue*, ca àmotzin, ca àmo
nicmati, &c. sic de çeteris.

    Auh inin, amotlateotoquiliztlacatecolo-
nahuatil, cuix ipampa in anquitacatia, anmomati,
auh ca zan hualaz ca çan hualmocuepaz in iquin
on, ca oc

[12 VERSO]

to surpass them, already are left very behind and
to the rear of people. That is done because you
still do not yet despise and forever bid farewell to
the remnants and works of idolatry that came and
took root in your grandfathers, the idolaters, who
lived in eternal darkness.

    When someone died—perhaps your relative
or maybe some other person—did you accompany, bury and wrap each one of them up with
henequen cloaks, tobacco, tumplines, sandals,
money, water, food, [and all] unbeknownst to the
priest? *Answer. (Affirmative)* Yes, it is true; we did
it. *(Negative)* No, I don't know, & sic de ceteris
[and the same as for the other questions].

    And as for this idolatrous and diabolical cus-
tom of yours: do you make provisions because of
it? You thinking: but he is just to come and return
one day, for

a viuir en algun tiempo acá en el mundo; porque va aora desta presente vida, á hazer penitencia en aquel lugar (á quien los viejos de la siega gentilidad, que nunca tuvieron lumbre de la verdadera Fè) llamauan Ximoayan?[7] *Respuesta.* Si Padre, l. no.

Tienes por costumbre, el yr enterrando tus dineros, presumiendo que as de voluer otra vez despues de muerto á gozarlos. *Respuesta.* Si Padre. l. no.

Si fueren mugeres, se les á de preguntar lo siguiente, que es lo que siempre acostumbran hazer, particularmente [13 verso] en los pueblos.

Quando murio tu hijo niño, y pequeñuelo, por ventura pusistele con cañutos tu leche, enterrandole con ellos, ò vas a derramarla en la sepultura donde está enterrado. *Respuesta.* Si Padre, l. no.

Aora pues oyeme, y abre los ojos de tu entendimiento,

to live again sometime here in the world, because he is going now from this present life to do penance in that place which the ancients of blind heathendom who never had the light of the true faith used to call Ximoayan?[8] *Answer.* Yes, Father / no.

Do you customarily go burying your money, presuming that you have to return after death to enjoy it? *Answer.* Yes, Father / no.

If they are women they have to be questioned about the following, which is what they are always used to doing, particularly in the small towns.

When your little son died, still very small, did you perhaps put your milk in small cane containers with him, burying him with them, or do you go pouring your milk into the grave where he is buried? *Answer.* Yes, Father / no.

Now then, hear me and open your eyes in understanding,

---

7. To the right in the margin: *Ximoayan, quiere dezir, ádonde todos van a parar* [sic].

8. To the right in the margin: *Ximoayan, which means "where everyone ends up"* [sic].

[13 RECTO]

zepa nemiquiuh in nican tlalticpac ca zan, oc tlamaçehuato, in canin ximoayan tlatenehuaya, in xolopitin huehuentoton, in àcan oquimahuiçotiaque in ilhuicac tlaneltoquiliztli, tlanextli? In ye axcan, oamolhuiltic oamomacehualtic. *Respuesta.* Ca quemacatzin. l. amotzin?

Cuix tictoca, in motomin cuix tictlatia? Cuix ticmolhuia ca oc cepa tihualmocuepaz in iquin on, intla otimic auh ca quin yquac in motech monequiz?

Auh intla çihuatzitzintin nican ca in motlatlanizque, in mochipa quimotequiuhtiani, oc qualca in altepetl ipan.

Cuix in yquac, omomiquili moconeuh, cuix acatica, otictlallilli in momemeyalo, in mochichihulayo?[29] Cuix ipan otictocac. Cuix noço, in campa toctoc? Cuix ompa tiauh, ticnoquiz ticpipiaçoz, in mochichihualayo.

In[30] axcan xiccaqui xictlapo in mix in moyolo, in cententica in ontentica nimi-

[13 RECTO]

he will come to live again here on earth. He has just gone to do penance where Ximoayan ([so]called by the fools and little old men who nowhere saw the divine faith and light) is. At this time you [presume you] have earned great merit. *Answer.* Yes / no.

Do you bury your money? Do you hide it? Do you say you will return one day after you have died, and that then you will have need of it? [*Answer.* Yes / no.]

And if they are women being questioned here, what they always are taking responsibility for [must be addressed], especially in the altepetls.

When your child died, did you put your breast milk on him with a reed? Did you bury it with him? Or where you buried him: do you go there to spill and pour your breast milk on him? [*Answer.* Yes / no.]

Now[31] listen and open your eyes in understanding to the few words

---

29. mochichihulayo: read *mochichihualayo.*

30. Although this marginalia actually begins on 13v, it would appear to more appropriately begin here: *Platica tercera, en que se les reprehende, a los Naturales, las supresticiones de idolatria que vsan el dia de oy con sus diffuntos enterrandolos con varias cosas, segun vsaban en su gentilidad, y el demonio se lo mandaua, como los ministros lo ven cada dia; pues en Atlapulco, que es seys leguas de Mexico, [14r] el año de [16]31. hallò mucho desto el ministro de doctrina, y dio parte a su Señoria, y otros muchos lo an visto. Tambien en esta platica se les da a entender breuemente, que cosa es, Cielo, purgatorio, Limbo, è Infierno segun los Doctores de la Iglesia.*

31. Although this marginalia actually begins on 13v, it would appear to more appropriately begin here: *Third speech, in which the natives are taken to task for the sins of idolatry that they practice nowadays with their deceased, burying them with things as they used to do in their heathendom and the devil commanded them to it, as the ministers see every day. In Atlapulco (which is 6 leagues from Mexico [City]) in 1631 the minister of doctrine found a lot of this and reported to His Lordship, and many others have seen [evidence of] it. Also in this speech they are briefly given to understand what sort of thing Heaven is, purgatory, limbo and hell, according to the doctors of the church.*

[13 VERSO]

que quiero con breues y concluyentes razones, despertarte del profundo sueño de ignorancia en que estás: aduirtiendote lo que estás obligado a creer, y sauer; muy contrario a esso en que el Demonio os trae engañados, y burlados, con quimeras, que dio a tragar, y beber en el pulque, y en el vino á vuestros antepasados en sus borracheras, y embriagueses. Ya eres muy otro que ellos, ya te á amanecido el Sol de la verdadera Fè, y eres Christiano, ya no viuees en aquella confußion, y se[14 recto]guera, en que ellos viuian; pues pertenceces a Dios verdadero, que tiene infinito poder, sobre la vida, y la muerte. Aquesto pues es lo que deues, y estás obligado a sauer, que es lo que está escrito por Dios en la Escritura sagrada, sciencia del cielo, y diuina. A tres lugares embia Dios las almas que van deste mundo: al Purgatorio, Limbo, ò Infierno: al Purgotorio⁹ van a parar, las animas de los Christianos, que avnque murieron confessados, no satisfacieron en este mundo

[14 RECTO]

por sus culpas: y assi cumplen alli primero, con castigos de fuego, que les pone Dios en aquel lugar, para purgar sus pecados, y satisfacer lo que en el mundo no satisfacieron, por el tiempo que su diuina Magestad es seruido. El Limbo, es vn lugar de perpetuas tinieblas, y aqui van a parar, las animas de [14 verso] de los niños inocentes, que murieron sin receuir agua de Baptismo. Y estas Almas tiene alli la Magestad de Dios, para lo que el es seruido, ni tienen pena, ni gloria, sino que siempre estan en vna continua obscuridad. El tercer lugar se llama Infierno, á quien vuestros antepasados llamaron lugar de la muerte, casa de fuego sin respiradero, ni chimenea, como el Demonio les enseñò, que le llamasen: aqui estan arrojados, y encerrados toda aquella maquina, y multitud de Demonios, que trayan engañados, a vuestros antepasados, y á vosotros os traen hasta el dia de oy, siegos, y perdidos:

[13 VERSO]

for with brief and conclusive reasons I want to waken you from the deep sleep of ignorance in which you lie, pointing out to you what you are obliged to believe and know, very contrary to that with which the devil brings you along, deceived and mocked with the fanciful notions he gave to your ancestors, to swallow and to drink in [during] their drunken sprees and bouts of intoxication. You are already very different from them, the sun of the true faith has already dawned on you, and you are a Christian, you no longer live in that confusion and blindness in which they used to live, since you belong to the true God who has infinite power over life and death. That then is what you have to and are obliged to know, which is that which is written by God in the Holy Scriptures, heavenly science, and divine. God sends the souls that go from this world to three places: to purgatory, limbo or hell. In purgatory end up the souls of those Christians who, although they died having made their confession, did not provide satisfaction in this world

[14 RECTO]

for their sins. And thus they fulfill their obligations there first with fiery punishments that God puts upon them in that place in order to purge [them of] their sins and provide satisfaction for that which they did not provide satisfaction in the world, for [whatever the amount of] time His Divine Majesty is pleased [to give]. Limbo is a place of perpetual darkness. There the souls of innocent children who died without receiving the water of baptism are destined. And God's Majesty has them there for whatever pleases Him. They have neither pain nor glory but are always in a continuous darkness. The third place is called hell, which your ancestors called the place of death, house of fire without an air vent nor a chimney, as the devil taught them to call it. Here were flung and shut up all that fanciful host and multitude of demons that went on deceiving your ancestors,

---

9. Purgotorio: read *Purgatorio*.

[13 VERSO]

tzizcalia nimitznonotza, auh in ma zan, yuhqui otiçenyaticochi ic nimitzixitia in huel nelli ticçenmatiz ticçenneltocaz, ca amo yehuatl, on, tlacatecolotl, iteixpopoyotiliz itecanecacayahualiz in ipan oquimiti oquintololti in huehuentoton in mixitl in tlapatl in tlahuanaliztli, ca in tehuatl ca ye toc çentlamantli ca ye o mopan tonac ca ye o mopan tlathuic, ca aocmo [tla]yohuayan in tinemi, ca ye tiChristiano, ca ye itetzinco otimopouh otimonetolti in çan huel içeltzin nelli teotl Dios in, onca izenhuelitzin in ipan in yoliliztli in ipan in miquiliztli, auh ca nican ca in monahuatil, in ticneltocaz in ticmatiz, in ipan ycuiliuhtoc in ilhuicac amoxtlamachiliztli in yehuatl huel nelli neltoconi. Ca yexcan in motetlalilia in Dios, *Purgatorio, Limbo, Infierno*, Purgatorio ca ompa yauh in inyolia in yehuantin Christianos, tlaquatequiltin in amo caxiltitihui in nican tlalticpac

[14 RECTO]

in intlamazehualiz, ca oc ompa quitzonquixtitiquiza; tletica quinmotlamaçehualmaquilia in Dios, oncan moçencauhtehua mochipauhtehua in ixquich cahuitl quinmotlatlalililia in *Limbo*, ca ompa in çemicac tlayohuayan, auh ca ompa quinmotlalilia in Dios in pipiltzitzintin in zan yuh momoquilia[32] in àtle quimomazehuitihui in nequatequiliztli in Sancto Baptismo, auh in yquein[33] ca ompa quinmopilia in Dios ca yehuatzin quimomachiltia, in tlen quinmochihuiliz, ca ayac aquin huel quimati, auh yeçe àmo tle ic motolinia àmo no tle ic papaqui çan tlayohuayan onoque. Auh inic yexcan ca ye ompa in *Infierno* in amocolhuan çemicac, oquitocayotique Mictlan, Atlecalocan, Apochquiahuayocan. In iuhqui quinmachti tlacatecolotl quitocayotizque auh ca ye oncan in in çentepeuhticate zentzauh[c]ticate in oquintlapololtitinenca in huehuet-

[13 VERSO]

with which I teach and correct you. Do not just be going to sleep, I will thus awaken you, and you will really and entirely understand and believe that it is not the blindness and mockery of the devil that he gave the little old men to drink and swallow in [during bouts of] inebriation and drunkenness. For you already are of a different sort, the sun [of the true faith] has come out upon you, [the true faith] has dawned on you, you no longer live in darkness for already you are a Christian, already belonging and promised to the only true deity, God, Who has total power over life and death. Here is what you are obliged to believe and know, written down in the heavenly book of wisdom and truly indeed worthy of belief. God puts people into three places: *purgatory, limbo*, and *hell*. There to purgatory go the souls of those baptized Christians who did not provide satisfaction here on earth

[14 RECTO]

[with] their penance, for they are still to bring it to a conclusion. God gives them a penance of fire, there to quickly prepare and purify themselves during the time He has set down for them. There in *limbo* it is a place of eternal darkness, and there God puts the little children who just died as such who did not enjoy the act of pouring water on one's head, holy baptism. And as to this: God has them there for [reasons only] He knows; no one really knows what will happen to them. However, they suffer nothing nor enjoy [any]thing but just lie in darkness. The third place is there in *hell*, what your grandfathers always called "Mictlan" [Place of the Dead] and "Atlecalocan, Apochquiahuayocan" [place without a chimney, place without a smoke vent], as the devil taught them to call it. There are scattered and locked up all the ancients your grandfathers whom the [devil] confused,

---

32. momoquilia: read *momiquilia*.
33. in yquein: perhaps to be read *inyc ye in*.

á estos llamaron vuestros mayores *Tzitzimime*, que quiere dezir, feissimos monstruos, *Coleletin*: dañadas, y asquerosas vestias, *Tzontemoctin*, aquellos que cayeron del Cielo pre[15 recto]cipitados assia abajo, con sus espantables melenas. Todos los quales dieron nombres, y apellidos a los idolos, que truxeron perdidos a vuestros antepasados, llamandolos. *Tetzauhteotl, Huitzilopoch, Tezcatlepocca [sic], Tlalocan, Tecuhtli*, &c. Y otra infinita multitud, que truxeron á la gentilidad engañada, haziendose Dioses: aqui van a parar tambien los idolatras, ereges, judios, luteranos, y todos los malos Christianos, que no cumplen, y quebrantan los Mandamientos de la ley de Dios, y mueren, y acauan en peccado, y en desgracia suya, sin confesarsse [sic], y hazer penitencia de sus culpas. Los quales para siempre van aborrecidos de la diuina Magestad, y los Demonios, los atormentarán, y castigarán eternamente en aquel lugar, que este sera el pago

que les daran [15 verso] por auerlos seruido, y ovedecido en este mundo.

El Cielo es morada, y Palacio Real de la Magestad de Dios, lugar de eterna, y soberana gloria, y descanso, donde xamas puede llegar ninguna pena, ni trauajo: es patria, y lugar de vida eterna. Aqui van a descansar los amados, queridos, y amigos de Dios, los que en aqueste mundo le siruieron, y ouedecieron, no quebrantando sus diuinos mandamientos, ni la Santa Fè que professaron. Y lo que contiene el Credo, que el dia del juicio, an de resucitar, no es porque aqui han de venir á viuir otra vez en el mundo en vida mortal, sino que con el poder soberano de Nuestro Señor Iesu Christo, han de resucitar los buenos en cuerpos gloriosos, y los ha de llevar consigo a su celestial Reyno. Y a los malos entonces los condenará, y echará

and who up until today bring you along, blind and lost. Your elders called these [demons] *Tzitzimime*, which means "very ugly monsters"; *Coleletin*, "rotten and loathsome beasts"; and, *Tzontemoctin*, "those who fell from heaven, cast downward with their dreadful long hair." To all of which they gave names, and surnames to their idols that brought along, lost, your ancestors, calling them *Tetzauhteotl, Huitzilopoch[tli], Tezcatlipoca, Tlalocan Tecuhtli*, etc. And another infinite multitude that brought about deception in their heathendom, making themselves gods. Here end up the idolaters, heretics, Jews, Lutherans, and all the bad Christians who do not fulfill [their religious obligations] and break the commandments of the law of God, and die and end in sin and in self-disgrace without making confession of and doing penance for their sins. Who also go about abhorred by the Divine Majesty. And the demons will torment and punish them for eternity in that place, for this will be the payment

that they will give them for having served and obeyed them in this world.

Heaven is the dwelling and royal palace of God's Majesty, place of eternal and supreme glory and rest, where no pain or labor can ever come; it is the fatherland and place of eternal life. Here go to rest God's loved ones, dear ones and friends, those who in this world served and obeyed Him, neither breaking His divine commandments nor the holy faith they professed. And what the Credo contains, that on the day of judgment they must come back to life, is not because they have to come here in the world to live a mortal life again, rather that by the supreme power of our Lord Jesus Christ the good will come back to life in glorious bodies and He will take them with Him to His celestial kingdom. And the bad He will then condemn and cast

que amocolhuan ihuan in oc noma amehuantin
axcan amechtlapololtia; auh ca yehuantin,
oquintocayotitehuaque tzitzimime Coleletin,
Tzontemoctin in inpan omixeuhtinenque in
aquique, tlalticpac tlaca cate Tezcatlepoca,
Tlalocan teacuhtli,[34] &c. Yhuan in oc çequintin
oquimiztlacahuitinenque in huehuetque, in çan
omoteonenequia in çan omoteotlapiquia; auh ca
ye ompa in ihui in mochintin, tlateotocanime
idolatras, yhuan, in ereges judios, luteranos,
yhuan in ixquichtin in ámo qualtin Christianos in
çan quitlacoa in zan quixpoloa, in iteotenahuatiltzin Dios in ipan tzonquiça in ipan miqui in
temictiani tlatlacolli in àmo moyolcuititihui in
ámo mopalehuitihui, moçencauhtihui auh ca
oncan ye içenmayan, oquinmoçemixnahuatili in
Dios ca aocmo oc cepa quiçazque ca zemicac
ompa tletica quintolinizque, quintlahiyo-
huiltizque in tlatla

catecolo in oquin, tlacamatque[35] in oquintla-
yecoltique in nican tlalticpac.

   Auh in ilhuicatl ca ytlatocatecpanchantzinco in
Dios, auh ca zemicac ompa papacoa, necuiltonolo
netlamachtilo ilhuitihua, àtle ompa huel açi in
tetolini in tecoco zemicac yolihua, auh ye oncan
in inhui in icniuhtzitzihuan in itlaçotzitzihuan
Dios in oquimotlacamachiltique, in
oquimotleyecoltilique,[36] in àtle ic oquitzotzonque
oquixopeuhque in iteotenahuatiltzin yhuan in
melahuac, otlaneltocaque. auh in quitoa neltoconi
Credo in oc zepa, mochi tlacatl yoliz mozcaliz, ca
àmo ipampa in nican oz cepa nemiquihuÉ
tlalticpac ca, y, huelitilizticatzinco[37] in totlaçotemaquixticatzin IESV Christo mozcalizque, auh
in qualtin yectin quinmohuiquiliz in ompa
ilhuicatl ytec gloria in itlatocachantzinco, auh in
yehuantin ámo qualtin içenmayan quinmix.

and he still confuses you today. They called "tzitzimime," "coleletin" and "tzontemoctin" the [dev-
ils] who represented themselves as being those
who are people of the earth [with names like]
Tezcatlipoca, Tlalocan Tecuhtli, etc., and the others who went about lying to the ancients, just pre-
tending to be gods, just falsely claiming to be
gods. And there likewise [go] all who worship
things as gods, the idolaters, and the heretics, the
Jews, the Lutherans, and all the bad Christians
who just damage and ruin God's divine commandments, who come to an end and die in mortal sin without confessing, without helping and
preparing themselves. And there once and for all
God bids farewell forever to those who will never
again emerge, for the devils will forever afflict
them there with fire, making suffer

those who obeyed and served them here on earth.

   Heaven is the royal palace of God, and there all
are eternally enjoying themselves, rich and pros-
perous and enjoying [their just] rewards. No
affliction and pain reaches there; all live forever.
There go the friends and beloved ones of God
who obeyed and served Him, who doubted and
rejected not His divine commandments and who
truly believed. All the people who say what is worthy of belief, the Credo, will live and stir to life
again, not because they will again come to live on
earth for it is with the power of our beloved
Savior Jesus Christ that they will be resurrected,
and He will accompany the good and righteous
there into Heaven and glory, His royal palace. And
those who are bad He will dismiss once and for
all,

---

34. teacuhtli: read *tecuhtli*.
35. oquin, tlacamatque: read *oquintlacamatque*.
36. oquimotleyecoltilique: read *oquimotlayecoltilique*.
37. y, huelitilizticatzinco: read *yhuelitilizticatzinco*.

[15 VERSO]

para siem[16 recto]pre jamas al infierno; en compañia de los abobinables[10] monstruos, y dañados
espiritus, y de los que aora andan por el mundo, y
os hazen pecar, que entonces seran encarcelados
para siempre xamas, juntamente con los conde-
nados.

As creydo en sueños, en el Peyote, Ololiuque, en
el fuego, en los Buhos, Lechusas, ò Culebras, &c. O
en otros abusos que tuvieron tus antepasados.

¶ *PREGVNTAS*, Acerca del segundo, que es no
jurar su Santo nombre en vano.

AS jurado alguna vez el nombre de Dios, en vano,
poniendo la Cruz, haziendo juramento, affir-
mando con el lo que no fue cierto, solamente á fin
de hazer mal, ò vengarte de alguno,

[16 RECTO]

ó porque te pagaron, ó te emborracharon para
que fuesses testigo [16 verso] contra alguno?
Respuesta. Si Padre, si he sido testigo, y caydo en
esta pecado, l. no Padre.

As sido testigo en fauor de los que quieren
casarsse [sic], afirmando, y jurando, que no tienen
impedimento para contraher Matrimonio, siendo
mentira? Y sauiendo al contrario, ò no cono-
ciendo los contraientes? Porque vosotros los
Naturales siempre lo acostumbrais hazer, y os
vays a poner ante la justicia, ó ministro, y á testi-
ficar lo que ni es cierto, ni os paßa por la imagina-
cion? Ante emborrachado, ó pagado porque
hiziesses esto?

Algun mal Christiano Español, te á cohechado,
para que jurases falso contra algun Sacerdote, ó
otra persona honrada, que mediante tu dicho, y
por ti le quieren, y pretenden quitar la honra, que
por este camino algun minis[[17 recto]tro del
diablo

[15 VERSO]

into hell forever and ever, in company with
abominable monsters and wicked spirits. And as
for those who now walk through the world and
make you sin, they will then be shut up forever
and ever, together with the condemned.

Have you believed in dreams, in peyote, in
ololiuhqui, in fire, in eagle owls and barn owls, or
serpents, etc.? Or in other superstitions that your
ancestors had?

QUESTIONS concerning the second [command-
ment], which is not taking His holy name in vain.

Have you sometimes sworn the name of God
on the cross in vain making an oath, affirming
thereby that which was not certain, only with the
aim of doing evil or taking your revenge on
someone,

[16 RECTO]

or because they paid you or got you drunk so that
you were a witness against someone? *Answer.* Yes,
Father, I have been a witness and fallen into this
sin / No, Father.

Have you been a witness in favor of those who
want to marry, affirming and swearing that they
have no impediment in contracting matrimony, it
being a lie and knowing the contrary [to be true],
or not [even] being acquainted with those contracting matrimony? Because you natives always
are accustomed to doing it and you put yourselves
before the legal authorities or minister and bear
witness to what is neither certain nor even imagined by you. Did they make you drunk or pay you
to do this?

Has some bad Spanish Christian bribed you to
falsely swear against some priest or other honorable person, that by means of your statement and
through you they want and attempt to destroy his
honor, that by this way some servant of the devil

---

10. abobinables: read *abominables*.

[15 VERSO]

nahuatiliz, mictlan quinmotepehuiliz, mochin, quinmohuicaltiliz in tzitzimime coleletin tzontemoctin, tlatlacatecolo in axcan yohualli cecatl[38] quimonahualotitinemi in amechtlapololtia ic zentzaqualozque aocquic oc cepa quizazque.

Cuix ticneltoca in temictli in Peyotl, Ololiuhqui, Tletl, Tecolotl, Chiquatli. coatl nozo itla oc centlamantli quimoteotiaya in mocolhuan huehuetque.

TETLAT[L]ANIliztli yn itechpa in Amo motlapictenehuaz in itocatzin Dios.

CVIX quenmanian otictlapicteneuh in imahuiztocatzin Dios? Oticchiuh Cruz? Otican juramento, juramentotica, oticneltilli in tlen ámo melahuac ticmati in azo zan ic otitecocoli, in aço aca

[16 RECTO]

omitztlaxtlahui omitztlahuanti, inic tehuicpa testigo otimochiuh? *Respuesta*. Ca neli ca melahuac, ca onicchiuh ca onicnotequiuhti, l. àmotzin.

Cuix nozo testigo otimochiuh in ipampa monamictique in zan tlapic oticyto oticteneuh in ca ticmati in ca átle ic tzotzoni in teoyotl nenamictiliztli, yhuan ca tiquimiximati in monamictique auh zan moch iztlacatiliztli ypampa in amehuantin anmazehualtin, mochipa yuhqui anquichihuani; ompa teixpan anmoquetztinemi, anquineltilia in tlen amo anquimati; auh cuix omitztlahuantique omitztlatecontilique in iuhqui oticchiuh?

Cuix noço aca àmo quali Christiano caxtiltecatl, omitztlaxtlahui inic yhuipca timojuramentotiz, in àço teopixqui in àço aca oc çe mahuiztic tlacatl in çan moca in çan mopampa quimahuizpoloznequi in çan aquin Diablo ixiptla,

---

throwing them down into hell, making them accompany the tzitzimime, coleletin, tzontemoctin and [other] devils [like] Night Wind who now go around casting evil spells[39] confusing you. Thus they will all be locked up, never again to emerge.

Do you believe in dreams, peyote, ololiuhqui, fire, owls, barn owls, snakes or some other thing your grandfathers the ancients used to worship?

QUESTIONS concerning not taking the name of God in vain.

HAVE you sometime falsely sworn the honored name of God? You did it on a cross? You took an oath, by means of swearing, and you verified what you know is not true? Did you do it just because you hated people? Or someone

[16 RECTO]

paid you, got you drunk so that you would become a witness against others? *Answer*. It is certain and true, I did it, I was responsible for it / no.

Did you become a witness because of those who were married, just falsely saying and declaring that you know there is no impediment to holy matrimony and that you know those who got married-and it was all just a lie? Because you natives always are accustomed to doing such; there in public you get up verifying what you do not know. Did they get you drunk giving you a little glass of something so you would do so?

Perhaps some bad Spanish Christian paid you so that you would take an oath against a priest or some other honorable person, or someone who is a representative of the devil—through and because of you—wants to dishonor him,

---

38. cecatl: read *e[h]ecatl*.

39. *casting evil spells:* tentative translation.

[16 VERSO]

pretende vengarse de la tal persona. *Respuesta*. Si Padre, l. no.

Quantos Christianos ay en el mundo (si assi se puede dezir) se admiran de vosotros y avn otros se rien, y hazen donayre, en ver que por vna xicara de pulque, ó tecomate de vino, echeys vuestras almas al infierno, y las days al Demonio. Y avn los Negros, Chinos, y Iapones[es], se admiran, y os lo tienen á mal, viendo quan facil, y mudable sea vuestra condicion, que algunos malos Christianos, os hazen dezir, y afirmar de otros, todo lo que quieren, y pretenden; por lo qual no os tienen en nada, y perdeys la honra y estimacion que pudierades tener acá en el mundo: pues que sera ante el diuino Acatamiento de Dios Nuestro Señor? Y de lo que mas nos admiramos, y espantamos de vosotros, es ver que [17 verso] no eran assi vuestros antepasados

[17 RECTO]

los viejos: porque eran muy otros de lo que aora soys: tenian aviso, cordura, miedo, y verguença, y criança: pero los que aora viuis, que teneys? Que ha de ser de vosotros? Hasta quando? De verdad os digo, que no es otra cosa lo que assi os tiene conuertidos en vestias, sino la borrachera, y embriagues, que os va, ya quitando el vso de la razon, y lumbre natural del entendimiento que el soberano Dios os dio, porque ya no criais a vuestros hijos con otra cosa, ni les days mas doctrina desde que nacen sino la del vino, y el pulque, y avnque los viejos vuestros mayores lo vebian, era con moderacion, y templança (como lo hazen aora vuestros proximos, los Españoles) y si por ventura hallauan alguna vez, algun vorracho, le quitavan luego la vida por ello, y aora [18 recto] en nuestros tiempos, es, porque nadie os va a la mano, con pena de muerte,

[16 VERSO]

attempts to take revenge on such a person? *Answer*. Yes, Father / no.

All the Christians in the world (if it can be so said) marvel at you and some even laugh and make jokes in seeing that for a gourd of pulque or a cup of wine you cast your souls to hell and give them to the devil. And even the Blacks, Chinese, and Japanese marvel and think it improper of you, seeing how easy and changeable your condition is, that some bad Christians make you say and affirm about others all that they want and attempt. As a result of this they have no regard for you and you lose the honor and esteem that you could have had in the world. What will it be like before the divine reverence of God our Lord? And what we most marvel at, and are astonished by concerning you, is that your ancestors the ancients were not thus,

[17 RECTO]

because they were very different from what you are now. They had discretion, prudence, fear and shame and good breeding. But you who live now: What's wrong with you? What will become of you? How long can you go on like this? Truthfully I say to you, that it is nothing other than drunkenness and intoxication that has turned you into beasts, that has gone on taking away from you the use of reason and the natural light of knowledge that sovereign God gave you. Because you no longer raise your children with anything else nor give them more doctrine from the time they are born but that of wine and pulque. And even though the ancients your elders drank, it was with moderation and restraint (as your neighbors the Spaniards do today). And if by chance they sometimes used to discover some drunkard, they immediately took away his life for it. And now in our times it exists because nobody restrains you with the death penalty,

[16 VERSO]

in çan ic motzoncui motlahuelquixtia. *Respuesta.*
Ca quemacatzin, l. ámotzin.

In⁴⁰ ixquichtin Christianos çemanahuac, huel
amechmotetzahuia yhuan çequintin, zan amoca
huetzca amoca paqui in quita quimahuiçoa in zan
ce xicali, octli noço çentecontontli, vino ic
anquimictlantlaça, in amoyolia, yhuan ipampa
anquimaca in tlacatecolotl. Auh in manel
Cacatzactin, Chinotin noço Iapontin, mochintin
amoca huetzca amoca paqui ic amechtlatzohuilia,
in quita quimahuiçoa in amoyeliz in zan
cuecuepqui ipampa in çaço quexquich
quinequizque, in amo qualtin Christianos, in teca
anquitozque, anquineltilizque ixquich quichihua,
yeica in átle ipan amito anmacho, moch ic
anquipoloa in mahuiçotl in nican tlalticpac, quen
mache in ilhuicatl itec ixpantzinco Dios, auh in
huel ic titotetzahuia, in amo yuhque catca in
amechcauh-

[17 RECTO]

tihui ámocolhuan, huel oc zentlamantin catca
mimatia ixtlamatque catca tlamauhcaytaya,
momahuiztiliaya. Auh in axcan ye annemi, tle
oàmaxque? Quen oanmochiuhque? Tle
anquimati? Huel nelli àmo itla oc çentlamantli in
yuh amechchihua, in amechmanenencatilia,
intlacamo yehuatl in mixitl, in tlapatl,
tlahuanaliztli, in ye ic anquipoloa in
yollizmachiliztli, yoliztlanextli, in oamechmo-
maquili in ipalnemoaloni Dios. Ca noço za
yehuatl in ipan anhualmohuapahua, anhual-
mozcaltia in octli in tepach auh maçiihui [sic], in
quia in àmotahuan huehuetque ca çan
tlaixyeyecoliztica, in quia ca çan motlamachiaya,
(in yuhqui axcan amohuanpohuan caxtilteca,)
auh intla, aca quenmanian, quitaya tlahuanqui
niman quimictiaya quipopoloaya, auh in axcan
cuix ipampa in, ayac amechtlacahualtia,
miquiliztica in ancuecuenoti, in ye anmo

[16 VERSO]

just taking his revenege and anger out on him?
Answer. Yes / no.

All⁴¹ the Christians in the world are scandalized by you and some just laugh at and enjoy your
misfortunes, seeing and observing that for just
one gourd vessel of pulque or one little clay pot of
wine you cast your souls into hell and because of
it you give them to the devil. And even the Blacks,
the Chinese or the Japanese all laugh at you and
enjoy your misfortunes with which you are
ensnared, seeing and observing how changeable is
your state of being. Because whatever bad
Christians want you to say about people, you
verify all that they do, wherefore you are held in
very low esteem, losing with it all honor here on
earth. And how will it be in Heaven before God?
And what we are very much scandalized by is that
those who went leaving you behind, your grandfathers, were not so,

[17 RECTO]

they were another thing altogether: prudent, wise,
fearful, and honoring and respecting each other.
And you who now live: what have you done?
What have you made of yourselves? What do you
know? Truly indeed there is no other thing that
makes you beasts than the drunkenness and
intoxication with which you destroy the ingenuity
and living light [of reason] that God, the Giver of
Life, gave you. Is it just in pulque and tepache that
you are raised and instructed? And even though
your fathers the ancients used to drink, it was just
with moderation, they used to drink just to enjoy
themselves (as do your neighbors the Spaniards
today). And if sometimes someone used to see a
drunkard then they killed and destroyed him. But
now: is it because no one restrains you with [the
penalty of] death that you are proud and presumptuous,

---

40. Beginning with this line and paralleling this text to the
left, is the following marginalia: *Platica Quarta, en que se reprehenden los testigos falsos inducidos por algunos malos
Christianos, por la facilidad que hallan en los Naturales mediante el emborracharlos.*

---

41. Beginning with this line and paralleling this text to the
left, is the following marginalia: *Fourth speech, in which are
reproved the witnesses who are induced to be false by bad
Christians, on account of the ease that they find [in this type of
inducement] among the natives by means of getting them drunk.*

[17 VERSO]

os dexais ir por el camino de la perdicion: pero es possible, que esteys tan ciegos, que no vereys el castigo de Dios, su ira, y su enojo, que sobre vosotros embia con que os vays ya acabando sin remedio, con inumerables persecuciones, y traba-jos de sujecion, y esclauitud, que no ay otra nacion en el mu[n]do que los tenga mayores que vosotros: pues que es esto, á que se podra atribuyr, si no al castigo del Cielo, por muchos, y muy atroces pecados que tragays con el pulque, y hazeys estando borrachos, como se dirá en su lugar.

PREGVNTAS Acerca del tercer Mandamiento.

OIste Missa los dias de Domingos, y fiestas de [18 verso] guarda, ò

[17 VERSO]

you let yourselves go down the road to perdition. But is it possible that you are so blind that you do not see God's punishment, His ire and anger that He sends upon you, with which you are now coming to an inevitable end, with innumerable persecutions and cares of subjection and servi-tude, that there is no other nation in the world that has greater ones than you? Well, what is this? To what can it be attributed, if not to the punish-ment of Heaven on account of the many and very atrocious sins that you drink in with pulque and commit being drunk, as will be said in its place.

QUESTIONS concerning the third commandment.

Did you hear Mass on Sundays and obligatory feast days, or

[17 VERSO]

nenquixtia, in ye anmonenpoloa, yeçe quien⁴²
mach in amixpopoyome? In amo anquita in
içomaltzin in itlahueltzin Dios, in amopan ca, in
amotech, timalihui, in itetzin in iquauhtzin in
ijusticiatzin, in ye amechonçencahua,
amechontlatlamia, ihuan in oc cequi nepapan
tecoco, tetoneuh tequiotl, tlacoyotl, in ayaque oc
çequintin oncate çemanahuac, in iuhqui inpan
mochihua, netoliniliztli, in iuhqui amehuantin
auh tlen quitoznequi, in, àmo noço yehuatl in
ilhuicac tetlatzaquitiliztli [sic], ca noço ypan
anqui, anqui, toloa,⁴³ in mixitl in tlapatl
tlahuanaliztli, in nepapan tlatlacolli in iuh mitoz,
in iyeyan.
¶ *TETLATLANIliztli* in itechpa inic yey teotenahuatilli.

CVIX ⁴⁴ oticcac Missa in Domingo yhuan huey
ilhuitl ipan cuix noço quen-

wasting and destroying yourselves in vain? Yet
how blind you are to not see the anger and wrath
of God upon you, His castigation and justice
swelled up on you! Already it is leaving you totally
destroyed. And the other diverse afflictions and
travails, work and servitude that happen to you,
sufferings that no others in the world [endure]
like you: what does it mean? Is it not perhaps the
punishment of Heaven? Did you not drink and
swallow them in (as will be said in its place) in
[your bouts of] drunkenness and intoxication?

¶ *QUESTIONS* concerning the third commandment.

*HAVE*⁴⁵ you heard Mass on Sundays and feast
days? Or sometimes

---

42. quien: read *quen*.
43. anqui, toloa: read *anquitoloa*.
44. The following marginalia begins to the left of this
word: *Las platicas que pertenecen al [18r] Tercero. Quarto.
Quinto. Sexto. Septimo. y Octauo Mandamiento, se remiten á
vna sola, que es con que gravemente se á de reprehender el
pecado de la Gula, y embriaguez porque con este cometen los
naturales, los otros seys pecados mortales, y otros muy graues, y
enormes, contra los diez Mandamientos [18v] de la ley de Dios,
y para hazer qualquier pecado graue, de proposito se emborrachan y les es puerta, y entra de todo genero de vicios, y pecados, la borrachera. Y assi el prudente Confessor, la hallarà a
donde corresponde esta señal + que en vna sola platica ay materia para todo lo que quisiere acomodar a su propo[19r]sito, assi
para reprehender este vicio como los demas, que se cometen con
solo este pecado.*

45. The following marginalia begins to the left of this word:
*The speeches that pertain to the third, fourth, fifth, sixth, seventh
and eighth commandments are consigned to one only, that is, the
sin of gluttony, and drunkenness must be gravely criticized,
because with this the natives commit the other six mortal sins,
and others—very grave and enormous—against the ten commandments of the law of God. And in order to commit any grave
sin, they intentionally get themselves drunk, and drunkenness is
the door and entry for them of all types of vices and sins. And
thus the prudent confessor will find it wherever it fits in with this
mark "+," that in a single speech there is all that he might want
to accommodate to his purposes, both for criticizing this sin and
all the rest that are committed with only this sin.*

[18 RECTO]

as quebrantado alguno? *Respuesta.* Si Padre,
quebrantè los Domingos, fiestas &c.

Quantas Missas quebrantaste, y dexaste de oyr.
Respuesta. Cinco, l. seis &c.

Que fiestas quebrantaste fueron Domingos, ò
algunas de las que estays obligados a guardar?
Respuesta. Si Padre VerbiGracia dos Domingos, y
vna Pasqua.

Y essa Pasqua, en que dexaste de oyr Mißa, fue
el primero, ò el segundo dia? *Respuesta.* el
primero dexè de oyr Missa.

Por que caussa dexaste de oyr Missa? fue á no
poder mas? O porque estauas enfermo, ó te avia
acontecido otro impedimento semejante?
Respuesta. no Padre sino que de floxedad, y por
andarme emborrachando con otros, dexè de oyr
Missa, y la quebranté.

Dexastela de oyr por alguna enfermedad? ó
por no tener quien mirase por tu ca[19 recto]sa, ò
por

[18 VERSO]

estar muy desnudo, y ser muy pobre. *Respuesta.* Si
Padre, por no tener quien me guardase mi cassa, y
estoy muy pobre, y muy solo y desnudo, y desar-
rapado.

Eres por ventura Tepachera, ò vendes pulque, y
por esso eres caussa de que dexen muchos de oyr
Missa los Domingos, y Pasquas, por estar
veuiendo todo el dia en tu casa. *Respuesta.* Si. l.
no.

Causaste floxedad, a alguno para que no fuesse
a oyr Missa, ò fuiste caussa para que la dexasen de
oyr tus hijos, y todas aquellas personas, que te son
a cargo, haziendolos trabaxar, y seruirte con que
dexaron de oyr Missa. *Respuesta.* si, l. no.

Quando estás oyendo Missa, la oyes con toda
atencion, ò estás diuertido en otras cosas mientras
la oyes. *Respuesta.* si, l. no.

[18 RECTO]

did you miss some? *Answer.* Yes, Father, I missed
Sundays, feast days, etc.

How many Masses did you miss and neglect to
hear? *Answer.* Five / six, etc.

What feast days did you miss? Were they
Sundays or some of those that you are obliged to
observe? *Answer.* Yes, Father, for example, two
Sundays and a day in Easter week.

And that day in Easter which you failed to hear
Mass, was it on the first or second day? *Answer.* I
neglected to hear Mass the first.

Why did you fail to hear Mass? Was it because
you were unable to? Or because you were sick or
some other similar impediment had happened to
you? *Answer.* No, Father, rather that from negligence and on account of getting myself drunk
with others I neglected to hear Mass and I missed
it.

Did you fail to hear it on account of some
sickness? Or on account of not having someone
to keep an eye on your house, or

[18 VERSO]

being bereft of clothing and very poor? *Answer.*
Yes, Father, as a result of having no one who
might keep an eye on my house for me, and
because I am very poor, and very alone and lacking clothes and shabby.

Are you perhaps a maker/seller of tepache, or
do you sell pulque, and are you the reason why
many fail to hear Mass on Sundays and feast days,
on account of drinking all day in your house?
Answer. Yes / no.

Did you cause someone to fail to hear Mass, or
were you the reason why your children and all
those for whom you are responsible failed to hear
it, making them work and serve such that they
failed to hear Mass. *Answer.* Yes / no.

When you are hearing Mass: do you listen to it
attentively or are you distracted by other things
while you hear it? *Answer.* Yes / no.

[18 RECTO]

manian oticytlaco? *Respuesta*. Ca quemaca ca onicitlaco.

Quezqui in Misa oticitlaco? *Respuesta*. Ca nahui macuili &c.

Tlen ilhuitl cuix Domingo? Cuix yehuatl in huel ámonahuatil? *Respuesta*. Ca quemaca ca ome Domingo, VerbiGracia yhuan çe pascoa.

Cuix yehuatl in achto ilhuitl pascoa? Cuix noço ye inic ome ilhuitl paschoa [sic]? *Respuesta*. Ca yehuatl in huel acachto ilhuitl pascoa in huel yancuican.

Tleyca in oticcauh, in Missa in àmo ticcac in àmo ticmocuitlahui? cuix ypampa in amo tihuelit? In aço otimococoticatca, in anoço o [sic] itla o mopan mochiuhca? *Respuesta*. Ca àmotzin ca onitlatziuh ca onitlatlahuantinen; ca tecnihuan onechtlahuantique auh ipampa in onic[c]auh in Missa ámo niccac çan onicitlaco.

Cuix noço çan otimococoaya, cuix noço ipampa in ayac oncatca mitztlapializ? Cuix noço ypampa in huel ticnotlacatl in

[18 VERSO]

atle onca motzotzomatzin: idé: monechichiuh. *Respuesta*. Ca ipampa in ayac tlapia, in ayac nechtlapializ nochan ca huel ninotolinia ca nicnotlacatzintli, ca zan nozel nica, yhuan ca za nipetlauhtinemi ca za àchica notzotzomatzin.

Cuix titepachtlalia? Cuix tocnamacac? cuix ipampa in miac tlacatl, ticcahualtia in Missa, in Domingotica, in pasco[a]tica in zan mochan quixcahuiticate tlahuana, ze çemilhuitl? *Respuesta*. Ca quemaca l. ámo.

Cuix aca otictlatzihuizmauh inic quicahuaz Missa? Cuix noço otinquincahualti[46] in monencahuan, in mopilhuan, in momamalhuan, mochihua? Cuix otiquintlatequipanolti? Cuix omitztlayecoltique? Cuix ipampa in oquixiccauhque in teoyotl yhuan in Missa? *Respuesta*. Ca quemaca. l, ámo.

Cuix in iquac ticcaqui, in iMissatzin Dios, cuix mochi yca, in moyollo? Cuix noço zan tlen ticyilnamiqui? *Respuesta*. Ca quemaca. l. amo-

[18 RECTO]

miss it? *Answer*. Yes, I missed it.

How many Masses did you miss? *Answer*. Four, five, etc.

What feast days? Sundays? Those for which you were very obligated [to attend]? *Answer*. Yes, two Sundays, for example, and one Easter.

Was it the first day of Easter? Or was it the second day of Easter? *Answer*. It was the very first day of Easter for the very first time.

Why did you neglect Mass, not hearing [or] taking care of it? Was it because you couldn't? Perhaps you were ill or something happened to you? *Answer*. No, I was lazy and drunk; friends got me drunk and because of it I abandoned Mass, not hearing it, just missing it.

Were you perhaps ill? Was it because there perhaps was no one to look after things for you? Was it because perhaps you are very poor

[18 VERSO]

and had no rags [or] adornment? *Answer*. Because there is no one to guard things, no one to keep an eye on things for me in my home; I am very miserable and poor, there is only me and I go about bereft of clothing, often just in rags.

Do you sell tepache? Do you sell pulque? Because of this do you impede others from the Mass on Sundays and Easters, they just occupying themselves in getting drunk all day in your home? *Answer*. Yes / no.

Did you infect someone with laziness so that he abandoned Mass? Did you restrain from it those who have become your burden of responsibility, your domestic help and children? Did you make them work? Because of it did they neglect the divine offices and the Mass? *Answer*. Yes / no.

When you heard God's Mass: was it with all your heart? Or were you thinking of [other] things? *Answer*. Yes / no.

---

46. otinquincahualti: read *otiquincahualti*.

[19 RECTO]

Los dias de fiesta, y Domingos, los as guardado co[19 verso]mo Dios manda, teniendo oracion, y dandole gracias, y lo mesmo quando le as hecho dezir a tu Santo alguna Missa? As sido caussa para emborracharte todo el dia, y emborrachar a otros. *Respuesta.* si, l. no.

Trabaxaste tu, por ganar dineros, hilando, texiendo, arando, o trabaxando de otra manera, con que dexaste de yr a la Doctrina, y a la Iglesia. [*Respuesta.*] Si Padre, l. no.

*A LOS QVE SIR*ven, y estan con Españoles, se les a de preguntar assi.

Que tanto tiempo a que no oyes Missa. *Respuesta.* Seys meses á, siete, &c. l. vn año, l. alguna vez.

Porque? que caussa ay para ello? *Respuesta.* Soy pastor, guardo ganado, soy boyero, y no me dexa mi amo, y no puedo dexar las obejas, l. los bueyes, &c. [20 recto]

Tu solo eres el que

[19 VERSO]

guardas el ganado, ó tienes otro compañero que te ayude. *Respuesta.* Si Padre otros compañeros tengo que me ayuden.

Pues porque no os trocays para poderla oyr todos: debes de ser alguno floxo, peresoso mal Christiano, y que no temes a Dios: Aora pues te mando, que nunca dexeis de oyr Missa, sino que os troqueis

PREGVNTAS, para las personas, que tienen á su cargo vna Republica.

Tubiste cuydado de la Doctrina, y procuraste que acudiesen a ella. *Respuesta.* si Padre. l. no.

Al tiempo, y quando contaste la gente en la Iglesia, escondiste algunos criados tuyos, ò otras personas, que por tu caussa no se hallaron en la Iglesia, y Doctrina, y bien de sus almas. *Respuesta.* Si Padre. l. no.

Castigas, y reprehender los [20 verso] que tienen floxedad, y no acuden a la doctrina. *Respuesta.* si,

[19 RECTO]

Have you observed feast days and Sundays as God orders, praying and giving Him thanks, and the same when you have a Mass said for the saint [after whom you are named]? Have you been the reason why you were drunk all day, and making others drunk? *Answer.* Yes / no.

Did you work to make money, spinning, weaving, plowing or working in some other way, and so you failed to go to the doctrine and the church? [*Answer.*] Yes, Father / no.

THOSE WHO SERVE and are with Spaniards must be questioned thus.

How long since you've heard Mass? *Answer.* It's been six months, seven, etc. / one year / a while.

Why? What reason is there for that? *Answer.* I am a shepherd, I watch over livestock, I am a drover, and my employer doesn't let me, and I cannot leave the sheep / the oxen, etc.

Are you the only one who

[19 VERSO]

guards the livestock, or do you have another workmate who helps you? *Answer.* Yes, Father, I have other workmates who help me.

Well, why don't you switch around among yourselves so that everyone can hear it? You must be some weak person, a bad and lazy Christian, who doesn't fear God! Now then, I order you to never neglect hearing Mass, rather that [the whole lot of you] switch [the work] around among yourselves.

QUESTIONS for those persons who are in charge of a municipality.

Did you tend to religious instruction and take care that they came to it? *Answer.* Yes, Father / no.

At the time, and when, you counted the people in the church, did you hide some of your servants or other persons who because of you were not found in the church and doctrine and [attending to] the good of their souls? *Answer.* Yes, Father / no.

Do you punish and reprimand those who are negligent and do not come to the doctrine? *Answer.* Yes /

[19 RECTO]

tzin.

Cuix otitlateoma in ilhuitl ipan, in Domingotica, yn iquac octicteochiuh noço Missa oticytlanili in moSancto? Cuix noço çemilhuitl otitlahuan? Yhuan otitetlahuanti? *Respuesta*. Ca quemacatzin. l. amo.

Cuix otitlatequipano in tehuatl otimotlayecolti? cuix otitzauh otiquit otelemic ànoço ytla oc zentlamantli tequitl oticchiuh, inic oticxic[c]auh in teoyotl *Respuesta*. Ca quemaca. l. àmotzin.

IN TETLAN NEnenque yehuatl, in, in motlatlanizque.

Ye quexquich cahuitl in ámo ticcaqui Missa. *Respuesta*. Ca yc chiquazen metztli, l. chicome, l. ye çe xihuitl, l. zan quenman.

Tleyca tle ipampa. *Respuesta*. Ca nichcapia, ca nipitzopia ca niquaquauhpia, ca ámo nechcahua in noteco, ca àhuel niquincahua in ichcame in quaquahueque.

Cuix moçel in tichca-
[19 VERSO]
pia, cuix noço oncate in mitzpalehuia? *Respuesta*. Ca oncate in nechpalehuia.

Auh tleyca in ámo anmopapatla, inic huel anquicaquizque? Ca çan titllatziuhqui[47] ca ámo quali tichristiano, àmo ticmimacaxilia in Dios axcan, nimitznahuatia, aoquic xiccahua in iMissatzin Dios, ximopapatlacan.
TLATOQVE IC motlatlanizque in aço Gouernador, in àço Alcalde.

Cuix o ypan titlato in teoyotl? Cuix omitztequipacho? Cuix oticmocuitlahui? *Respuesta*. Ca quemaca. l. àmo.

Cuix in yquac teopan otitepouh, cuix aca oticixpacho, in aço monencauh in anoço, oc çe tlacatl in mopampa, oquicauh teoyotl in ipalehuiloca in ianima? *Respuesta*. Ca quemaca. l. amotzin.

Cuix tiquinnonotza, cuix tiquin, tlatzacuiltia[48] in tlatziuhtinemi in quitlacotinemi in teoyotl? *Respuesta*. Ca quemaca.

[19 RECTO]

Did you occupy yourself in spiritual matters on feast days and Sundays when you prayed or asked for a Mass for your saint? Or were you drunk the whole day? And you made others drunk? *Answer*. Yes / no.

Did you work making a living? Did you spin, weave, till the soil or do some other work, for which reason you neglected what pertains to God? *Answer*. Yes / no.

THESE WILL BE asked of those who are lowly household dependents [of Spaniards?].

How long has it been since you heard Mass? *Answer*. It already has been six months / seven / already one year / a while.

Why? On account of what? *Answer*. I guard sheep, I guard pigs, I guard cattle, and my boss doesn't let me, for I am unable to leave the sheep and cattle.

Do you alone guard the sheep,
[19 VERSO]
or are there others who help you? *Answer*. There are those who help me.

Why don't [all of] you switch around so that [each one of] you can hear it? You are just lazy and a bad Christian! You do not fearfully respect God. I order you now to never neglect God's Mass. Switch around [among yourselves]! *RULERS* or governors or alcaldes will be questioned thus.

Did you speak on behalf of that which pertains to God? Did it preoccupy you? Did you take care of it? *Answer*. Yes / no.

When you counted people in the church, did you hide someone, perhaps your servant or maybe some other person, who on account of you abandoned what pertains to God and to the aid of his soul? *Answer*. Yes / no.

Did you admonish and punish those who went around lazy and damaging that which pertains to God? *Answer*. Yes

---

47. titllatziuhqui: read *titlatziuhqui*.
48. tiquin, tlatzacuiltia: read *tiquintlatzacuiltia*.

[20 RECTO]

l. no.

Tienes cuydado, y diligencia en enseñar las oraciones y doctrina a tus hijos, y subditos, y que acudan a la Iglesia. *Respuesta.* Si, l. no.

PREGVNTAS, Acerca del quarto Mandamiento.

*HO*nraste a tu Padre, y a tu Madre, a tus mayores, á los viejos, y ancianos. *Respuesta.* Si Padre, l. no.

Perdiste el respeto alguna vez a tu Padre, y a tu Madre? quando estubiste borracho: los aporreaste, les diste de bofetadas, cozes, o trataste mal de otra qualquiera manera, arrancandoles las barbas los cabellos, como siempre lo soleis hazer estando borrachos. *Respuesta.* Si. l. no.

[20 VERSO]

Obedistelos quando te mandaron alguna cosa. Ayudastelos (pudiendo) en sus [21 recto] necessidades, fauoresistelos, estando enfermos, ó te los dexaste solos, desamparandolos por yrte a emborrachar. *Respuesta.* Si Padre, l. no.

Y quando te reprehenden, (porque te van a la mano) de algun pecado, respondesles con rabia, y con enojo a sus palabras, y razones, ayrandote contra ellos demasiadamente, de tal manera que si posible fuera te los tragaras, segun te ves ayrado. *Respuesta.* si. l. no.

Quando los viste muy rotos, y con grande necessidad de vestido, te mouieron a compasion, vistiendolos, y cubriendoles sus carnes (pudiendo) ò con la auaricia, y cudicia que tienes endurreciste de tal manera tu coraçon, que no distribuyes los bienes que Dios Nuestro Señor a sido seruido de darte.

[20 RECTO]

/ no.

Are you careful and diligent in teaching the prayers and doctrine to your children and subordinates and that they come to church? *Answer.* Yes / no.

QUESTIONS concerning the fourth commandment.

DID you honor your father and your mother, your elders, the old people and the ancient ones? *Answer.* Yes, Father / no.

Did you once lose respect for your father and your mother? When you were drunk: did you beat them up, hit them, kick them or mistreat them in any other way, pulling out their beard or hair as you always are accustomed to do when you are drunk? *Answer.* Yes / no.

[20 VERSO]

Did you obey them when they ordered you to do something? Did you aid them (being able) in their time of need? Did you help them when they were sick or did you abandon them, leaving them helpless so you could go get drunk? *Answer.* Yes, Father / no.

And when they reprimand you (because they are restraining you from some sin), do you respond to their words and arguments with rage and annoyance, becoming so excessively angry with them that you look so angry that, if it were possible, you would swallow them up? *Answer.* Yes / no.

When you see them very wretched and in great need of clothing, do they move you to compassion, [you then] dressing them and covering their flesh (being able), or, with the avarice and greed you have, you hardened your heart in such a way that you do not distribute the goods that our Lord God has been pleased to give you?

[20 RECTO]

l. amotzin.

Cuix ipan titlatoa, in quimatizque teoyotl, in mopilhuan in motlapacholhuan, ynic hualazque teopan. *Respuesta.* Ca quemaca. l. amo.

¶ *TETLATLANI*lliztli, in itechcopa, ic nahui teotenahuatilli, in tiquinmahuiztilizque in tonantzin totatzin &c.

CVIX otiquinmahuiztili, in monantzin, in motatzin motiachcahuan in huehuetque, in ilamatque in acachtopa otlacatque? *Respuesta.* Ca quemaca. l. amo.

Cuix quenmanian, ixco i[c]pac otinen, in monantzin in motatzin? Cuix in yquac otitlahuan, cuix otiquinmimimicti? Cuix otiquinmiyxtetlatzini? Cuix otiquintetetelicçac? cuix noço quen otiquinchiuh? In aço otiquintentzonhuihuitlac, in aço intzon itech otiquiman in iuh anquichihuani? *Respuesta.* Ca quemaca. l. amo.

[20 VERSO]

Cuix otiquintlacama in iquac, tlen omitz-nahuatique? Cuix otiquinpalehui in in, netolini-lizpan,[49] cuix o inca timochiuh, in yquac cocoliztli inpan, ohuala? Cuix noço zan otiquintlaztiquiz in ipampa in motlahuanaliz in moxixicuiyo in yuh anquichihuani. *Respuesta.* Ca quemaca. l. amo.

Auh in quenmanian in áço omitznonotza, in aço mitztlacahualtia, cuix zan ic tiquinnananquilia in tlen amo qualli tlatolli ic tiquinpinauhtia ic tiquincuepilia in i, miyo[50] in intlatol, in çan ic otimoçoneuh in zan ic opozon in mochichicauh, in ticnequi ma xiquinqua. *Respuesta.* Ca quemaca. l. amo.

In yquac otiquimitac in çá áchica, intatapatzin, cuix omitztlaocoltique? Cuix otiquintlaquenti? Cuix otiquintlapachilhui in innacayotzin? In ça pani, ócatca, cuix noço zan omitztlapololti in maxca motlatqui in omitzmopialtilli in Dios in tictetlaocoliz, cuix zan ilhuiz oquitepitzo in

[20 RECTO]

/ no.

Have you spoken on behalf of your children and subordinates knowing what pertains to God so that they will come to church? *Answer.* Yes / no.

¶ *QUESTIONS* concerning the fourth divine commandment: we shall honor our mother and our father.

Did you honor your mother and your father, your elder brothers, the elderly men and women who were born first? *Answer.* Yes / no.

Did you sometime offend your mother and your father? Did you repeatedly beat them when you were drunk? Did you slap them in the face? Did you repeatedly kick them? Perhaps you disturbed them? Perhaps you pulled out their facial hair or grabbed them by their hair as you are wont to do? *Answer.* Yes / no

[20 VERSO]

Did you obey them when they ordered you [to do something]? Did you help them in their time of affliction? Did you take care of them when some sickness came upon them? Perhaps you just quickly cast them aside because of your drunkenness and gluttony, as you are wont to do? *Answer.* Yes / no.

Perhaps they admonish and restrain you sometimes: do you frequently respond to their [parental] correction [by] shaming them and returning their fine words with bad language, getting so excited and your bile and bitterness boiling over so, that you want to eat them up? *Answer.* Yes / no.

Did they make you feel pity when you saw their rags, threadbare and patched? Did you clothe them? Did you cover [the parts of] their bodies that showed? Or did your goods and property (which God provided you for safekeeping to have mercy on others) just confuse you? Did avarice just especially harden

---

49. in, netolinilizpan: read *innetolinilizpan.*

50. i, miyo: read *imiyo.*

[21 RECTO]

Respuesta. Si Padre, l. no.

PREGVNTAS a[21 verso]cerca del quinto Mandamiento.

AS matado a alguno, hiriendole, dandole bocado, hechizandolo, ò echandolo en alguna barranca, ò rio. *Respuesta.* Si Padre. l. no.

As desseado la muerte á alguno, hechando modos, y traças como quitarle la vida. Y esto te duro por mucho tiempo. *Respuesta.* Si Padre, l. no.

Aste desseado la muerte, desesperadamente. *Respuesta.* Si. l. no.

Tienes aora odio, y enemistad con alguna persona, con todo tu coraçon. *Respuesta.* si. l. no.

[21 VERSO]

PREGVNTAS, para las doncellas.

Tomaste algun veuediso estando preñada, para echar la criatura. *Respuesta.* Si Padre. l. no.

Recibio el agua del Baptismo, ó murio sin ella. *Respuesta.* Si Padre. l. no.

Quantas vezes as hecho [22 recto] este pecado. *Respuesta.* Quatro, ò cinco, &c.

PREGVNTAS, para las parteras.

Diste alguna veuida a alguna doncella, o persona preñada, á fin de que echase la criatura. *Respuesta.* Si, l. no.

Quantas vezes lo as hecho. *Respuesta.* dos, tres, &c.

Pues aora te mando, que otra vez, no te acontesca tal, porque as cometido vn grauisimo pecado, perdiendose por tu caussa la crivtura[11] de Dios, sin receuir el medio de su saluacion, que es el Santo Baptismo y si

[21 RECTO]

Answer. Yes, Father / no.

QUESTIONS concerning the fifth commandment.

Have you murdered someone, wounding him, giving him [some poisoned?] morsel, casting a spell on him, or throwing him into some ravine or river? *Answer.* Yes, Father / no.

Have you desired death for someone, contriving ways and plans how to take his life away? And this continued with you for some time? *Answer.* Yes, Father / no.

Have you desperately desired to die? *Answer.* Yes / no.

Do you now bear (with all your heart) hatred and enmity for some person? *Answer.* Yes / no.

[21 VERSO]

QUESTIONS for young women.

Being pregnant, did you take some potion in order to expel the baby? *Answer.* Yes, Father / no.

Did he receive the water of baptism, or did he die without it? *Answer.* Yes, Father / no.

How many times have you committed this sin? *Answer.* Four or five, etc.

QUESTIONS for the midwives.

Did you give some drink to some young woman, or a pregnant person, in order that she expel the baby? *Answer.* Yes / no.

How many times have you done it? *Answer.* Two, three, etc.

Now then, I order you that such will not happen to you again because you have committed a very grave sin; because of you a creature of God was lost without receiving the means of his salvation (which is holy baptism). If

---

11. crivtura: read *criatura*.

[21 RECTO]

moyolo in tzotzocatiliztli *Respuesta.* Ca quemaca. l. amo.

❡ *TETLATLANIliztli,* in itechcopa inic macuiltetl, teotenahuatilli, in amo titetopehuaz titemictiz.

CVIX aca oticmicti, in huel o momac mic? In aço oticyxil, in aço oticpayti in àço otictlachihui, in àço oticatlacomolhui octictepexihui, in otictla[z], in otla⁵¹ tictocac. *Respuesta.* Ca quemacatzin, l. amotzin.

Cuix otitemiquizelehui? Cuix oticnemilitinen, in quenin, titemictiz, in huel momac miquiz, in aquin? Cuix huecauhtica, in o yuh ticilnamictinen. *Respuesta.* Ca quemacatzin, l. amo.

Cuix otimomiquizelehui, otitlaçentlami in quenmanian? *Respuesta.* Ca quemaca. l. amo.

Cuix aca ticçentelchiuhtinemi, ticcocolitinemi? *Respuesta.* Ca quemaca. l. amo.

[21 VERSO]

NICAN CA IC motlatlanizque ichpopochtin.

Cuix otimopayti in iquac totztli in ipampa timotlatlaxiliz, in huetziz moconeuh? *Respuesta.* Ca quemaca. l. amo.

Cuix amo quatequitia? cuix noço zan yuh omic? *Respuesta.* Ca quemaca. l. amo.

Quezquipa in yuhqui, oticchiuh *[Respuesta.]* çepa opa &c.

NICAN CA IC motlatlania in titiçi.

Cuix aca ichpochtli otic, payti⁵² oticmacac patli, inic huetziz yconeuh motlatlaxiliz. *Respuesta.* Ca quemaca. l. amo.

Quezquipa in ye yuh ticchihua? *Respuesta.* Ca ye opa yexpa.

Axcan nimitznahuatia áocmo, oc cepa yuhqui ticchihuaz, ca zenca huei tlatlacolli, ca mopampa nenpolihui in itlachihualtzin Dios, in amo quimomacehuitiuh in nemaquixtiliztli Sancto Baptizmo, ca tehuatl mictlan tiaz, intla

[21 RECTO]

your heart? *Answer.* Yes / no.

❡ *QUESTIONS* concerning the fifth divine commandment: not to contend against and kill people.

HAVE you killed someone? Someone died at your hands? Did you stab him or give him a deadly poison or bewitch him or throw him down into a well, hurl him down from on high, cast him into water, bury him? *Answer.* Yes / no.

Did you desire the death of others? Did you go about thinking how to kill people, how he could die at your hands, and who it would be? Did you think [this] for a long time? *Answer.* Yes / no.

Did you desire your own death, sometime wishing to bring it all to an end? *Answer.* Yes / no.

Have you despised and hated someone? *Answer.* Yes / no.

[21 VERSO]

HERE IS WHAT young unmarried women will be asked.

Did you take some medicine when you were pregnant in order to abort the baby, your child falling [stillborn]? *Answer.* Yes / no.

He was not baptized? Or did he die just as he was? *Answer.* Yes / no.

How many times have you done such? *[Answer.]* Once, twice, etc.

HERE IS WHAT midwives will be asked.

Did you give medicine [or] a potion to a young unmarried woman so that her baby would fall [stillborn] and be aborted? *Answer.* Yes / no.

How many times have you done it? *Answer.* Two, three times already.

Now I order you to never again do so for it is a very great sin. On account of you a creature of God, who did not enjoy salvation and holy baptism, perished in vain. You will go to hell if

---

51. otla: perhaps to be read *atlan.*
52. otic, payti: read *oticpayti.*

otra vez lo hizieres te as de ir al infierno.

PREGVNTAS, Acerca del Sexto Mandamiento.

AS estado amançebado, te as entregado a los vicios de la sensualidad, y deleyte carnal. As tenido ex[22 verso]cesso[12] con alguna, ò algunas mugeres. *Respuesta*. Si Padre. l. no.

Con quantas mugeres as pecado, teniendo con ellas parte. *Respuesta*. Con quatro, l. cinco &c.

Son casadas, viudas, solteras, ò doncellas. *Respuesta*. VerbiGracia la vna casada, la otra viuda, la otra soltera, y la otra doncella.

Es alguna dellas, tu parienta cercana, tu hermana, tu

cuñada, tu sobrina, ó finalmente deuda tuya, dentro del primero, segundo, tercero quarto grado. *Respuesta*. Si Padre. l. no.

Quando llegaste a tu parienta, estabas borracho, ó no. *Respuesta*. Si, l. no.

La doncella que dizes con quien pecastes, quitastele la honra tu, estrupandola. *Respuesta*. Si Padre, l. no.

Y para cometer este pecado forçastela, con violencia, y amenaças, arrastrandola, y haziendola fuerça, resistien[23 recto]dose ella con muchas veras. *Respuesta*. Si Padre, l. no.

Quantas vezes tubiste acto con cada vna de las mugers que carnalmente as conocido. *Respuesta*. Con la vna VerbiGracia dos, con la otra tres, &c.

Con quantas mugeres casadas pecaste, y quantas vezes con cada vna. *Respuesta*. con dos ò tres &c.

AQVI SE LES HA de aduertir a los penitentes,

you do it again you have to go to hell.

QUESTIONS concerning the sixth commandment.

HAVE you had concubines, have you delivered yourself up to the vices of sensuality and carnal delight? Have you had carnal access to one, or some, women? *Answer*. Yes, Father / no.

How many women have you sinned with, having relations with them? *Answer*. With four / five, etc.

Are they married women, widows, single women or virgins? *Answer*. For example, one is married, the other is a widow, the other single, and the other a virgin.

Is one of them your close female relative, your sister, your

sister-in-law, your niece, or (finally) your relative within the first, second, third [or] fourth degree [of consanguinity]? *Answer*. Yes, Father / no.

When you got to your female relative, were you drunk or not? *Answer*. Yes / no.

The virgin with whom you say you sinned: did you steal her honor, raping her? *Answer*. Yes, Father / no.

And in order to commit this sin you coerced her with violence and threats, dragging her around and raping her, she being completely unwilling? *Answer*. Yes, Father / no.

How many times did you do it with each one of the women whom you have known in a carnal manner? *Answer*. With the one, for example, two, with the other three, etc.

With how many married women did you sin, and how many times with each one? *Answer*. With two or three, etc.

HERE THE penitents have to be cautioned

---

12. excesso: here and elsewhere (e.g., 24v and 34v) probably to be read (given the context) as *accesso* "carnal access."

[22 RECTO]
oc çepa yuhqui ticchihuaz.

¶ *TETLATLANIliztli*, in itechcopa chiquaçentetl, teotenahuatilli.

CVIX otimomecati? Cuix otaàhuilnen? Cuix otimomecati in tlalticpac tlatlacolli tlailpaquiliztli? Cuix àca noço acame çihua ó intech tacic in innahuac otitlatlaco. *Respuesta*. Ca quemaca. l. amo.

Quezquintin in çihua o intech taçic o innahuac titlatlaco. *Respuesta*. Ca nahui, macuilli, &c.

Cuix namiqueque? cuix icnoçihua? Cuix zan yuh nemi? Cuix nozo huel oc maçiticate ichpopochtin. *Respuesta*. VerbiGracia ca in ce namique, in oc ce icnoçihuatl, in oc çe zan yuh nemi auh in oc ce ichpochlti.[53] &c.

Cuix ma çeme mohuayolque in aço quen ticnotza in aço mohueltiuh mo
[22 VERSO]
huepol momach in anoço zentlamampan ontlamampan yetlamampan mohuayolqui meço motlapalo. *Respuesta*. Ca quemaca. l. amo.

In iquac o ytech taçic mohuayolqui, cuix otitlahuan noço amo. *Respuesta*. Ca quemaca. l. amo.

In ichpochtli ticytoa o ynahuac, titlatlaco, cuix quin tehuatl yancuican oticmahuizpolo, oticxapotlac oticcuilli in iichpochyo *Respuesta*. Ca quemaca. l. amo.

Cuix oticcuicuitlahuilti? Cuix temamauhtiliztica in o itech taçic, cuix acachtopa, otichuihuilan? Cuix huel àmo quinequia, cuix omomapatlaya? *Respuesta*. Ca quemaca. l. amo.

Quequezquipa innahuac otaçic in çeceme çihua otiquinnotz? *Respuesta*. Ca in çe VerbiGracia opa in itech onaçic auh in oc ce yexpa, &c.

Quezqui in namique itech otaçic, yhuan quezquipa. *Respuesta*. Ca ome, yey, &c.

NICAN MONEMAchtiz, in moyolcuitiani

[22 RECTO]
you again do so.

¶ *QUESTIONS* concerning the sixth divine commandment.

HAVE you had conbubines? Have you licentiously enjoyed yourself? Have you given yourself over to earthly sin and lust? Or did you have sexual relations and sin with one or a few woman? *Answer*. Yes / no.

How many women did you have sexual relations and sin with? *Answer*. Four, five, etc.

Married women? Widows? Single women? Or completely virgin maidens? *Answer*. For example, the one is married, the other a widow, the other single, and the other a maiden, etc.

Is one of them your relative or relation or your older sister, your
[22 VERSO]
sister-in-law, your niece or your relative or offspring within the first, second [or] third degree [of consanguinity]? *Answer*. Yes / no.

When you had sexual relations with your relatives: were you drunk or not? *Answer*. Yes / no.

The maiden you are saying you sinned with: did you just now for the first time disgrace her, deflowering and spoiling her and taking her virginity from her? *Answer*. Yes / no.

Did you repeatedly force her? Did you have sexual relations with her by means of fear and terror? Did you first repeatedly drag her around? She absolutely did not want it? She was resisting? *Answer*. Yes / no.

How many times did you have sexual relations with each one of the women you mentioned? *Answer*. The one, for example, I had sexual relations with two times, and the other three times, etc.

How many married women have you had sexual relations with, and how many times? *Answer*. Two, three, etc.

HERE THE PENITENT will be advised

---

53. ichpochlti: read *ichpochtli*.

[23 RECTO]

que es muy necessario, asignar el numero cierto de los pecados, y en esta Platica, se les dá a entender vastantemente el orden, que para ello an de tener.

Teneys ya de costumbre, vosotros los Naturales, que si estays metidos con vna muger de dia, y de noche, vn año, ò dos, llegado el Confessor, á preguntaros, que quantas vezes habeis, llegado a ella, respondeys que dos ò tres. Y este mo[23 verso]do de responder, es en todos vosotros vniuersalmente, con lo qual hazeis las confessiones defectuosas: por quanto es muy necessario, dezir el numero cierto de las vezes, que cometeis vn pecado, y haueys de declarar, y dezir señaladamente el numero de vezes que llegays a cada vna de las mugeres que confessais; porque cada acto es vn pecado distinto numero, y avnque no os acordeis del numero cierto de pecados, por auer pasado mucho tiempo, y vosotros aumentadolos en gran manera:

[23 VERSO]

pero id recorriendo, y trayendo a la memoria, por el discurso de los dias, de las noches, de las semanas, de los meses, y de los años, contando con maizes vn dia con otro, hasta llegar a vn año, a dos, &c. Y si desta manera no estays muy ciertos en el vltimo numero, cumplireis con [24 recto] dezirle al Confessor, no estoy cierto en el numero, Padre de los pecados, que he cometido en el discurso del año: pero me parece, que tantas vezes poco mas a[13] menos, quatrocientas, ò aquel numero que jusgais ser el mas cierto, y desta manera hazeis buena confession.

Por ventura, quando te embriagaste, perdiendo tus sentidos, caiste en el abominable pecado de la sodomia, teniendo que ver con otro.
Respuesta. Si Padre. l. no.

O as cometido el pecado contra naturaleza,

[23 RECTO]

that it is very necessary to determine the exact number [of each one] of the sins, and in this speech they are given to broadly understand the order that they have to observe in this.

You natives already have the habit that if you are involved with a woman day and night [for] a year or two, once the confessor has arrived to question you how many times you have gotten to her, you respond two or three times. And this way of responding is universal in all of you, whereupon you make defective confessions. Hence it is very necessary to say the exact number of times you committed a sin, and you must declare and state specifically the number of times you got to each one of the women about whom you are confessing, because each act is a sin distinct in number. And although you do not know the exact number of sins because a great deal of time has passed and you have greatly increased them:

[23 VERSO]

but go remembering and recalling through the passage of the days, the nights, the weeks, the months and the years, counting up with kernels of corn one day after another, until reaching a year, two, etc. And if in this way you are [still] not very sure of the final number, you comply [with your obligations] by saying to the confessor: "Father, I am not sure of the number of sins I have committed in the period of a year, but it seems to me that it was about 400 times, a little more or less, or that number that you judge to be most certain." And in this way you make a good confession .

Perhaps when you got drunk and lost your senses you fell into the abominable sin of sodomy, having something to do with another man?
Answer. Yes, Father / no.

Or have you committed the sin against nature,

---

13. a: read *o*.

[23 RECTO]

inic huel quimelauhcaytoz in izquipa tlatlacoa inahuac çe cihuatl, in çaco[54] quexquich cahuitl.

In amehuantin anmaçehualtin, in manel ye oxihuitl, ye xihuitl, anquimomecatititcate çe çihuatl, in çeçemilhuitl in çeçeyohual ytech antlatlacoticate, in iquac amechtlatlania, in teopixqui teyolcuitiani in quezquipa inahua[c] oantlatlacoque; zan anquinanquilia, ca opa, yexpa, auh huel amoçentlatol in anmochtin, auh ca yehuatl in huel ic anquitlacoa in ámoneyol-cuitiliz. Yeyca huel monequi, in mopoaz molnamiquiz in ipan neyolcuitiliztli, in quezquipa mochihua tlatlacolli, ypampa in izquipa itech amaçi ce çihuatl, ca no yzqui temictiani, tlatlacolli anquichihua, auh in manel aocmo anquilnamiquizque in yzquipa, ipampa, in ye huel huecauh antlatlacoa, yhuan huel oanquitlapehuilique

[23 VERSO]

in tlatlacolli yecce[55] ic anquitepotztocazque, ic anquilnamiquizque, in çeçemilhuitl, in zeçeyohual in çecenmetztli in çeçexihuitl, auh anquitlaolpoazque, in çeçemilhuitl tlatlacolli, auh zan yuh anquitzonquixtihue in çe xihuitl, in onxihuitl, &c. Auh intlacamo huel, amoyolo pachihui, in yzquipa, anquilhuizque in amotei-olcuiticauh, ca ámo huel nicilnamiqui, in huel quezquipa onicchiuh tlatlacolli, in çe xihuitl, yece [ni]nomati yzquipa, in in aço centzompa, in anoço izquipa in achi, anquixyeyecoa, anquipantilia, in izquipa, auh iuhqui, in, inic melahuac anmoyolcuitizque.

Cuix in iquac otitlahuan, cuix ó ipan tihuetz, in temamauhti tlatlacolli? In motenehua cuiloyotl? In aca oc ze in zan moquichpo o ytech taçic. *Respuesta.* Ca quemaca. l. amo.

Cuix noço oticmotequiti, in áchihualoni tetzauhtlatlacolli, in aço itla ma-

[23 RECTO]

so that he will be able to truthfully say all the times he sinned with a woman and for how much time it was.

You natives, even though you are cohabiting for two [or] three years already with a woman and sinning with her every day and every night, when the priest and confessor questions you about how many times you have sinned with her, you just reply: "Two times, three times." And you all make the same [sort of] statement, and with this you really damage your confession. Because it is very necessary to count and remember in confession how many times the sin was done, because all the times you have sexual relations with a woman, you also commit as many mortal sins. And even though you will not remember how many times it was because you have been sinning for a long time and greatly increased the

[23 VERSO]

sins; yet investigate and remember them by each day and night, each month and year, counting the sins of each day with dried kernels of maize, just so bringing to a conclusion one year, two years, etc. And if you are not satisfied of all the times, say to your confessor: "I cannot remember absolutely all the times I committed this sin in one year, yet I think it was this many times, perhaps 400 times, or as many times, more or less, as you discretely deem certain all the times to be." And it is in this way that you will rightly confess.

When you were drunk: did you fall into the frightful sin, when you have had sexual relations with your fellow man, called sodomy? *Answer.* Yes / no.

Perhaps you were responsible for the frightful sin, unworthy of being done,

[24 RECTO]

teniendo acto con algun animal. *Respuesta.* Si Padre, l. no.

As tenido tactos con tus mesmas carnes, teniendo el objeto en alguna muger. Y si fuere muger, se le preguntará. Teniendo el objeto en algun hombre, teniendo polucion, y derramamiento de [24 verso] semen, como si verdaderamente tubieses acto con la tal persona. *Respuesta.* Si. Padre. l. no.

Y essos hombres. Y si es muger. Y essa muger en quien pensauas, es casada, soltera, viuda, ò doncella, quantas vezes te á sucedido esso? *Respuesta.* Es casada, viuda, soltera, doncella, y lo [he] hecho, quatro, cinco [vezes], &c.

As hecho burla de alguna muger? (Y si fuere muger) De algun hombre, poniendote alguna mala cosa en la parte natural, quando llegaste á ella, de lo qual le procedio alguna enfermedad? *Respuesta.* Si Padre, l. no.

Quando llegaste a tu muger, ò a otra qualquiera, estaba con su costumbre? *Respuesta.* si. l. no.

[24 VERSO]

PREGVNTAS, para solas las mugeres.

Llegò alguua[14] vez tu marido, ó otro a ti estando con tu costumbre. *Respuesta.* Si Padre. l. no. [25 recto]

Tubiste tacto con ti mesma, teniendo por objeto algun hombre, de tal manera que cumpliste, y consumaste el acto. *Respuesta.* Si l. no.

Tubiste acto carnal, con otra muger como tu, ó ella contigo. *Respuesta.* Si l. no.

Quando tu marido tubo excesso contigo, estando borracho, fue por el vaso comun, ò hizo el pecado nefando, trocando la parte, y tu no se lo impediste. *Respuesta.* Si Padre. l. no.

As vsado de palabras desonestas, para mouer a las mugeres? *Respuesta.* Si Padre. l. no.

Quando pecaste con

[24 RECTO]

committing a carnal act with some animal? *Answer.* Yes, Father / no.

Have you felt your own flesh, having [as] the object [of your desire] some woman? And if it were a woman she will be asked [see below]: having [as] the object [of your desire] some man, did the emission and spilling of semen occur as if you truly had had a carnal act with this person? *Answer.* Yes, Father / no.

And those [are] the men. And if it is a woman: and that woman whom you thought about, is she a married woman, single, widow, or virgin? How many times has this happened to you? *Answer.* She is a married woman, widow, single, virgin, and I have done it four, five times, etc.

Have you deceived and made fun of some woman? And if it were a woman: [Did you deceive and make fun] of some man, putting something on your private parts, [so that] when you got to him, because of this some sickness happened to him? *Answer.* Yes, Father / no.

When you got to your wife or any other woman, was she menstruating? *Answer.* Yes / no.

[24 VERSO]

QUESTIONS for women only.

Did your husband or some other man come to you while you were menstruating? *Answer.* Yes, Father / no.

Did you touch yourself, having as the object [of your desire] some man, in such a way that you completed and consummated the carnal act? *Answer.* Yes / no.

Did you commit a carnal act with another woman like you, or she with you? *Answer.* Yes / no.

When your husband had carnal access with you (being drunk), was it in the common vessel [i.e., vagina] or did he commit the unspeakable and abominable sin, switching parts [i.e., anal sex], and you did not stop him? *Answer.* Yes, Father / no.

Have you used lewd words to provoke women? *Answer.* Yes, Father / no.

When you sinned with

---

14. alguua: read *alguna.*

[24 RECTO]

nenenqui yolcatl itech otaçic. *Respuesta.* Ca quemaca. l. amo.

Cuix quenmanian oticmatocac in monacayo, in aca çihuatl, ticilnamictica. Auh intla çihuatl molhuiz. In aca oquichtli ticilnamicticac. Auh cuix oticnoqui in motlacaxinachyo, in yuhqui in huel o ytech taçic timomati. *Respuesta.* Ca quemaca. l. amo.

Auh tleinon çihuatl? Cuix namique? Cuix icnoçihuatl? cuix ichpochtli, cuix zan yuu[56] nemi, quezquipa, in yuh oticchiuh? *Respuesta.* Ca namique &c. Auh ca na[u]hpa in onicchiuh.

Cuix aca cihuatl o yca timoca[ca]yauh. Auh intla cihuatl motlatlaniz. Cuix aca oquichtli o yca timoca[ca]yauh itla otictlalili, in monacayo, in yquac itech otacic noço motech oaçic inic ococolizcui. *Respuesta.* Ca quemaca. l. amo.

In yquac ytech otaçic monamic noço aca çe çihuatl, cuix moçihuacocoa? Cuix mezhuia? *Respuesta.* Ca quemaca. l. amo.

[24 VERSO]

NICAN CA, IC motlatlanizque in çihuatzitzintin.

Cuix quemanian timezhuia, in iquac motech oaçic monamic noço oc ze tlacatl? *Respuesta.* Ca quemaca. l. amo.

Cuix oticmamatocac, in monacayo, in oquichtli ticilnamiqui, in ticnequi ma monahuac tlacaco.[57] Auh cuix otimommahui, in otictzonquixti in tlaylpaquiliztli. *Respuesta.* Ca quemacatzin, l. amo.

Cuix ma quenmanian, otimopatlachhui in çan no mocihuapo ytech taçic, noço motech oaçic? *Respuesta.* Ca quemaca. l. amo.

Cuix in iquac tlahuanqui monamic motech açic cuix oncan inic tiçihuatl? Cuix noço quenmanian o motech quichiuh in tetlaylti tlatlacolli? In amo tictlacahualti? *Respuesta.* Ca quemac[a] l. amotzin.

Cuix oticmotequiuhti, in tlailpaquiliztlatolli inic otiquinyoleuh in çihua? *Respuesta.* Ca quemaca. l. amo.

Cuix in yquac aca otic-

[24 RECTO]

of having sexual relations with a four-legged animal [or] a beast? *Answer.* Yes / no.

Did you sometime touch your body thinking of some woman? And if it is a woman she will be told: you thought of some man. Did you [then] spill your semen, you thinking that it was just as if you had really had sexual relations with that person? *Answer.* Yes / no.

What was that woman's status? Was she married? A widow? A maiden? Single? How many times did you do so? *Answer.* She is married, etc., and I did it four times.

Did you deceive some woman? And if it is a woman, she will be asked: did you deceive some man, putting something on your body so that he caught some illness when you had sexual relations with him or he had sexual relations with you? *Answer.* Yes / no.

When you had sexual relations with your wife or some other woman: was she menstruating? Was she with her monthlies? *Answer.* Yes / no.

[24 VERSO]

HERE IS WHAT the women will be asked.

Were you menstruating sometime when your husband or some other man had sexual relations with you? *Answer.* Yes / no.

Did you repeatedly feel your body, thinking of a man, and wanting him to sin with you? Did you do it to yourself with your hands, bringing to a conclusion your lust? *Answer.* Yes / no.

Did you sometime commit a carnal act, you having sexual relations with another woman or she likewise having sexual relations with you? *Answer.* Yes / no.

When your husband was drunk: did he have sex with you where you are a woman, or sometime did he do the disgusting sin to you? Did you restrain him? *Answer.* Yes / no.

Were you responsible for dirty words with which you provoked and excited women? *Answer.* Yes / no.

When you cohabited

---

56. yuu: read *yuh.*
57. tlacaco: read *i[h]tlacoco.*

[25 RECTO]

mugeres fue delante de algunos a quienes diste mal exemplo; porque hasta entonces no sabian pecar con mugeres, y por tu mala nota se lo enseñaste. *Respuesta.* Si Padre l. no.

As sido tercero, ò alcaguete de alguno, ó alguna, que por ti se ayan conocido, y pe[25 verso]cado mouiendo tu a alguna muger para otro.

Eres consentidor, ò consientes que estèn amancebados tu padre, ó tu madre, hijos, parientes, y criados, sin yrles a la mano, y reprehenderlos. *Respuesta.* Si. l. no.

Quando con la borrachera, y embriaguez, se caen sin sentido en tu casa algunos, y hazen en tu presencia abominables pecados, no les vas a la mano? o te los estas mirando. *Respuesta.* Si Padre. l. no.

PREGVNTAS, Acerca del Septimo Mandamiento.

[25 VERSO]

As hurtado los bienes de tus proximos. *Respuesta.* Si. l. no.

Que es lo que as hurtado dineros, mantas, bueyes, caballos, obejas, puercos, gallinas, ó otra cosa de mucho valor, y precio. *Respuesta.* Si Padre. l. no. [26 recto]

A quien hurtaste lo que dizes, es persona pobre, y nesecitada? *Respuesta.* Si Padre. l. no.

Fuiste a robar alguna noche, agujerando la casa, echando sueño a los dueños della, con palabras diabolicas, de hechizo, ò encantam[i]ento, con lo qual facilmente tubiste lugar de traerte todo lo que hallaste? *Respuesta.* Si Padre. l. no.

Tienes de costumbre, el hurtar? *Respuesta.* No Padre. si alguna vez hurto, no son sino vnos elotes, calabaças, &c.

Tienes en tu casa, algunos hurtos que has hecho. *Respuesta.* Si l. no.

PREGVNTAS Acerca del

[25 RECTO]

women: was it in front of some to whom you gave a bad example? Because until then they did not know how to sin with women, and on account of your notoriousness you showed it to them? *Answer.* Yes, Father / no.

Have you been the procurer or pimp of some man or woman, who because of you might have gotten acquainted and sinned, you provoking some woman to another man?

Were you complaisant or did you consent that your father or your mother, children, relatives and servants cohabit, without restraining and reprimanding them? *Answer.* Yes / no.

When some fell senselessly in your house because of drunkenness and intoxication and in your presence committed abominable sins: didn't you restrain them? Or were you [just] looking at them? *Answer.* Yes, Father / no.

QUESTIONS concerning the seventh commandment.

[25 VERSO]

Have you stolen your neighbors' property? *Answer.* Yes / no.

What is it that you have stolen: money, blankets, cattle, horses, sheep, pigs, fowl, or something else of great value and price? *Answer.* Yes, Father / no.

Is the one you say you stole from a poor and needy person? *Answer.* Yes, Father / no.

Did you go to rob some night, making a hole in a house and casting sleep upon the owners of it with diabolical words of magic and enchantment, whereupon you easily had the opportunity to carry away all that you found? *Answer.* Yes, Father / no.

Do you have a habit of stealing? *Answer.* No, Father. If sometimes I steal, it is nothing but some ears of green roasting corn, gourds, etc.

Do you have in your house some of the things you have stolen? *Answer.* Yes / no.

QUESTIONS concerning the

[25 RECTO]

momecati, çihuatl, cuix àcame, imixpan in,
ayamo quitta tlatlacolli in tehuatl, otiquimititi?
otiquin, nextili,[58] in amo qualli. *Respuesta.* Ca
quemacatzin, l. amotzin.

Cuix quenmanian aca otictlanahualnochili? In
mopampa, omiximatque tlatlacoltica, in huel
tehuatl, oticyoleuh çihuatl, in otictenochili?

Cuix ticmachilitica, in aço monantzin? in aço
motatzin? mopilhuan mohuayolque?
monencahuan inic momecatitiezque? cuix amo
tiquintlacahualtia?

Cuix in yquac mochan tlahuanticate, in
xoxocomiqui, in o[n]can mixpan quichihua, in
áchihualoni tlatlacolli, cuix amo tiquintlacahualtia? Cuix zan tiquimiyta? *Respuesta.* Ca
quema[ca]tzin, l. amotzin.

¶ *TETLATLAN*Iliztli in itechcopa ic chicontetl,
teotenahuatili in amo tichtequiz.

[25 VERSO]

CVIX otichtec? Cuix oticcuic in teaxca in
tetlatqui? *Respuesta.* Ca quemaca. l. amo.

Tlen oticichtec? Cuix tomi[n]? Cuix tilmatli?
Quaquahue, caballo, ychcame, totoltin, pitzome,
noço ytla oc zentlamantli huel patio? *Respuesta.*
Ca quemaca. l amo.

Cuix in aquin, o yca timoca[ca]yauh otictlach-
tequili, cuix huel icnotlacatzintli? *Respuesta.* Ca
quemaca. l. amo.

Cuix quenmanian otitecalcoyoni? yohualtica
tepan oticalac? otitecochtlaz, in motlacate-
colotlatol yca? inic otichtequito inic oticmamato
in teaxca in tetlatqui? *Respuesta.* Ca quemaca. l.
amotzin.

Cuix ye motequiuh, in tichtequi? *Respuesta.* Ca
ámotzin. ca çan elotzintli ayotzintli &c.
Quenmanian nicelehuia.

Cuix zà ye noma, mochan ticpixtica in teaxca
tetlatqui oticichtec. *Respuesta.* Ca quema[ca]tzin,
l. amotzin.

¶ *TETLATLAN*Iliztlatolli in itechcopa,

[25 RECTO]

with some woman: did you show and reveal what
was bad in front of those who had not yet seen
the sin? *Answer.* Yes / no.

Did you sometime pimp for somebody? On
account of you did they know themselves through
sin, you yourself provoking a woman for whom
you had summoned someone?

Did you know the failings of your mother or
your father, your children and your relatives, your
household dependents, that they were cohabiting,
and you did not restrain them? [*Answer.* Yes / no.]

When they were drunk and intoxicated in your
home, there committing before you sins unworthy of doing: didn't you restrain them? Did you
just look at them? *Answer.* Yes / no.

¶ *QUESTIONS* concerning the seventh divine
commandment: you shall not steal.

[25 VERSO]

HAVE you stolen? Have you taken other people's
goods and property? *Answer.* Yes / no.

What have you stolen? Money? Blankets?
Cattle, horses, sheep, domestic fowl, pigs, or some
other thing of great value? *Answer.* Yes / no.

The one you deceived and stole from: is he
really poor and miserable? *Answer.* Yes / no.

Did you sometime make a hole in a house,
entering in on people during the night and casting them into sleep with your diabolical words of
enchantment so that you stole and carried away
the goods and property of others? *Answer.* Yes /
no.

Is stealing your profession? *Answer.* No, it is
just a little bit of fresh green maize, gourds, etc.,
that I sometimes desire.

Do you still have in your home the goods and
property you stole from others? *Answer.* Yes / no.

¶ *QUESTIONS* concerning the

---

58. otiquin, nextili: *otiquinnextili.*

[26 RECTO]

Octauo Mandamiento.

AS mentido, ò leuantado falso testimonio?
Respuesta. Si Padre, l. no.

Y a quien leuantaste falso testimonio, fue por ello ignominado, y afrentado, y fue [26 verso] delante de muchas personas el leuantarle testimonio, y quitarle la honra: siguiosele por ello algun castigo, ygnominioso. *Respuesta.* Si l. no.

PREGVNTAS, Acerca del noueno Mandamiento.

*DE*seaste, y procuraste la muger de tu proximo.
Respuesta. Si Padre, l. no.

PREGVNTAS, Acerca del decimo Mandamiento.

[26 VERSO]

*CV*diciaste los bienes de tus proximos, teniendo ambicion dellos. *Respuesta.* Si l. no.

ESTOS SON LOS cinco Mandamientos de nuestra Madre la Yglesia.

El primero, oyr Missa entera los Domingos, y fiestas de guardar.
El segundo confessar en la Quaresma, ò quando ay [27 recto] necesidad.
El tercero, comulgar el Iueues Santo ó Pasqua, &c.
El quarto, ayunar quando lo manda la Yglesia.
El quinto, pagar los diesmos, y primicias.

*PREGVNTAS SO*bre estos cinco Mandamientos de la Sancta Yglesia.

[26 RECTO]

eighth commandment.

HAVE you lied or given perjured evidence?
Answer. Yes, Father / no.

And the one against whom you gave perjured evidence: was he disgraced because of it? And the bearing of false witness against him and the taking away of his honor: was it in front of many people? Did some disgraceful punishment follow him because of it? *Answer.* Yes / no.

QUESTIONS concerning the ninth commandment.

DID you desire and endeavor to get the wife of your neighbor? *Answer.* Yes, Father / no.

QUESTIONS concerning the tenth commandment.

[26 VERSO]

DID you covet the property of your neighbors, seeking it? *Answer.* Yes / no.

THESE ARE THE five commandments of our mother the Church.

The first: hear an entire Mass on Sundays and feast days.
The second: confess during Lent or when it is necessary.
The third: take communion Maundy Thursday or Easter, etc.
The fourth: fast when the Church orders it.
The fifth: pay tithes and first fruits.

QUESTIONS concerning these five commandments of the holy Church.

inic chicuei teotenahuatilli in amo tiztlacatiz titetentlapiquiz.

CVIX otiztlacat? cuix otitetátlapiqui?[59] *Respuesta.* Ca quemaca. l. amo.

Auh in aquin otictentlapiqui. Cuix huel zenca ic omahuizpololoz? Auh cuix teixpan, in tlen zan tlapic oticecahuilti, in itech otictlami, in huel ic oticpinauhti in huel ic oticmahuizpolo, cuix otoliniloc, omecahuitecoc opinauhtiloc? *Respuesta.* Ca quemaca. l. amo.

¶ *TETLATLANI*liztli in [i]tec[h]pa, 9.

CVIX huel oticmotequiuhti oticelehui in teçihuauh? in tenamic? Cuix huel oticmo-mactocac [sic]? *Respuesta.* Ca quemaca. l. amo.

¶ *TETLATLANI*liztli in itechpa 10.
CVIX oticamic oticteoçiuh, in teaxca in tetlatqui? in teytonal in tetetlapalihuiliz? *Respuesta.* Ca quemacatzin l. amo.

¶ *NICAN CA, IN* macuiltetl yteotenahuatiltzin Sancta Yglesia.

Inic çentetl, in Domingo, yhuan in ilhuitl ipan Missa mocaquiz, in huel maçitiez çe missa.
Inic ontetl neyolcuitiloz in yquac Quaresma, &c.
Inic etetl tlaçeliloz, in yquac Iueues Sancto, noço in inezcalilitzin, noço in imonecyan.

Inic nauhtetl nezahualoz in iquac motlana-huatilia in Sancta Yglesia.
Inic macuiltetl tlamanaloz in iquac imonecyan.
¶ *TETLATLANI*liztli in itechcopa, in macuiltetl, yteotenahuatiltzin Sa[n]cta Yglesia.

eighth divine commandment: you shall not lie, you shall not bear false witness against others.

HAVE you lied? Have you borne false witness against others? *Answer.* Yes / no.

And the one you bore false witness against: was he completely dishonored? Did you publicly cast a shadow on him and impute sin to him, greatly shaming and defaming him? Was he made miserable, whipped and shamed [because of it]? *Answer.* Yes / no.

¶ *QUESTIONS* concerning the ninth.

WERE you responsible for desiring the woman and wife of another? Did you get her to fondle you? *Answer.* Yes / no.

¶ *QUESTIONS* concerning the tenth.
DID you thirst and hunger after other people's goods and property, [the products of] other people's sweat and effort? *Answer.* Yes / no.

¶ *HERE ARE THE* five divine commandments of the holy Church.

First: on Sundays and feast days a Mass will be heard, one entire Mass.
Second: confess when it is Lent, etc.

Third: take communion when it is Maundy Thursday or His resurrection or when it is necessary.
Fourth: fast when the holy Church orders it.

Fifth: make offerings when it is necessary.

¶ *QUESTIONS* concerning the five divine commandments of the holy Church.

---

59. otitetátlapiqui: read *otitetentlapiqui.*

[27 RECTO]

Acerca del primero.

Oiste Missa entera los Domingos, y fiestas, no yendo á la mitad, ó al fin della. *Respuesta.* Si l. no.

Acerca del segundo.

AS confessado todas las Quaresmas, ò te á engañado e[l] diablo, dexando de confessar alguna dellas. *Respuesta.* Si l. no.

Acerca del tercero.

As comulgado el Iueues Santo ó Pasqua de Resurreccion. *Respuesta.* Si l. no.

Acerca del quarto.

Ayunaste los viernes, y vi[27 verso]gilias que tienes obligacion, ò te engañò el diablo, y comiste carne en algunos. *Respuesta.* Si l. no.

[27 VERSO]

Acerca del quinto.

Pagaste, y ofreciste lo que debes a la Yglesia. *Respuesta.* Si l. no.

PREGVNTAS, sobre las catorze obras de Misericordia.

QVando fue a tu casa algun pobre, con ambre, y necesidad a pedirte, que le partiesses vn pedaço de pan, distele de comer, socorristelo ò en otra parte que te lo pidio? *Respuesta.* Si l. no.

Diste de veber al necesitado de agua, y fatigado de sed? *Respuesta.* Si l. no.

Mouieronte á lastima, y compasion los desnudos, y rotos, hizistesles algun socorro? *Respuesta.* Si l. no.

Visitaste a los enfermos, consolandolos,

[27 RECTO]

Concerning the first.

Did you hear an entire Mass on Sundays and feast days, not going in the middle or at the end of it? *Answer.* Yes / no.

Concerning the second.

Have you confessed every Lent or has the devil deceived you, failing to confess on some of them? *Answer.* Yes / no.

Concerning the third.

Have you taken communion on Maunday Thursday or Easter? *Answer.* Yes / no.

Concerning the fourth.

Did you fast on the Fridays and vigils which you are obligated to observe or did the devil deceive you, and you ate meat on some? *Answer.* Yes / no.

[27 VERSO]

Concerning the fifth.

Did you pay and present what you owe to the church? *Answer.* Yes / no.

QUESTIONS about the fourteen works of charity.

When some poor person, hungry and needy, went to your house to ask you to share a little bread with him, did you feed him, succor him or [provide] in some other way what he begged of you? *Answer.* Yes / no.

Did you give drink to him who needed water and was weary of thirst? *Answer.* Yes / no.

Did the naked and ragged move you to pity and compassion? Did you give them some succor? *Answer.* Yes / no.

Did you visit the sick, consoling them

[27 RECTO]
In itechcopa yc ce.

CVIX oticcac mochipa, Domingotica, in Missa, yhuan in pialloni ilhuite[60] ipan, in amo zan oticcoton, oticytlaco. *Respuesta.* Ca quemacatzin, l. amotzin.

In itechcopa ic ome.

CVIX otimoyolcuiti. in Quaresmatica? cuix noço quenmanian, omitztlapololti in tlacatecolot[l], inic otic[c]auh? *Respuesta.* Ca quemaca. l. amo.

In itechcopa yc ei.

CVIX otitlazelli in Iueves Sancto? anoço in inezcalilitzin, pascoa. *Respuesta,* Ca quemacatzin. l. amo.

In itechcopa ic nahui.

CVIX otimozauh, in viernes, yhuan vigilia ipan? cuix noço quenmanian omitztlapololti in tlacatecolotl inic oticqua, in nacatl? *Respuesta.* Ca quemaca. l. amo.

[27 VERSO]
In itechcopa ic macuilli
CVIX otitlaman otimohuenti in imonecyan. *Respuesta.* Ca quemaca. l. amo.

❡ *TETLATLAN*liztli, in itechcopa in matlactli onnahui tetlaocoliliztli, in motenehua obras de Misericordia.
CVIX in yquac àca cocoxcatzintli, motolinicatzintli, moquiahuac omoquetzato, in mitzytlanilitiuh, motlaxcal, cuix otictlapani? cuix otictlaocolli in noço çaço campa oticipantili? *Respuesta.* Ca quemaca. l. amo.
Cuix oticàtliti in ça ytentzin huahuactiuh, in aço quenmanian omitzaytlani? *Respuesta.* Ca quemaca. l. amo.
Cuix omitztlaocoltique in mopetlahuiltitinemi, in iquac otihuelit, cuix o ytla tzotzomatzintli tiquintlaocolli? *Respuesta.* Ca quemaca. l. amo.
Cuix otiquinyolalito, cuix otiquintlapaloto? in

[27 RECTO]
About the first.

HAVE you always heard a Mass on Sundays and on the feast days that one is obliged to observe, not just cutting it off and missing it? *Answer.* Yes / no.

About the second.

DID you confess during Lent? Or perhaps sometime the devil confused you so that you abandoned it? *Answer.* Yes / no.

About the third.

HAVE you taken communion on Maunday Thursday or on His resurrection, Easter? *Answer.* Yes / no.

About the fourth.

DID you fast on Fridays and vigils? Or did the devil sometime confuse you so that you ate meat? *Answer.* Yes / no.

[27 VERSO]
About the fifth.
DID you make offerings when it was necessary? *Answer.* Yes / no.

❡ *QUESTIONS* concerning the fourteen acts of compassion, called "works of mercy."

WHEN some sick and poor person showed up at your door to beg bread of you: did you break it with him? Did you have mercy on him or in any other place find for him [the succor] he was searching for? *Answer.* Yes / no.
Did you give drink to him whose lips were dry or who perhaps sometime begged water of you? *Answer.* Yes / no.
Did those who go about naked and uncovered move you to compassion? Did you have mercy on them (when you were able) with some rags? *Answer.* Yes / no.
Did you go to console and greet the

---

60. ilhuite: read *ilhuitl.*

y animando[28 recto]los. *Respuesta.* Si l. no.

Ayudaste a los cautiuos tus proximos, rogaste por ellos a Dios nuestro Señor, que les fauoresca, *Respuesta.* Si l. no.

A los pobres peregrinos y pasajeros, quando fueron a dar a tu casa, dieronte lastima, los ospedaste, y recebiste?

Ayudaste a enterrar a los pobres difuntos, quando se ofrecio ocasion tubiste caridad con ellos. *Respuesta.* Si l. n.

Enseñaste, y auisaste, a aquellos que iuan errados, y despeñandose en cosas de la ofensa de Dios? *Respuesta.* Si l. no.

Correxiste al que lo vbo menester? *Respuesta.* Si l. no.

Consolaste a los afligidos, y tristes. *Respuesta.* Si l. no.

Perdonaste a los que te ofendieron, rogando a Dios nuestro Señor por ellos como lo manda su diuina Magestad, para que merescays? *Respuesta.* Si l. no. [28 verso]

Tubiste paciencia, y sufrimiento en las inurias que te hizieron tus proximos. *Respuesta.* Si l. no.

Enseñaste a los que no saben. *Respuesta.* Si l. no.
Pediste a Dios, por los que te tratan mal. *Respuesta.* Si l. n.

*SENTIDOS COR*porales.

Ofendiste a Dios con los ojos, y con la vista, teniendo con ella deleytacion en cosas desonestas, y malas? *Respuesta.* Si l. no.

Ofendiste con el oyr, atendiendo, y oyendo con voluntad, y deleyte las cosas que son en su ofensa, y contra la ley diuina. *Respuesta.* Si l. no.

Ofendistele con el gusto, no

and cheering them up? *Answer.* Yes / no.

Did you help your neighbors the prisoners, praying for them to God our Lord that He favor them? *Answer.* Yes / no.

When the poor pilgrims and travelers come upon your house: do they rouse you to pity? Do you welcome them and give them shelter?

Did you help bury the poor deceased when the occasion arose? Were you charitable with them? *Answer.* Yes / no.

Did you instruct and advise those going astray and falling headlong down into things offensive to God? *Answer.* Yes / no.

Did you rebuke him who needed it? *Answer.* Yes / no.

Did you console those who were afflicted and miserable? *Answer.* Yes / no.

Did you forgive those who offended you, praying for them to God our Lord as His Divine Majesty orders, so that you have merit? *Answer.* Yes / no.

Were you patient and long-suffering in the offenses that your neighbors gave you? *Answer.* Yes / no.

Did you teach the ignorant? *Answer.* Yes / no.
Did you pray to God for those who mistreat you? *Answer.* Yes / no.

BODILY Senses

Did you offend God with your eyes and sight, taking delight with it in lewd and evil things? *Answer.* Yes / no.

Did you offend with hearing, willingly and with pleasure heeding and listening to things which are an offense to Him and against the divine law? *Answer.* Yes / no.

Did you offend with the sense of taste, not

[28 RECTO]

cocoxque, cuix otiquinçiauhquetzato? cuix otiquimelaquahuato? *Respuesta*. Ca quemaca. l. amo.

Cuix otiquinpalehui? cuix otiquinmanahui in tlatlacotzitzintin, l. (falten) [sic] cuix inpampa otitlatlauhti otimohuenti? *Respuesta*. Ca quemaca. l. amo.

Cuix in nenencatzitzintin, in yquac o mopan calaque, cuix omitztlaocoltique? cuix otiquin-caloti, cuix otiquintlaocolli?

Cuix in iquac, aca icnotlacatzintli, omomiquili in ayac yca, cuix oicnoyoac in moyolo inic ticpalehuiz motocaz. *Respuesta*. Ca quemaca. l. amo.

Cuix in mopilhuan yhuan in amo quimati, cuix otiquimizcali, cuix otiquinnonotz in tlen itechcopa, tlatlacoa? *Respuesta*. Ca quemaca. l. amo.

Cuix otiquintlacahualti in amo quali quichiuhtinemi? *Respuesta*. Ca quemaca. l. amo.

Cuix otiquimelaquauh cuix otiquinyolalli in tlaocoxtinemi, motequipachotinemi. *Respuesta*. Ca quemaca. l. amo.

[28 VERSO]

Cuix otiquintlapopolhui in motecocolicahuan? cuix inpampa otitlatlauhti? in yuh mitzmon-ahuatilia Dios inic titlacnopilhuiz. *Respuesta*. Ca quemaca. l. amo.

Cuix otichiyohui tlapacahiyohuiliztica, in tecoco tetoneuh? inic mixco mocpac onenque in mohuanpohuan? [*Respuesta*.] Ca quemaca. l. amo.

Cuix otiquinmachti in aquique, ámo quimati. *Respuesta*. Ca quemaca. l. amo.

Cuix inpampa, otitlatlauhti, in ixquichtin mitztolin[i]a. *Respuesta*. Ca quemaca. l. amo.

CIRCA SENSVS.
CVIX ic oticmoteopohuili in Dios in mixtelolo in motlachializ, in tlen amo quali? Cuix tlachializtica itech otitlailpac? *Respuesta*. Ca quemaca. l. amo.

Cuix ic oticmoteohuilli, in moteotzin in ica monacaz, in amo qualli, yyolitlacolocatzin, otichuelcac? o ic tictlamachti, in monacaz? *Respuesta*. Ca quemaca. l. amo.

Cuix ic oticmoteopo-

[28 RECTO]

sick? Did you go to greet, strengthen and encourage them? *Answer*. Yes / no.

Did you help them? Did you defend those who were slaves (text lacking here)? Did you pray and make offerings because of them? *Answer*. Yes / no.

Did pilgrims move you to compassion when they visited you? Did you give them shelter, taking mercy on them?

When some unfortunate died who had no one to take care of him: did your heart become compassionate and pious so that you helped to bury him? *Answer*. Yes / no.

Did you instruct, did you admonish your children and those who were ignorant concerning what sins they were committing? *Answer*. Yes / no.

Did you restrain those who were doing evil? *Answer*. Yes / no.

Did you strengthen, encourage and console those who went about sad and troubled? *Answer*. Yes / no.

[28 VERSO]

·Did you pardon your enemies? Did you pray for them as God orders you to so that you will achieve blessedness? *Answer*. Yes / no.

Did you patiently suffer the pains and afflictions with which your neighbors offended you? [*Answer*.] Yes / no.

Did you teach those who were ignorant? *Answer*. Yes / no.

Did you pray for all those who mistreat you? *Answer*. Yes / no.

ABOUT THE SENSES.
DID you offend God with your eyes and sense of sight? With the sense of sight: did you enjoy yourself with carnal delight in something evil? *Answer*. Yes / no.

Did you offend your God with your ears, you enjoying hearing what is offensive to Him and evil? Or you enjoyed it with your ears? *Answer*. Yes / no.

Did you offend God with

[29 RECTO]

buscando, ni dandote otra cosa cuydado mas de cosas de tu gusto. *Respuesta.* Si. l. no.

Ofendiste con el olfacto, no siruiendo mas de a solos [29 recto] los olores. *Respuesta.* Si l. no.

Ofendistele con el tacto, deleitandote en cosas que pertenecen a este sentido. *Respuesta.* Si l. no.

LAS POTENCIAS.

Ofendiste a su diuina Magestad con la memoria, acordandote de los pecados pasados? *Respuesta.* Si l. no.

Ofendistele con el entendimiento, vsando mal del? *Respuesta.* Si l. no.

Ofendistele con la voluntad, cometiendo luego sin resistencia de las cosas de su ofensa? *Respuesta.* Si l. no.

Resistes los pensamientos del mundo, y sençualidad? *Respuesta.* Si l. no.

El Demonio quando te tienta con algun pecado,

[29 VERSO]

defiendeste con las palabras de Dios? *Respuesta.* Si l. no.

Quando la carne te tienta resistesle con instancia, y cuydado, de suerte que te li[29 verso]bres della. *Respuesta.* Si l. no.

ESTOS SON LOS siete Pecados Mortales, acuerdate quantos as cometido. El primero dellos, es la Soberuia. El segundo Auaricia. El tercero Luxuria. El quarto Yra. El quinto Gula. El sexto Inuidia. El septimo Pereça. *Respuesta.* Si Padre, acusome que los he cometido todos.

PLATICA SOBRE los siete Pecados Mortales, particularmente el de la embriaguez y borrachera, que es la principal causa de cometer todos los generos, y especies de pecados que ay con que

searching out nor being concerned about anything except for things related to your sense of taste? *Answer.* Yes / no.

Did you offend with the sense of smell, it not serving any other purpose than [smelling] nice scents? *Answer.* Yes / no.

Did you offend with the sense of touch, taking pleasure in things that pertain to this sense? *Answer.* Yes / no.

THE FACULTIES

Did you offend His Divine Majesty with your memory, remembering past sins? *Answer.* Yes / no.

Did you offend Him with your understanding, making evil use of it? *Answer.* Yes / no.

Did you offend with your will, committing then without resistance things in offense to Him? *Answer.* Yes / no.

Did you resist thoughts of the world and sensuality? *Answer.* Yes / no.

When the devil tempts you with some sin,

[29 VERSO]

do you defend yourself with the words of God? *Answer.* Yes / no.

When the flesh tempts you, do you insistently and carefully resist it in such a way that you free yourself of it? *Answer.* Yes / no.

THESE ARE THE seven mortal sins: remember how many you have committed. The first of them is pride. The second, avarice. The third, lust. The fourth, anger. The fifth, gluttony. The sixth, envy. The seventh, sloth. *Answer.* Yes, Father, I confess that I have committed all [of them].

SPEECH ABOUT the seven deadly sins, particularly that of intoxication and drunkenness, which is the principal cause for committing all the types and kinds of sins that there are with which

huili in Dios in motlahuelmatiliz in zan yehuatl otictlayecolti.

Cuix ica [sic] oticmoteopohuilli in Dios in yca motlanecuiliz in huel omitzotlapololti [sic] in xochitl in heytl?

Cuix ic oticmoteopohuili in in ica moma in amo quali oticmatocac, in huel omitztlapololti?

CIRCA POTENCIAS

Cuix ic oticmoteopohuili in Dios in motlalnamiquiliz in tlen àmo quali ticilnamiqui. *Respuesta*. [Ca quemaca.] l. amo.

Cuix ic oticmoyolytlacalhui in mixtlamachiliz in motlacaquiliz, in amo qualli otimotequiuhti.

Cuix ic oticmoyolytlacalhui in moçializ in motlanequiliz in niman oticzelitihuetz in iteopoalocatzin. *Respuesta*. Ca quemaca. l. amo.

Cuix, in tlalticpacayotl in tlaylpaquiliztli Cuix àmo ixquich motlapal ticchihua in ihuicpa timicali? *Respuesta*. [Ca quemaca.] l. [amo.]

In tlacatecolotl in yquac mitztlapololtiznequi, cuix

ica in teotlatoli timomapatla timopalehuia. *Respuesta*. Ca quemaca. l. amo.

In monacayo icquac [sic], mitztlapololtia, cuix ixquich motlapal ticchihua inic yhuicpa timomaquixtia, inic amo quitlacoz moyolia?
§ *NICAN CA IN* chicontetl temictiani tlatlacolli Xicyta xicilnamiqui catlehuatl, in oticchiuh in ypan otihuetz? Inic çe Nepoaliztli, inic ome, Teoyehuacatiliztli inic yey Tlailpaquiliztli, inic nahui Tlahuelli, in[ic] macuilli Xixicuiyotl, inic chiquaçen, Nexicolliztli, inic chicome Tlatzi-huillztli?[61] *Respuesta*. Ca quemaca ca onicchiuh ca ipan onihuetz in izqui oticmotenehuilli Tlatlacolli.
§ *TENONOTZAliztli* in itechcopa in izquiquitetl, omoteneuh temictiani tlatlacolli, oc cenca qualca in tlahuanaliztli in quiçenhuica, in ixquich in nepapá tlatlacolli inic mo

your sense of taste, you just serving [this particular sense]? [*Answer*. Yes / no.]

Did you offend God with and through your sense of smell, [the odors of] flowers and tobacco greatly confusing you? [*Answer*. Yes / no.]

Did you offend Him with and through your hands when you touched something evil with your hands that greatly confused you? [*Answer*. Yes / no.]

ABOUT THE FACULTIES.

Have you offended God with your memory, you thinking of what was evil? *Answer*. [Yes] / no.

Have you offended Him with your understanding, you being responsible for what is evil? [*Answer*. Yes / no.]

Have you offended Him with your will and volition, quickly accepting then what is in offense of Him? *Answer*. Yes / no.

You did not exert every effort to fight against earthly things and lust? *Answer*. [Yes] / [no].

When the devil wants to confuse you: do

you defend and aid yourself with words of God? *Answer*. Yes / no.

When your flesh confuses you: do you exert every effort to save yourself from it so that it will not harm your soul? [*Answer*. Yes / no.]
§ *HERE ARE THE* seven mortal sins. See and remember which of them you have committed and fallen into. First, pride. Second, avarice. Third, lust. Fourth, anger. Fifth, gluttony. Sixth, envy. Seventh, laziness. *Answer*. Yes, I have committed and fallen into all the sins you have mentioned.

§ *ADMONITORY* speech concerning all the aforementioned mortal sins, especially drunkenness, which thoroughly accompanies all the various sins with which

---

61. Tlatzihuillzltli: read *Tlatzihuiliztli*.

[30 RECTO]

se quebrantan los diez mandamientos de la ley de Dios. [30 recto]

OYDME con atencion todos los que dezis ser Christianos, y aduertid, y tened por cosa muy cierta: como vuestra voca, y vientre trae perdida vuestra alma, y la echa sin remision al infierno, a quien no tan solamente entriega a los siete pecados mortales, sino á otros infinitos mas, sin quento ni numero grauissimos y enormes, en que os haze caer la infernal veuida del pulque &c. Porque vn borracho, vn hombre sin juizio, quantos pecados cometerá al dia? Concideralde quando va por essas calles, que no ay viuora, ni sierpe tan hinchada, y engreida, tirando flechas de venenosa ponçoña a la honra de quantos topa, ò como perro que va rabiando, que a los que encuentra daña, á quien no ay cosa que iguele en presuncion, [30 verso] y soberuia, ya no ay mas sino sus tripas, y vientre,

[30 VERSO]

no dá a su alma ni vna blanca ni vn marauedi, todo lo que junta y adquiere en la semana, y en el mes, y lo niega y esconde a los necesitados y pobres, en vn rato lo va a gastar en la taberna, y se lo echa en el vientre. Y como esta priuado de la lumbre natural del entendimiento: aunque sea con su mesma madre, hermana, parienta, y su sangre grauissimos insextos. Y sucede topa con otro borracho como el, y incurrir en el de la sodomia, o cometer el pecado contra naturaleza, teniendo parte con algun animal, y esta mesma infernal veuida va hirbiendo en sus entrañas, y le va causando rabia y enejo[15]: de tal manera, que en llegando a su casa, aporrea y maltrata a [31 recto] su muger è hijos, dandoles de coses, y arrojandolos por aquel suelo. Y apenas ha amanecido otra vez quando va a la taberna, y donde se vende el pulque, y tepach,

[30 RECTO]

the ten commandments of the law of God are violated.

LISTEN attentively, all of you who say you are Christians, and note and take for a certainty how your mouth and belly cause your soul to be lost and cast it without forgiveness into hell; not only is it handed over to the seven deadly sins but to infinitely more (without count or number) very grave and enormous ones into which the infernal drink of pulque makes you fall, etc. For how many sins will a drunkard, a man lacking good judgment, commit in a day? Consider him when he goes along those streets: there is no viper nor serpent so swollen and conceited, shooting arrows of venomous poison at the honor of as many as he comes across, or like a dog rabidly going along hurting those whom it encounters; there is nothing which equals him in presumption and pride, now there is nothing but his guts and belly.

[30 VERSO]

He gives nothing of value to his soul. All that he accumulates and acquires in a week and in a month he denies and hides from the needy and poor, spending it in a moment in the tavern and tossing it down into his belly. And as he is deprived of the natural light of understanding, although it might be with his very own mother, sister, female relative and those of his bloodline, [he commits] very serious acts of incest. And [so] it happens: he bumps into another drunk like himself and commits the sin of sodomy, or commits the sin against nature having relations with some animal. And this infernal brew goes bubbling in his innards and making him furious and angry, in such a way that upon arriving at his house he beats and mistreats his wife and children, kicking them and knocking them down onto the ground. And hardly has it dawned again when he goes to the tavern where pulque and tepach is sold

---

15. enejo: read *enojo*.

[30 RECTO]

tlacoa, in izpuitetl,[62] teotenahuatilli.

*MA XIC*caquican in amixquichtin, anmotenehua
anChristiauos[63] ca yehuatl in amocuitlaxcol in ye
huel cohuetilia in àmanima, ca yehuatl in ye
quimictlantlaça, quitepexihuia in amo çan
ixquich in chicontetl temictiani tlatlacolli
quicuitia yecce,[64] in ixquich in quexquich, onca in
temamauhti teyçahui in ámo çan tlapoali ipan
amehctlaça[65] in mictlan Atl, yeyca in tlahuanqui
in xocomiqui, in aocmo quimati; quexquich in
quimotequiuhtia? In quichihua, in çemilhuitl,
intla otli quitocatiuh, yuhqui in coatl
moçoneuhtiuh, quipotztiuh, quiztlacmintiuh in
temahuiço, noçe yuhqui, in chcihi,[66] iztlac
ytenqualac çemotlica quihuihuilantiuh, aoctle
yuhqui inic mopouhtiuh moçoneuhtiuh. Auh
aocac aquin, quicnelia quitlaocolia ça ixquich in
ycamac ycuitlaxcol,

[30 VERSO]

in quiçenmati quitlayecoltia, atle çe melio çe
cacahuatl, ic quicnelia in iyolia in ixquich
quitlapehuilia in çe semana in çe metztli in çan
quintlatilitica in ihuanpohuan icnotlaca, çan
achitonca in tepachnamacoyan huinonamacoyan,
compopoloa, concuitlaxcoltema. Auh in quenin
aocmo quimati, in manel ynantzin, noço
yhueltiuh noço in çan huel yhuayolqui yeço
ytlapalo ytech açi quichihua in temanauhti[67]
tlatlacolli, nel ye aço çan no, yoquichpo
ytlahuancapo monepanoa, noço quimotequiuhtia
in achihualoni tetzauhtlatlacolli, in campa
manenenqui quinamiqui, in ytech tlatlacoa. Auh
çan no yehuatl in in mictlan, atl, ytec popoço-
catiuh quitlahuelcuititiuh, çan ic onaçi in ichan in
quimictia in inamic in ipilhuan, quintetelicça
tlalli ic quinmotla, auh çan ic ontlathui in oc çepa
yauh in tepachnamacoyan in vinonamacoyan in
on-

[30 RECTO]

all the divine commandments are broken.
LISTEN, ALL of you who called yourselves
Christians, your innards are putting your souls in
great danger, for they are casting them down into
hell and hurling them down [there] as from a
height, not just making [your souls] catch the
seven mortal sins but all and how[ever] many and
countless frightening and terrifying things infernal drink casts you into. Because how many
things is the drunkard and the intoxicated person
who is ignorant responsible for doing in a day? If
he goes following along the road he excites and
upsets himself like a snake, throwing up at and
shooting poison at other people's honor, or like a
dog who goes repeatedly dragging his poisonous
spittle down the entire street, there being nothing
else as proud [or] excited as him. He shows no
favor, has pity on no one, his mouth and his
innards are all

[30 VERSO]

he pays close attention to and serves. With not
one coin of little value, with not one cacao bean,
does he favor his soul. All that he adds in a week
[or] a month he just hides from his neighbors the
poor, in a short while spending it in the place
where tepache and wine are sold, filling his guts
with it. And how can it be that he no longer has
the use of reason? Even though it is his [own]
mother or his older sister or just a relative [or] his
[own] offspring: he has sexual relations with her,
doing the frightful sin to her. Indeed, he perhaps
couples with a man like himself, a fellow drunkard, or he is responsible for the frightful sin
(unworthy of doing) wher[ever] he encounters an
animal, sinning with it. And likewise this infernal
drink goes boiling along in him, causing him to
become enraged. [Then] frequently [upon] reaching his home he beats his wife and children, kicking and kicking them, throwing earth at them.[68]
And just when it dawns he again goes to the place
where tepache and wine is sold, there

---

62. izpuitetl: read *izquitetl.*
63. anChristiauos: read *anChristianos.*
64. yecce: read *yece.*
65. amehctlaça: read *amechtlaça*
66. chcihi: read *chichi.*
67. temanauhti: read *temamauhti.*

---

68. *throwing earth at them*: tentative translation.

y se entriega a ello hinchiendo el vientre, y
estando repleto y ahito, comiença a trocar, y enlo-
darse como vn puerco ó animal en lo que echa. Y
es de manera, que si se va a caer en alguna calle, a
toda vna ciudad causa asco, y aun hasta los mesmos brutos quedan espantados en verlo, y le van
rodeando para pasar la calle, y de aqui nace la
inuidia, y rencor que tiene con otros: ya no se
acuerda de la doctrina, de su casa, de su muger, de
sus hijos, tierras, y simenteras, todo se le va en
veuer y emborracharse, oluidado de Dios que le
crio, teniendo a su vientre por Idolo, y al tepach, y
pulque por [31 verso] su Dios, y si mientan a Dios
no es para honrarle, y bendecirle, sino para blas-
femarle, tomando en su sacriliga voca el nombre
de Dios, diziendo juro a Dios, &c.

Y que sean Domingos, dias de fiesta, o Pascoas,
nunca oye Missa, porque no entiende en otra
cosa, sino en seruir al diablo, emborrachandose
con lo qual ya no guarda respeto a nadie, ni a su
madre, ni a su padre, porque les dá de bofetadas,
les arranca las barbas, los maltrata y ofrenta, y se
vuelue como perro (quando está herido de
ponçoña o yerba) acometiendo a todos, con que
biene a matar a su muger, o a vno de sus proximos, o el mismo se viene a matar ahogandose en
alguna asequia o poço, que quando le vienen a
sacar está hinchado como vna vestia, que todos
tienen que ver en el [32 recto] en quantos pecados
de sodomias, y adulterios acabará el desdichado?
Quantos latrocinios lleuará a su cargo, sangre y
sudor de pobres? Quantos testimonios dexaria
por restituir, con que quitò la honra de sus
proximos?

and gives himself over to it filling his belly, and
being gorged and full he begins to vomit and soil
himself like a pig or animal with what he is dis-
charging. It is such that if he goes falling down in
some street he disgusts the whole city, and even
the brute [animals] are appalled at seeing him;
they make a detour around him in order to cross
the street. And from here is born the envy and
rancor he has for others: he no longer remembers
the doctrine, his house, his wife, his children,
lands and sown fields—everything slips away
from him in drinking and getting drunk, forgotten by God Who created him, taking his belly for
an idol and tepach and pulque for his god. And if
he mentions God it is not to honor and bless Him
but rather to blaspheme against Him, taking into
his sacrilegious mouth the name of God, saying "I
swear to God," etc.

And whether it is Sundays, feasts days or holy
days he never hears Mass because he occupies
himself in nothing else but serving the devil, getting himself drunk. Whereupon he no longer
shows respect to anyone, neither his mother nor
his father, because he hits them, pulls out their
hair, mistreats and offends them. He turns into a
dog (when it is hurt by poison or undomesticated
plants) attacking everyone, and so he ends up
killing his wife or one of his neighbors; or he ends
up killing himself, drowning himself in some
ditch or well. When they come to take him out he
is bloated like a wild animal in which everyone
has to see [the following]: in how many sins of
sodomy and adultery will the poor devil come to
an end? How many thefts (the blood and sweat of
poor people) is he responsible for? How much
perjured testimony may he have omitted making
restitution for, by which he destroyed the honor
of his neighbor?

[31 RECTO]

can moxixicuinpoloa quicuitlaxcolquetza in
ixquich in tep[a]ch in ixquich in oct[l]i, auh intla
oten in ma çan yuhqui cuetlaxtli, miçotla maxixa,
iyçotlal iaxix ic maltia in yuhqui pitzotl in yuhqui
manenenqui. Auh intla cana, otlica ohuetzito
oncan çemaltepetl in quitlayltia in manel ye
manenenque çan oquimotetzahuia, áocmo otli
quitoca, ça hueca quitlayahualhuia. Auh ye no
oncan in pehua in moxicoa in moyolcocoa in
tetlailyta. Auh aoctle quitequipachoa in ma
teoyotl. In ma ychan in ma inamic ypilhuan ymil
ycal çan quixcahuia, in tlahuantenemi [sic]
tlatziuhtinemi, quimoçemilcahuilia in
iteyocoxcatzin Dios ca yteouh in icuitlaxcol in
ixixicu[i]yo in ioc in itepach. Auh intla
quimotenehuiliz amo yca in quimotlatlauhtiliz
çan ipanpa in quimomahuizpolhuiz in quitoz yca
ytencuicuitl quimomachiltia in Dios, voto a Dios,
&c.

[31 VERSO]

Auh ma Domingo, ma huey ilhuitl ma huey
Pascoa aoquic quicaqui, in Missa ça quixcahuia in
quitlayecoltia in tlacatecolotl tlatlahuantinemi,
auh in itlahuanaliztica aocac quimahuiztilia, ma
ynantzin ma ytatzin quimixtetlatzinia, quinten-
tzonhuihuitla quinmimictia quinpinauhtia. Auh
yuhquin chichi yquac paqua mocuepa, quixilli
quitopehua in inamic noço çeme in ihuanpohuan, noço çan no yehuatl campa miquiliztli
quimonamictia in aço cana matlahuia, quiquixtia
o mach cuitlapoçahuac, yuhqui chichi, oncan
atenco tenechicoa tetlacaololoa: quexquich in
ipan miqui in ipan tzinquiça[70] in tetzauhtlatlacolli, in nemecatiliztli? quexquich in
tlachtequiliztli in ymamal mochiuhtiuh? In
imitonal in innecocol in çequintin icnotlaca?
Quexquich in temahuiço ytech yetiuh? In acan
quitecuepilitiuh, in tlatlacolli çan tlapic,

gluttonously destroying himself and swelling his
gut[69] with all the tepache and pulque; and if he is
filled up he is just like a tanned leather wineskin.
He [then] vomits and urinates on himself, wetting
himself with his [own] vomit and urine like a pig
and an animal. And if somewhere on the road he
falls down, he disgusts the whole altepetl there,
even the animals just are amazed at him, not following the road but circling around him from
afar. And there also begins his being envious and
in pain and his looking at people with disgust and
abhorrence. And nothing makes him anxious,
whether it is that which pertains to God or his
home or his wife and child, his fields and house;
he just occupies himself in going about drunk
and lazy, completely forgetting God, his Creator,
for his guts are his god and his pulque and his
tepache is his gluttony. And if he makes a
promise, he does not on some occasion pray but
[rather] on account of it destroys His honor, saying with his filthy mouth "God knows" or "I swear
to God," etc.

[31 VERSO]

And whether it is Sunday or a great feast day or
Easter he no longer hears Mass; he just occupies
himself, going around getting drunk, in serving
the devil. And in his drunkenness he no longer
honors [any]one; whether it is his mother or his
father he slaps them in the face, drags them
around by their lip hairs and repeatedly beats and
shames them. And like a dog when it drinks a poisoned liquid [then] he changes into [something
else], he stabs and shoves his wife or one of his
neighbors, or he likewise encounters death somewhere. Perhaps somewhere he drowns himself in
water and they [later] take him out: how swelled
up he was, like a dog! There on the bank they
gather and bring together the people, [who mur-
mur:] how many died and came to an end in
frightful sins and illicit sexual unions? How many
[acts of] thievery became his burden of responsibility? [How much] of the sweat and pain of some
poor people? How much of the honor of others
does he owe for which he has nowhere made
restitution, just falsely

---

70. tzinquiça: read *tzonquiça*.

69. *swelling his gut*: tentative translation.

[32 RECTO]

Que ambicion de los bienes axenos, y de las mugeres de sus proximos. Pero aduertid que no teneis ante Dios escusa ninguna, avnque digais que el vino, o el pulque lo haze: porque quando cometeys los pecados ya no sabeys lo que os hazeis; porque antes de emborracharos, y perder el vso de la razon, no alcançais con el, que oueis de incurrir en infinitos pecados, y tambien no tomais exemplo en los que se emborrachan, que incurren en grandes yerros.

[32 RECTO]

What striving after the property of others, and the wives of his neighbors? But bear in mind that you have no excuse before God, although you say that the wine or the pulque did it. Because when you commit sins you no longer remember what you are doing to yourselves. Because before getting yourself drunk and losing the use of reason you do not comprehend with it that you are about to fall into an infinite [number of] sins; also you do not take an example from those who get drunk, who fall into great errors.

[32 RECTO]

tetech quitlamitiuh? Quexquich in teaxca in tetlaltqui[71] capìzmictiuh, quiteoçiuhtiuh? Quexquich in tenamic in teçihuauh quelehuitiuh? Auh yeçe ma huel iuh xicmatican yhuan ma huel yuh ye in amoyolo, ca amo amechmaquixtia in in ixpantzinco in Dios, in anquitoa, ca yehuatl in octli quichihua, ca aocmo nicmati in tlen onicchiuh in tlen onicnotequiuhti? Yeyca in ayamo titlahuanqui in ayetle tocon, y,[72] in octli amo ticmati in ca çenca miac tlatlacolli in ipan mitztlaçaz àmo intech timixcuitia in tiquimita, tlahuanque, in ixquich ypan tihuetzi.

[32 RECTO]

imputing blame to others? How much of other people's goods and property does he thirst and hunger for? How many wives and women of others does he desire? Yet know well and be certain that it will not save you before God to say "the pulque did it, I no longer know what I did [or] what I was responsible for." Because before you were a drunkard, when you had not yet imbibed the pulque, you did not know the many sins into which it would cast you; you did not take an example from the drunkards you saw and all [the sins] into which they fell.

---

71. tetlaltqui: read *tetlatqui.*
72. tocon, y: read *tocony.*

CONFESSIONARIO MENOR

BREVE Y SVMARIO, DONDE SE
contienen todas las preguntas, y respuestas que se
requieren para los penitentes.

En lengua Mexicana, y Castellana.

TIenes Bula? *Respuesta.* Si Padre l. no. Padre.

Saues las quatro oraciones? *Respuesta.* Si Padre.
l. no.
Te has acordado de todos tus pecados?
Respuesta. Si Padre. l. no.
Confiessate aora con todo tu coraçon.
Respuesta. Si Padre Pesate sumamente de haver
offendido a tu Dios y Señor? Has hecho firmis-
simo proposito de no offenderle? *Respuesta.* Si
Padre l. no Padre.

SMALL GUIDE TO CONFESSION

BRIEF AND ABRIDGED,
wherein are contained all the questions and
answers needed for penitents.

In the Mexican and Spanish languages.

Do you have a [papal] bull? *Answer.* Yes, Father /
No, Father.
Do you know the four prayers? *Answer.* Yes,
Father / no.
Have you remembered all your sins? *Answer.*
Yes, Father / no.
Now confess with all your heart. *Answer.* Yes,
Father. Does it exceedingly grieve you to have
offended your God and Lord? Have you very
firmly resolved to not offend Him [again]?
Answer. Yes, Father / No, Father.

CONFESSIONARIO MENOR

BREVE Y SVMARIO, DONDE SE
contienen todas las preguntas, y respuestas que se
requieren para los penitentes.

En lengua Mexicana, y Castellana.

Ticpia Bula, *Respuesta.* Ca quemaca. l. amo.
   Ticmati in nauhtlamantli. *Respuesta.* Ca
quemaca l. amo.
   Oticçentlalli in motlatlacol o moch ticilnamic.
Respuesta. Ca quemaca. l. amo.
   Cuix moçeyolocacopa in timoyolcuitiznequi,
Cuix huel ic timoyoltonehua in oticmoyolytla-
calhui in moteotzin, motlatocatzin Dios?
Cuix o yuh tictlali in moyollo in ca aocmo
ticmoteopohuiliz. *Respuesta.* Ca quemaca. l. amo.

SMALL GUIDE TO CONFESSION

BRIEF AND ABRIDGED,
wherein are contained all the questions and
answers needed for penitents.

In the Mexican and Spanish languages.

Do you have a [papal] bull? *Answer.* Yes / no.
   Do you know the four [prayers]? *Answer.* Yes /
no.
   Have you gathered together and remembered
all your sins? *Answer.* Yes / no.
   Do you want to confess with all your heart?
Are you very regretful and sorry that you
offended God, your Deity and Ruler? Have you
firmly proposed to no longer offend Him?
Answer. Yes / no.

[33 RECTO]

Te as quitado ya de los malos passos en que andas y as propuesto de no pecar mas? *Respuesta.* Si. l. no.

Di aora pues, y confiessa tus pecados, no escondas, o niegues alguno. Persignate primero, y di luego en tu lengua el Pater noster, &c.

No confundas con multitud de palabras tu Confession. (como lo soleys hazer) Di luego claramente tus pecados, y todo aquello con que as quebrantado los Mandamientos de la ley de Dios. Dizien, do[16] primeramente, si no le has querido, y amado como debes. Si as puesto mas ayna tu Coraçon en otra criatura suya, atribuyendole Diuinidad, y adoracion.

Si has jurado su Sancto Nombre en vano muchas vezes, quantas con mentira, quantas con verdad, si alguna vez has jurado falço contra alguno.

[33 VERSO]

Si has quebrantado algunos Domingos, y dias de fiesta, particularmente los que estays obligados a guardar. Y porque los quebrantaste, si fue por vastante impedimento, no pudiendo mas, por estar enfermo, v por otra legitima causa, o las dexalle de oyr de malicia, por pereça que tubiste, y por emborracharte o andar en otras maldades. O si tu fuiste causa para que la dexasen de oyr tus Hijos, tus criados, y tus subditos, por emborracharte con ellos, les causaste floxedad. Si vendes tepach, o pulque: con lo qual hazes que muchos dexen de oyr Missa los Domingos, y dias de fiesta, por estarse veuiendo, y emborrachando todo el dia en tu casa.

Si has deshonrado a tu madre, a tu padre, y mayores, no teniendolos en nada.

Si has muerto a alguno, hiriendole, dandole vocado, hechiçandole, o qui-

[33 RECTO]

Have you already given up the bad things in which you were mixed up and resolved to sin no more? *Answer.* Yes / no.

Now then, say and confess your sins, not hiding or denying any. Cross yourself first and then say the Paternoster in your language, etc.

Do not confound your Confession with a multitude of words (as you are wont to do). Say your sins clearly then and everything with which you violated the commandments of the law of God. First saying if you have not loved Him as you must, if you have more quickly set your heart on some other creature of His, attributing divinity and worship to it.

If you many times have sworn His holy name in vain: how many times lyingly, how many times truthfully? If you have sworn falsely against someone.

[33 VERSO]

If you have missed some Sundays and feast days, particularly those you are obligated to observe. And why you missed them: if it was because of a sufficient impediment, being exhausted, on account of being ill or for another legitimate reason, or maliciously failing to hear them on account of your laziness and getting yourself drunk or getting mixed up in other kinds of evil. Or if you were the reason why your children, your servants and your subordinates neglected to hear it; on account of you getting drunk with them you made them lax. If you sell tepache or pulque: on account of it you make many fail to hear Mass on Sundays and feast days for they are drinking and getting drunk all day in your house.

If you have dishonored your mother, your father and [your] elders, thinking nothing of them.

If you have killed someone, wounding him, hitting him in the mouth, casting an evil spell on him, or

---

16. Dizien, do: read *Diziendo.*

[33 RECTO]

Cuix ye ticçemixnahuatia, in tlatlacolli, inic aocmo cepa ticmomacaz? *Respuesta.* Ca quemaca. l. amo.

Ca ye qualli xicytto, xicpoa, xicpantlaça, xicmocuiti àmo çe xictlati. Auh acachtopa, ximixycuilo, xiquito in motlatolcopa Pater noster &c.

Amo xictlapehuili in motlatol, in yuhqui mochipa quichihuani. çan niman yçiuhca, xicmelauhcaytotihuetzi, in motlatlacol in yehuatl huel conmati, in moyolo oticchiuh. Inic oticytlaco in izquitetl teotenahuatilli, in aço amo ticchiuh, moçeyolocacopa, in itlayecoltilocatzin Dios. In aço ytla oc qualca ytech otictlalli in moyollo, in aço ytla oc çentlamantli oticneltocac, oticteoma?

In aço miacpa otictlapicteneuhtinen in imahuiztocatzin, in Dios in quezquipa, iztla[ca]tiliztica, in quezquipa neltiliztica. In cuix quenmanian, çan tlapic tepan otitestigotic.

[33 VERSO]

Quezqui Missa oticytlaco in Domingo, yhuan in huey ilhuitl ipan in huel amonahuatil? Auh tleyca in oticcauh, cuix ahuel otimochiuh cuix timococoa, cuix noço ytla oc çentlamantli inic amo tihuelit? cuix noço çan ic otimoquelo çan otitlatziuh, çan otitlahuan, çan ytla oc çentlamantli motlahuelilocayo in omitzcahualti? Cuix noço tehuatl otiquincahualti, acame in, aço mopilhuan, in aço monencahuan motlapach-olhuan, in aço otiquintlahuanti, otiquintlatequipanolti, in anoço otiquintlatziuizmauh? in cuix ti, tepachtlallia,[73] in aço çenca miac tlacatl, ypampa ticahualtitia in Missa in Domingo ypan yhuan in huei ilhuitl in çan quixcahuia mochan tlahuana.

In aço otiquinmahuizpolo in monantzin motatzin, in motiachcahuan, in aço atle ypan otiquimitac?

In aço aca, otictopeuh, oticmicti, in huel momac omic, in aço oticpaqualti

[33 RECTO]

Do you cast sin out forever so that you will give yourself to it no more? *Answer.* Yes / no.

That is good. Speak, count, reveal and confess them; do not hide a one. But first make [the sign of the cross] on your face, saying the Paternoster in your language, etc.

Do not augment your words as you always are wont to do, but speedily tell your sins quickly and honestly, those you are certain you did, breaking all the divine commandments. Perhaps you did not completely willingly do what is service to God, or you especially set your heart on something [else besides His service], or you believed and judged to be a god some other thing?

Perhaps many times you falsely spoke the honored name of God: how many times with lies, how many with the truth? Were you sometime a false witness against people?

[33 VERSO]

How many Masses, Sundays and great feast days (for which you are greatly obligated) have you missed? And why did you abandon them? You could not get yourself to do it? You are sick? Or there was some other [reason] why you couldn't? Or did you do it intentionally, you were just lazy and drunk [or] just some other perversity of yours kept you back? Did you perhaps restrain [from attending] your children or your household dependents and subordinates, or you got them drunk, made them work, or you infected them with laziness? Do you sell tepache? Perhaps because of it you make many people abandon Mass on Sundays and great feast days, they just occupying themselves with getting drunk in your home.

Did you dishonor your mother and father and older brothers, having no respect for them?

Have you contended against and murdered someone (who died at your very hands), or did you give him a poisoned potion to consume,

---

73. ti, tepachtlallia: read *titepachtlallia.*

tandole la vida de otra qualquier manera. Si te has deseado la muerte, desesperadamente, o si la as deseado a tus proximos, teniendo odio y rencor con alguno, buscando medios como quitarle la vida. Si has dado algun veuediço a alguna preñada para prouocarle a ecgar[17] la criatura, o tu lo tomaste para lo mismo.

Si estás amançebado, y quanto tiempo ha que lo estas, y que estado tiene la muger, si es casada, viuda, o soltera, o doncella, y quantas vezes has reyterado con ella, y quantos actos carnales as tenido en el discurso de vn año, v de dos &c. Discurriendo por los dias, las semanas, los meses, y por los años. Y si la tal muger es tu parienta y en que grado? Si has tenido parte con otras mugeres, y quantas an sido, qual dellas es casada, qual viuda, qual doncella, y qual soltera? Y si a la doncella la estrupaste tu, y le quitaste la honra? Y quan-

tos excessos tubiste con cada vna dellas? Y si hiziste fuerza a la doncella, estás obligado a ayudarle para que se case, o si no eres casado, casarte con ella, y voluerle la honra que le quitaste, y si alguna es tu parienta.

Si has incurrido en el detestable pecado de la sodomia, o en el vestial, y contra naturaleza, teniendo acto con algun animal.

Si has hurtado, y si te es a cargo alguna hazienda ajena. Si has leuantado algun falso testimonio, con que has quitado la honra. Si has desseado con ambicion los bienes ajenos, y la muger ajena.

Si has tenido presuncion

taking away his life in any other fashion. If you desperately have desired death for yourself or for your neighbors, bearing hatred and ill will for someone [and] searching for the means to take his life. If you have given some potion to some pregnant woman in order to induce her to lose her baby, or you took it for the same reason.

If you are in an illicit union: how long have you been [in it] and what is the woman's status (if she is married, a widow, single or a young unmarried virgin), and how many times have you repeated with her, and how many carnal acts have you had in the course of a year, or in two, etc.? Going along by the days, the weeks, the months, and by the years. And if the said woman is your female relative and in what degree of consanguinity. If you have had relations with other women, and how many were they? Which is them is married, which a widow, which a maiden and which single? And if you raped the maiden and destroyed her honor. And how many

carnal acts did you commit with each one of them? And if you raped the maiden you are obligated to help her get married, or if you are not a married man, marry her yourself, and return to her the honor you took away. And if some woman is your female relative [apparently some text is inadvertently left out here].

If you have fallen into the detestable sin of sodomy, or into the bestial and unnatural one, having a carnal act with some animal.

If you have committed theft and you are in charge of somebody else's property. If you have given some perjured testimony with which you have destroyed honor. If you have self-seekingly desired somebody else's property, and somebody else's wife.

If you have been conceited

---

17. ecgar: read *echar*.

[34 RECTO]

otictlachihui in, quen oticchiuh, in anoço çan tehuatl, otimomiquizelehui, otitlaçentlami, noço otitemiquizelehui, otitecocoli oticnemili, in quien[74] in titemictiz titepopoloz, in anoço aca, otztli, çihuatl oticpayti in ica quitlaz yconeuh, noço tehuatl, otipa, yc inic ohuetzin, moconeuh.

In aço timomecatia, in ye quexquich cahuitl, timomecatitica, in tle çihuatl, in cuix namique? In cuix icnoçihuatl? In cuix ichpochtli, noço çan yuh nemi, in ye quezquipa ic timoyolcuitia? Auh in ye quezquipa ytech taçi in çe xihuitl in onxihuitl &c. Ic xicpoa ic xicilnamiqui, in çeçemilhuitl, in çeçe[se]mana çeçenmetztli, çeçenxihuitl in cuix mohuayolqui? In aço quen ticnotza, in noço quezquintin in çihua, in çan inca otimahuilti in çan intech otaçic, in catlehuatl namique? In catlehuatl, huel maçiticatca ichpochtli, in catlehuatl,

[34 VERSO]

icnoçihuatl, in catlehuatl in çan yuh nemi. Auh in huel oc maçiticatca, ichpochtli, in cuix quin tehuatl oticmahuizpolo, oticxapotlac, auh in quequezquipa, in çeçeme intech otitlatlaco? Auh in ichpochtli, intla, oticmahuizpolo momamal inic tic[c]uepiliz, in imahuiço, ytla, yc ticpalehuiz, inic monamictiz, noço, intlacamo tinamique ticmonamictiz. In aço çeme mohuayolque in aço quen ticnotzo,[75] in intech otitlatlaco cihua, in aço ypan otihue[t]z in ayc chihualoni in temamauhti tlatlacolli, cuiloyotl, in anoço yehuatl in tetzauhtlatlacolli, in ytla manenenqui oticnepano ytech otitlatlaco?

In cuix noço otichtec, in cuix, ytla momamal mochiuhtica in cuix noço quenmanian, aca otictetentlapiqui, oticmahuizpolo, in cuix noço, octicteoçiuh, in teaxca in tetlatqui yhuan in tenamic?

In cuix otimopouh oti-

[34 RECTO]

[or] did you bewitch him? [Or] how[ever] you did it. Did you desire your own death, to put an end to everything? Or did you desire the death of others, hating them and pondering how you will kill and destroy them? Or did you give medicine to some pregnant woman so that she would expel her child, or you took it so that your child would fall [stillborn]?

Perhaps you have a concubine. How long have you been in an illicit sexual union? What is the status of the woman? Is she married? Is she a widow? Is she young and unmarried or single? How many times with them are you confessing? And how many times do you have sexual relations with her in one year, two years, etc.? Count and remember with each one of the days, weeks, months and years. Is she a relative or a relation? Or how many women has it been that you have just enjoyed yourself with and had sexual relations with? Which is married? Which a completely intact maiden? Which

[34 VERSO]

a widow? Which single? And the maiden who was still completely intact: did you then dishonor her, deflowering her? And how many times did you sin with each one? And as for the maiden: if you dishonored her it is your burden of responsibility to return her honor to her helping her to get married, or if you are not married to marry her [yourself]. Perhaps one of the women you sinned with is your relative or relation? Perhaps you fell into the terrifying sin (never worthy of doing) of sodomy or the astonishingly frightful sin of joining and having sexual relations with some animal?

Did you perhaps steal? Has something [stolen] become your burden of responsibility? Did you perhaps sometime falsely accuse someone, dishonoring them? Or did you hunger after the goods and property of others and their wives?

Were you haughty

---

74. quien: read *quen.*
75. ticnotzo: read *ticnotza.*

[35 RECTO]

y soberbia, no teniendo en nada a tus proximos?
Si has sido lacerado, y avariento, no socorriendo a los pobres necesitados?
Si te has entregado desenfrenadamente a la sensualidad?
Si te has ayrado demasiadamente?
Si as tenido invidia de tus proximos?
Si has sido floxo y peresoço?
Si has comido, y veuido vestialmente, trocando, y vomitando lo que comistes, y quantas vezes?

Si has comido carne, en alguna Vigilia, Viernes, o Quaresma?
Si te acordabas que lo era o no, o si estauas enfermo entonces?
Si ayunaste los dias que estas obligado, o los quebrantaste?
Si alguna vez te engañó el diablo, no cumpliendo el mandato de la Santa Yglesia, dexando de confessar, y comulgar, algun Año, con que incurriste en

[35 VERSO]

descomunion.

PREGVNTAS BREves, y compendiossas, para confessar en casos de necesidad.

TIENES Sumo dolor y arrepentimiento de haber offendido a tu Dios y Señor? *Respuesta.* Si Padre.
Tienes proposito firmissimo de no pecar mas? *Respuesta.* Si Padre.
Te apartas, y desistes con todo tu coraçon de las ocasiones, y pecados que te impiden el seruicio de Dios *Respuesta.* Si Padre.
As viuido desenfrenadamente acerca de los pecados de la sensualidad? *Respuesta.* Si Padre.
Con quantas mugeres as pecado? *Respuesta.* Con quatro, o cinco &c.
Son casadas, viudas, doncellas, o solteras? *Respuesta.* Padre la vna casada, la otra viu-

[35 RECTO]

and proud, thinking nothing of your neighbor.
If you have been stingy and greedy, not giving succor to the needy poor.
If you have given yourself over without restraint to sensuality.
If you have been excessively angry.
If you have been envious of your neighbors.
If you have been lax and lazy.
If you have eaten and drunk like a beast, throwing up and vomiting what you ate. How many times [was it]?
If you have eaten meat on a vigil, Friday or [in] Lent.
If you remember that it was or not, or if you were sick then.
If you fasted the days you were obligated [to fast], or you broke [the fasts for those] days.
If some time the devil deceived you into not complying with the mandate of the holy Church: failing to confess and take communion some year, whereupon you brought upon yourself

[35 VERSO]

excommunication.

BRIEF AND SUCCINCT questions for confessing in cases of necessity.

DO YOU have great pain and regret for having offended your God and Lord? *Answer.* Yes, Father.
Have you very firmly resolved to sin no more? *Answer.* Yes, Father.
Move away and desist with all your heart from the causes and sins that deter you from God's service. *Answer.* Yes, Father.
Have you lived immoderately with respect to the sins of sensuality? *Answer.* Yes, Father.
With how many women have you sinned? *Answer.* With four, five, etc.
Are they married, widows, maidens or single women? *Answer.* Father, the one is married, the other a widow,

[35 RECTO]

mochamauh in atle ypan otiteytac, in cuix noço otiteoyehuacat, otitzotzocatic, in atle otiquin-tlaocolli in icnotlaca? In cuix noço çemicac otaahuilnen oticmoçenmacac in tlaylpaquiliztli, in cuix, noço otitlahuelcuic, oti, qualan,[76] in cuix noço, otimoxicotinen, otimoyolcocotinen, in cuix noço, otitlatziuh, in atle oticchiuh, in cuix noço, quenmanian otitequitlaquaca otimoxixicuino otimoxhuiti? In cuix noço otitequiatlic, otite-quitlahuan, otimiçotlac, in quezquipa, in cuix noço oti[c]qua nacatl Vigilia, Viernes, noço Quaresmatica in cuix oticilnamic noço amo, in cuix noço timococoa yn yquac: noço àmo in cuix otimoçauh, in yquac monahuatil? In cuix noço çan oticytlaco in neçahualiztli çan otitequitlaqua; in cuix noço quenmanian omitztlapololti in tlacatecolotl, in amo timoyolcuiti in Quaresma, in aço amo titlaçeli in aço

[35 RECTO]

and swelled up with arrogance, having no respect for others? Or were you stingy and avaricious, showing no mercy to the poor? Or did you always enjoy yourself, giving yourself over completely to lust? Or were you angry and furious? Or were you jealous and suffered envy? Or were you lazy, doing nothing? Or sometime did you eat excessively, practicing gluttony, stuffing yourself, and vomiting? How many times? Or did you eat meat on vigils, Fridays or during Lent? Have you remembered it or not? Or were you sick then or not? Did you fast when you were obligated to? Or did you just break the fast [by] overeating? Perhaps sometime the devil confused you, you did not confess in Lent or you did not take communion or

[35 VERSO]

ipan otihuetz in excomunion ytetelchihualitzin Santa Yglesia.

*NICAN MOTLA*lia, in çan quezquicamatl, monectihuetziz intla, ye tla, ohueti.[77]

CVIX, huel ic timoyoltonehua, in oticmoteopohuilli in moteotzin motlatocatzin Dios ? *Respuesta*. ca quemacatzin.
  Cuix yc tic, çemixnahuatia[78] in tlatlacolli? *Respuesta*. Ca quemacatzin.
  Cuix ye yçenmayan, tictelchihua in catlehuatl mitzcahualtia in itlayecoltilocatzin Dios? *Respuesta*. Ca quemacatzin.
  Cuix oticmoçenmacac, in tlaylpaquiliztli? Cuix otimomecati? *Respuesta*. Ca quemacatzin.
  Quezquintin in çihua otiquinmomecati? *Respuesta*. Ca nahui, macuilli, &c.
  Cuix namiqueque, icnoçihua, ichpopochtin, noço çan yuh nemi? *Respuesta*. Ca çe na

[35 VERSO]

you fell into excommunication, [becoming] the condemned one of the holy Church.

HERE IS SET DOWN in just a few words what is quickly needed if things are difficult and pose a danger.
HAVE you experienced heartfelt pain from having offended your God and Ruler? *Answer*. Yes.

  Do you bid farewell forever to sin? *Answer*. Yes.

  Do you once and for all despise whatever causes you to abstain from service to God? *Answer*. Yes.
  Have you given yourself over completely to lust? Have you cohabited illicitly? *Answer*. Yes.
  How many women have you cohabited with illicitly? *Answer*. Four, five, etc.
  Are they married women, widows, maidens, or single women? *Answer*. One is

---

76. oti, qualan: read *otiqualan*.
77. tla, ohueti: read *tlaohueti*.
78. tic, çemixnahuatia: read *ticçemixnahuatia*.

[36 RECTO]

da, la otra doncella, y la otra soltera.

Quantas vezes pecaste con cada vna dellas. *Respuesta.* Tres, quatro, &c.

Te has emborrachado, perdiendo el sentido, y trocando, y vomitando? *Respuesta.* Si Padre. Quantas vezes? *Respuesta.* quatro vezes &c.

As hurtado. *Respuesta.* Si Padre. Que fue lo que hurtaste, cosa de valor y precio, o no? *Respuesta.* Si Padre, l. no.

Quando estauas borracho tubiste acto carnal con alguna parienta suya? *Respuesta.* Si Padre, l. no.

Aora pues ten muy gran confiança en Dios Nuestro Señor, y no te diuiertas en otras cosas, que es el que ha de perdonarte, y di vna Aue Maria, &c.

AQVI SE PONE el modo imperfecto, que todos los Naturales tienen en confesarse.

PADRE mio aqui vengo a vuestra presencia,
[36 VERSO]
a labar, y vañar mis culpas y pecados, y ha manifestaros mis asquerosas llagas, porque soy vn gran pecador, a quien no te menosprecies de oyr, pues eres Ministro de Dios.

Peque como malo que soy, riendome de mis proximos, los mormure,[18] les achaque mis culpas.

Se me antojó comer carne en Vigilia &c. Y comi vna poquilla.

Y vna mala muger me persuadio, a que pecasse vna vez con ella.

Y he desseado pecar con algunas mugeres que he cudiciado, y les he dicho palabras deshonestas.

Y se me antojó hurtar vnos elotes, y calabaças, y hurté vna poca de lana &c Y muchas vezes he veuido pulque, con que me he emborrachado, y perdido los sentidos, y bomitado, y siempre riño con mi muger, y con mis hijos.

Y esto es lo que he hecho Padre mio.

[36 RECTO]

the other a maiden, and the other single.

How many times have you sinned with each one of them? *Answer.* Three, four, etc.

Have you gotten yourself senselessly drunk, and throwing up and vomiting? *Answer.* Yes, Father. How many times? *Answer.* Four times, etc.

Have you committed theft? *Answer.* Yes, Father. Was what you stole of great value and price or not? *Answer.* Yes, Father / no.

When you were drunk did you have a carnal act with some female relative of yours? *Answer.* Yes, Father / no.

Now then, have great confidence in God our Lord and do not amuse yourself in other things for it is He Who has to pardon you, and say an Ave Maria, etc.

HERE IS SET DOWN the faulty way that all the natives have in confessing.

MY FATHER, I come here to your presence
[36 VERSO]
to bathe and wash away my faults and sins and to reveal to you my loathsome sores, because I am a great sinner whom you should not despise upon hearing, since you are a minister of God.

I sinned like the evil man I am, laughing at my neighbors; I gossiped about them; I laid my sins on them.

I had a whim to eat meat on a vigil, etc. And I ate a little.

And an evil woman persuaded me to sin once with her.

And I have wanted to sin with some women I have coveted, and I have said lewd words to them.

And I had a whim to steal some green ears of roasting corn and gourds, and I stole a bit of wool, etc. And I have drunk pulque many times, and so I have gotten drunk and lost my senses and vomited, and I always quarrel with my wife and my children.

And this is what I have done, my Father.

---

18. mormure: read *murmure.*

[36 RECTO]

mique çe icnoçihuatl, çe çan yuh nemi ce ychpochtli.

Quequezquipa, in innahuac otitlatlaco? *Respuesta.* Ca oopa ye yexpa &c.

Cuix otitlahuan, cuix huel oticpolo in tlalli, cuix otimiçotlac? *Respuesta.* Ca quemacatzin. Quezquipa? *Respuesta.* Ca nauhpa, macuilpa &c.

Cuix otichtec? *Respuesta.* Ca quemaca. Tlen oticychtec, cuix huel patio? *Respuesta.* Ca quemaca, l. amo.

Cuix aca, mohuayolqui çihuatl ytech otitlatlaco, in yquac titlahuanqui? *Respuesta.* Ca quemaca, l. amo.

Axcan, ça xicmoçenmachiltitie, in moteotzin, in motlatocatzin Dios macatle mitztlapololtiz, ca nelli in çenca mitzmocnoytiliz xicyto çe Aue Maria. &c.

*NICAN MOTLA*lia in yuhqui ic moyolcuitia in mochintin maçehualtin.

*NO*tlaçotatzine, ca nican mixpantzinco o-

[36 VERSO]

nihuala, in ninopapacaco in ninoçencahuaco, in mixpantzinco nictlallico, in niyaca in nopalanca, in nehuatl nitlatlacoanipol, campa nel noço tinechmotlaxiliz, canel titlatenquixticatzin in Dios, ca onicchiuh, ca onitlatlacopollo, ca teca onihuetzcac teca onicamanalo, teca oninonotz, tlatlacolli tetech, onictlami. Auh onicelehui nacatzintli çan tepitzin onicquac in Vigilia &c. Yhuan çe tlacatl, onechcuitlahuilti tlatlacolli onicchiuh, çepa çe çihuatl, ytech onaçic, yhuan oniteyxelehui, yhuan oniquincamanalhui cequintin çihua Auh onicelihui elotl, ayotli, yhuan tepitzin onicychtec ychcatl: auh miacpa in onoconyc in octli huel onitlahuan, huel onicpolo in, tlalli, onicchiuh in chicontetl temictiani tlatlacolli. Auh mochipa nicahua in nonamic, yhuan nopilhuan o ca yehuatl, in in onicchiuh, ca ye yxquich notlaçotatzine.

[36 RECTO]

a married woman, one a widow, one is single, and one is a maiden.

How many times did you sin with each one? *Answer.* Two, three times already, etc.

Were you drunk? Were you senselessly drunk? Did you throw up? *Answer.* Yes. How many times? *Answer.* Four times, five times, etc.

Did you steal? *Answer.* Yes. What did you steal? Was it expensive? *Answer.* Yes / no.

Did you sin with some female relative of yours when you were drunk? *Answer.* Yes / no.

Now, have complete confidence in God, your Deity and Ruler, and do not let anything confuse you, for truly He will take great pity on you. Say an Ave Maria, etc.

HERE IS SET DOWN the fashion with which the natives make their confession.

O my beloved Father, here before you

[36 VERSO]

I come to cleanse and prepare myself, setting down my sinful stink and rottenness before you. I am a big, wretched sinner. Where else [but here] perhaps would you cast me, for truly you are God's spokesman. I have done it, I have wretchedly sinned, I have laughed at people, told jokes about people, spoken ill of others and imputed my sins to others. And I desired a little meat and I ate just a little on a vigil, etc. And a person provoked me to sin and I did it, I had sexual relations once with a woman. And I coveted and told [dirty] jokes to some women. And I desired corn on the cob and gourds and I stole a little bit of wool. And many times I drank pulque; I became very intoxicated, senselessly drunk, and I committed the seven mortal sins. And I always quarrel with my wife and children. O, this is all that I have done! I am finished speaking, my beloved Father.

[37 RECTO]

Hijo mio, esta Confession que as hecho, en ninguna manera me satisfaze: porque dizes en ella tan confusos tus pecados, que no se dexan entender. Y siendo tu como el enfermo, que no descubre al medico su enfermedad, como puedo entender el remedio que te tengo de aplicar, para la salud de tu alma. Aora pues esta atento, que assi te as de confessar: discurriendo siempre por los ma[n]damientos, como aqui va escrito.

Habiendote hincado de rodillas, y persignado, y dicho el Pater noster, y el Ave maria, y la Confession &c. Iuntaras las manos, y començarás con toda atencion a confessarte. Diziendo: Acusome acerca del primer mandamiento, que es, Amar a Dios sobre todas las cosas, que no le he amado; porque la [sic] he offendido, con infinitas offensas, y no he cumplido con las cosas de la Santa Fee como debo. He creydo las locuras, y desatinos de la

[37 VERSO]

antigua gentilidad.

Assi mismo me acuso acerca del segundo, que es no jurar su Sancto Nombre en vano, que muchas, y diversas vezes lo he jurado con mentira: algunas 15. 20. vezes &c. Y he jurado falso, haziendome testigo dos, tres vezes &c.

Y acerca del tercero, que es sanctificar las fiestas: Acusome que no las he santificado; porque he trabajado los Domingos, y dias de guardar, y dexé de oyr quatro Missas al año &c.

Y acerca del quarto, que es honrar a nuestros padres no lo he hecho, sino que antes los he desonrado, poniendoles las manos quando estube borracho, dos, tres vezes.

Y acerca del quinto, que es no matar: muchas vezes he desseado la muerte a mis proximos.

Y acerca del sexto, que es no fornicar: Acusome que he fornicado, teniendo parte con quatro mugeres, &c. La vna casada, la otra

[37 RECTO]

My son, this Confession you have made in no way satisfies me, because in it you speak of such a confused jumble of sins that they cannot be understood. And you being like the sick person who does not reveal his sickness to the doctors, how can I come to know the remedy I have to apply to you for the health of your soul? Now then, pay attention, for you have to confess in this manner, always going through the commandments, as is written here.

Having knelt down and crossed yourself, and having said the Paternoster and the Ave Maria and the [general] confession, etc., put your hands together and with great care begin to confess, saying: I confess (concerning the first commandment which is to love God above all things) that I have not loved Him, because I have offended Him with an infinity of offenses, and I have not complied with my obligations toward the things of the holy faith as I should. I have believed the lunacies and follies of

[37 VERSO]

ancient heathendom.

Likewise I confess concerning the second (which is not to swear His holy name in vain) that many times and on diverse occasions I have sworn it in vain: some 15, 20 times, etc. And I have taken a false oath, making myself a witness, two, three times, etc.

And concerning the third (which is to observe feast days) I confess that I have not observed them, because I have worked on Sundays and feast days and neglected to hear four Masses a year, etc.

And concerning the fourth (which is to honor our parents): I have not done it. Rather on the contrary I have dishonored them, laying my hands on them when I was drunk two, three times.

And concerning the fifth (which is not to kill): many times I have desired the death of my neighbors.

And concerning the sixth (which is not to fornicate): I confess that I have fornicated, having relations with four women, etc. The one married, the other

[37 RECTO]

Nopiltze in octicteneuh moneyolcuitiliz, ca niman ámo can teyolpachihuilti ca çan yuhqui in tlay[o]hua[ya]n mextecomac tictlalia, in motlatlacol, auh in ma çan yuhqui ticocoxqui ca amo huel tinechnextilia, in mococoliz inic huel nicytaz yhuan nicmatiz in catlehuatl patle nicnamictiz inic huel tipatiz. Auh in axcan xicyta ca yuhqui yn in timoyolcuitiz, çan tictepotztocaz, inican[79] micuiloa in teotenahuatilli.

Intla otimotlanquaquetz, intla otimixicuilo, intla otiquito in Pater noster, noço Aue Maria, noço Confession, &c. Niman timomanepanoa, huel ticçeyolocacopahuitiaz in tlen tictenehuaz ticytoz ninoyolcuitia in itechcopa, inic çe teotenahuatili in tictoçentlaçotilizque in Dios, ca amo onicnoçentlaçotilli, ca çenca miac inic onicnoyolitlacalhui: ca àmo melahuac onicchiuh in iteomachocatzin, ca tlen inxolopitlatol huehuentoton,

[37 VERSO]

onicchichiconeltocac.

Auh in itechcopa, ic ome teotenahuatilli, in amo tictlapictenehuaz, in itocatzin Dios, ca nicnocuitia, ca çenca miacpa, in çen[80] tlapic, onicteneuh, aço caxtolpa, çenpoalpa, yhuan testigo, çan tlapic oninochiuh opa yexpa, &c.

Auh, inic yey, teotenahuatili, in titlateomatizque, ca, amo nicchiuh, ca çan onitlaatequipano, in ilhuitl ypan yhuan onitlahuan, auh in çexiuhtica, onic[c]auh nahui Missa &c.

Auh in ytechcopa, ic nahui, in ticmahuiztilizque in tonantzin, totatzin &c. Ca amo nicchiuh, ca çenca oniquinmahuizpollo, ca oniquinmimicti, in yquac nitlahuanqui, opa yexpa.

Auh in itechpa ic macuilli in amo, titem[i]ctizque. Ca miacpa, in onitecocolli onitemiquizelehui.

Auh in ytechcopa ic chiquaçen in amo ta, ahuilnemizque.[81] Ca nicnocuita ca onaahuilen, ca nahui, in çihuatl, onicnomecati o-

[37 RECTO]

My child, the confession you have made to me is in no way satisfying. It is just as if you have set your statement down in darkness and obscurity; it is just like you are a sick person who cannot show me his sickness so that I can see and know which medicine I shall apply to it so that you can be cured. Now look: it is in this fashion that you shall confess; just go following along the divine commandments written down here.

If you have knelt, crossed yourself and said the Paternoster or the Ave Maria or the [general] confession, etc., then put your hands together and completely willingly do what you shall declare and say: I confess concerning the first divine commandment—we shall completely love God—I did not completely love Him, for I offended Him with a great many [things], I dishonestly performed devotions to Him, for I perversely believed the foolish words of the miserable little old men.

[37 VERSO]

And concerning the second divine commandment—you shall not take God's name in vain—I confess I took it completely in vain perhaps 15 times, 20 times, and I became a false witness two times, three times, etc.

And the third divine commandment—we shall engage in spiritual exercises and ceremonies —I did not do it, I just worked on feast days and I got drunk, and during the year I missed four Masses, etc.

And concerning the fourth—we shall honor our mother and our father, etc.—I did not do it, for I greatly dishonored them, beat them repeatedly when I was drunk, two times, three times.

And concerning the fifth—we shall not kill— many times I have hated people and desired their death.

And concerning the sixth—we shall not frivolously indulge ourselves in pleasure—I confess I engaged in licentiousness, I cohabited with four women,

---

79. inican: read *in nican*.
80. çen: probably to be read *çan*.
81. ta, ahuilnemizque: read *taahuilnemizque*.

viuda, la otra doncella, y la otra soltera. Y aquella muger que he tenido por mançeba, por mucho tiempo, he pecado diuersissimas vezes con ella, que abran sido mas de quatrocientas. Y las demas que no son mis mançebas, pequé con cada vna, dos, tres vezes, &c. Acusome, que vna destas mugeres con quien he pecado, es mi parienta muy cercana, dentro del segundo grado, tercero, y quarto grado &c. Acusome grauissimamente, que he incurrido en otros muchos, y diversissimos pecados, acerca de la carne: como son teniendo tactos deshonestos, poluciones, y otras miserias. Y he sido alcahuete, y por mi causa han pecado mucgos,[19] y se han conocido carnalmente. Y tambien me acuso, que he dado muy mal exemplo á mis hijos, á mis parientes, y criados, y â todos mis subditos, y á todos aquellos que les debiera dar buen exemplo.

Y acerca del septimo, que es no hurtar. Acusome que he hurtado cosa de valor, y precio, como son dineros, gallinas, mantas &c.

Y acerca del octauo, me acuso, que he mentido infinitas vezes, y he leuantado testimonio, en cosas graues, y de honra.

Y acerca del noueno, y dezimo, me acuso, que he desseado con ambicion, y cudicia los bienes ajenos, y las mugeres ajenas.

Acusome acerca de los siete pecados mortales, que los he cometido, teniendo presuncion, y soberuia, y he sido lacerado y abariento, y me he entregado vestialmente a los vicios carnales, y ayrado demasiadamente, y en la comida, y veuida no he tenido tasa como hombre racional, sino que he comido, y veuido vestialmente hasta vomitar, dos, tres vezes &c. Y he tenido embidia de mis proximos, y he sido peresoço. Acusome tambien, que

he quebrantado los Mandamientos de la Santa Yglesia comiendo carne en Vigilia, y Quaresma, sin tener necesidad, y no he ayunado como Dios manda. Acusome finalmente de todo aquello en que he offendido a Dios, con el pensamiento, con la palabra, y con la obra, y digo a Dios mi culpa.

a widow, the other a maiden, and the other single. And that woman that I had as a mistress for a long time: I sinned with her on many and diverse occasions, coming to more than 400 times. And the rest that are not my mistresses: I sinned with each one two, three times, etc. I confess that one of these women with whom I sinned is my very close female relative within the second degree [of consanguinity], the third and fourth degree, etc. I confess most gravely that I have fallen into many other and most diverse sins concerning the flesh, as are having lewd touches, emissions of semen, and other miseries. And I have been a procurer, and because of me many have sinned and carnally known each other. And I also confess that I have set a very bad example for my children, for my parents and servants, and to all my subordinates, and to all those for whom I ought to set a good example.

And concerning the seventh (which is to not steal), I confess that I have stolen something of value and worth, money, chickens, blankets, etc.

And concerning the eighth, I confess that I have lied infinite times, and given perjured testimony in grave matters concerning honor.

And concerning the ninth and tenth I confess that I have desired with a spirit of self-seeking and covetousness the property and wives of others.

I confess (concerning the seven mortal sins) that I have committed them, being presumptuous and haughty and I have been stingy and greedy, and I have given myself over like a brute animal to the carnal vices, and been excessively angry, and in eating and drinking I have had no limit like a rational man but rather I have eaten and drunk like a wild animal until vomiting, two, three times, etc. And I have been envious of my neighbors, and I have been lazy. I confess also that

I have violated the commandments of the holy Church, eating meat on a vigil and Lent when there was no necessity, and I have not fasted as God orders. I confess finally about all that in which I offended God with thought, word and deed, and I address my sin to God.

---

19. mucgos: read *muchos.*

[38 RECTO]

onicyxima tlatlacoltica, in çe namique, in çe icnoçihuatl, in çe ichpochtli, in çe çan yuh nemi. Auh in huel nomecauh, ocatca, ca çenca miacpa in itech, onacic, in aço çentzonpa, auh, in oc, cequintin, in amo nomecauan, oopa ye, expa, intech onaçic; Auh nicnocuitia, in çeme intech, initlatlaco[82] ca çan nohuayolqui, ontlamampan, yetlamampan &c. Auh nicnohueicuitia, ca qualca çenca miac, in onicchiuh, tlatlacolli, in itechcopa, in tlalticpacayotl, in onicnahuilti, in nonacayo, in onicnoqui in notlacaxinacho. Yhuan in tlen mach amo quali onicnotequiuhti, auh miacpa in, onitetlanahualnochilli, auh nopampa miaquintin, intlatlacoltica, omiximatque, yhuan ic ninoyolcutia, ca amo qualli, oniquimititi, in nopilhuan, in nohuayolque, nonencahuan, notlapacholhuan, yhuan in mochintin in quali, oniquimititizquia.

[38 VERSO]

Auh inic chicontetl ninoyolcutia, ca onichtec, auh huel patio in onicychtec, tomin, totoltin, tilmatli &c.

Auh in ytechcopa inic chicuei nicnocuitia, ca huel çenca miacpa in oniztlacat, yhuan onitetentlapiqui temahuizpololiztica.

Auh in itechcopa ic chiuhnahui yhuan matlactli, nicmocuitia ca onicteoçiuh ca onicapizmic, in teaxca in tenococol, yhuan in innamichuan in nohuanpohuan.

Auh, no ninoyolcuitia, in itechcopa in chicontetl temictiani tlatlacolli ca onicchiuh ca onicnotequiuhti, ca oninopouh, ca oninochamauh, ca oniteoyehuacat, ca onicnotequimacac in tlaylpaquiliztli, ca oninotlahuelpolo, oniqualan, auh nicnocuitia, ca oninoxixicuino, oninoxixicuinpolo, oniniçotlac opa yexpa, yhuan oninoyolcoco, auh çenca onitlat[z]iuh.

Auh ca on[83] onicytlaco in

[39 RECTO]

izquitetl, yteotenahuatiltzin in Santa Yglesia oninacaqua in Vigilia in Quaresma, in çan onicnec, auh aic ninoçahua in yuhqui techmonehuatilia,[84] in Totecuiyo Dios, auh yequene moch ic ninoyolcuitia, in ixquich ic onicnoyolytlacalhui, in Dios in ica in notlalnamiquiliz in notlatol in notlachihual, çenca onihueytlatlaco.

[38 RECTO]

I sinfully fornicated with them, one being a married woman, one a widow, one a maiden and one single. And many times I have sexual relations with her who was my mistress, perhaps 400 times, and the others who were not my mistresses I had sexual relations with two times, three times already. And I confess that one of those that I sinned with is my relative within the second degree of consanguinity, third degree of consanguinity, etc. And I greatly confess I committed an especially great number of sins concerning the things of the earth: I gave pleasure to my body, spilling my semen. And what in the world that is evil have I [not] been responsible for? Many times I have procured for people and because of me many have known each other through sin. And I confess that I have shown evil to my children, my relatives, my servants and my subordinates, and I should have shown them all that is good.

[38 VERSO]

And as to the seventh—I confess I have stolen. What I have stolen (money, domestic fowl, blankets, etc.) is costly.

And concerning the eighth I confess I lied many times, and through the dishonoring of others I raised false testimony.

And concerning the ninth and tenth I confess I have hungered and thirsted after the property and things entrusted to me by others, and the wives of my neighbors.

I also confess concerning the seven mortal sins that I have committed and been responsible for them, for I was haughty and swelled up with arrogance, I was avaricious, I excessively gave myself over to lust, I was desperately angry and furious. And I confess I was gluttonous and wretchedly voracious—I threw up two, three times—and I suffer envy, and I was very lazy.

And I also have broken

[39 RECTO]

all the divine commandments of the holy Church. I ate meat on vigils and during Lent; I just wanted it. I never fast as our Lord God orders me to. And moreover I confess to all with which I offended God in my thoughts, my words and my works; very greatly I have sinned.

---

82. initlatlaco: read *onitlatlaco*.
83. on: read *no*.
84. techmonehuatilia: read *techmonahuatilia*.

PLATICAS

*PARA ADMINISTRAR LOS SAN*tos Sacramentos:
con las quales se les da a entender a los Naturales
lo que pertenece a esta materia:
assi para su inteligencia como para
disposicion de receuirlos.
¶ *PLATICA VNI*versal, sobre todos los Siete
Sacramentos.

[39 VERSO]

IESV Christo Nuestro Saluador constituyó siete
Sacramentos, que son los siguientes.

El primero, Baptizmo.

El segundo, Confirmacion.

El tercero, Penitencia.

El quarto, Comunion.

El quinto, Extremauncion.

El sexto, Orden Sacerdotal.

El septimo, matrimonio.

Y constituyó su Magestad estos siete
Sacramentos, para santifficar el Alma, y con ellos
dalle la gracia que avia perdido, por medio del
primer pecado que cometio nuestro primer Padre
Adan, el qual fue el principio y origen de todos los
demas pecados, siendo el primer humano que
cayò en los sienos de la culpa, con que enlodò a
toda la generacion humana. Y como quedo sucia,
y afeada con la culpa: fue conuenientissimo, de
que otra vez se labasse, y hermoseasse. Y no vbo
otro que tubiesse poder para hazer esto, sino el

[40 RECTO]

mismo Dios Nuestro Salvador.

Y esto hizo por medio de los siete Sacramentos
referidos; con los quales fue seruido de remediar
la generacion humana, que estava tan perdida con
la culpa original, que quedó toda como herida, y
emponçoñada del mortifero veneno de la
Serpiente, dexandonos su Magestad, el eficaz
remedio, en los siete Sacramentos.

Con el Baptismo, se remedia la culpa original,
renovandosse, y tornandosse en su primer estado
de gracia la naturaleza humana:

La Confirmacion, da firmeza, y constancia en
las cosas de Fee.

La Penitencia, laba, y limpia el Alma, de todo
genero de pecado, y culpa.

El Sanctissimo Sacramento del Altar, da fuerça,
y vida Eterna al alma.

La Extremauncion, alibia la salud del Alma, y
del cuerpo

SPEECHES

FOR ADMINISTERING THE HOLY Sacraments:
with which the natives are given to understand
what pertains to this material,
both for their understanding and for the [proper]
disposition of receiving them.
¶ *GENERAL SPEECH* about all seven Sacraments.

[39 VERSO]

OUR Lord Jesus Christ established seven
Sacraments, which are the following:

The first, baptism.

The second, confirmation.

The third, penance.

The fourth, communion.

The fifth, extreme unction.

The sixth, priesthood.

The seventh, marriage.

And His Majesty established these seven
Sacraments in order to sanctify the soul and give
it the grace it had lost through the first sin that
our first father Adam had committed which was
the beginning and origin of all the rest of the sins,
he being the first human being who fell into the
muck of sin, and so he stained all human lineages.
And as it was left foul and disfigured with sin, it
was most fitting that it again be washed clean and
beautified. And there was no other who had the
power to effect this except

[40 RECTO]

the same God our Savior.

And this He did by means of the seven
Sacraments referred to, with which He was
pleased to remedy the human lineage that was so
lost with original sin that it all turned out to be as
if it were wounded and poisoned with the deadly
venom of the serpent, His Majesty leaving us the
efficacious remedy in the seven Sacraments.

With baptism the original sin is remedied,
human nature restoring itself and returning to its
first state of grace.

Confirmation gives firmness and constancy in
matters of faith.

Penance washes and cleanses the soul of all
manner of sin and offense.

The most holy Sacrament of the Altar gives
vigor and eternal life to the soul.

Extreme unction quickens the health of the
soul and body.

PLATICAS

*PARA ADMINISTRAR LOS SAN*tos Sacramentos:
con las quales se les da a entender a los
Naturales lo que pertenece a esta materia:
assi para su inteligencia como para
disposicion de receuirlos.

¶ ZENTENONOtzaliztli, in mochi ytechcopa in
chicome Sacramentos

[39 VERSO]

IN yehuatzin Iesu Christo totlaçotemaquixticatzin,
chicontetl Sacramentos, oquimotlallilico. Inyc ce,
Nequatequiliztli. Inyc ome: Tlaneltoquilizchica-
hualiztli. Inyc, yei: Neyolcuitiliztli. Inyc nahui:
Tlaçeliliztli. Inyc macuili: Temachiotiliztli. Inyc
chicuaçen: Teopixcatiliztli. Inyc chicome:
Nenamictiliztli.

Auh ipampa oquimotecpanilli, in chicome
Sacramentos, in quiqualtiliz, in toyolia, in
tlatlacoltica, oytlacauhca in yquac otlatlaco in
achto totatzin, Adan in oquipehualti, in tlatlacolli,
in iuhqui yehuatl yancuican, omalauh,
omoçoquipetzco, oquiçoquinelo in tlalticpac
tlaca, in tlacamecayot[l]. Auh in quenin
tlatlacoltica, ocatzahuac, oyxpoliuh: huel çenca
omonec, inyc oc cepa mopapacaz, moqualnextiz.
Auh ayac aquin huel oquichihuazquia, in,
intlacamo yehuatzin oqcimonomahuilico,[85] in
Iesu Christo

[40 RECTO]

totemaquixticatzin, in Dios itlaçomahuizpiltzin.

Auh yehuatl in chicontetl, Sacramentos, in
omoteneuh, inyc oquimopatilico, inyc oc cepa
yehuatzin, oquimoyectililico, in tlalticpac tlacamecayotl, in tlatlacoltica, oixpoliuhca, auh in
ma çan yuhqui tequan, coatl[86] oquipotz, oquiz-
tlacmin, oquicocolizcuiti; ca yehuatzin otechmoc-
ahuitilitehuac, in itech in chicontetl, Sacramentos,
in patli ic mopatiz. In Nequatequiliztli, ca yehuatl,
in hue[i] tlatlacolli, in motenehua, pecado original.
quipatia in yuhqui oc cepa, quipilcuepa quiyan-
cuilia, in tlalticpac tlacamecayotl. In Tlanelto-
quilizteoyoticatechicahuiliztli, ca yehuatl, in
quinenelhuayotia, quitlaaquilotia, in tlaneltoquiliztlachihualli. In Neyolcuitiliztli, quipapaca,
quiçencahua, quitlatlacolquixtia, in toyolia in
içeliloca in inacayotzin, in Iesu Christo quitemaca
in çemicac, yotilitztli.[87] In

SPEECHES

FOR ADMINISTERING THE HOLY Sacraments:
with which the natives are given to understand
what pertains to this material,
both for their understanding and for the [proper]
disposition of receiving them.

¶ *ADMONITORY* speech for everyone concerning all seven Sacraments.

[39 VERSO]

OUR beloved Savior Jesus Christ came to establish seven Sacraments. The first is baptism. The
second is confirmation. The third is confession.
The fourth is communion. The fifth is extreme
unction. The sixth is priesthood. The seventh is
marriage.

The reason He established the seven
Sacraments was to restore our souls, damaged by
sin when our first father Adam (who began sin)
sinned, as he was the one who for the first time
slipped [into it], making the lineage of earthly
people slide into the muck [of sin] and get mixed
up in it. And as it was through sin that it was
dirtied and defaced, it was very necessary that it
again be cleansed and beautified. No one could
have done this except our Savior Himself, Jesus
Christ, beloved and honored Son of God Who
came here personally to do it.

[40 RECTO]

It is with the aforementioned seven Sacraments
that He came to cure and again restore earthly
lineages. It is just as if a poisonous snake spewed
out and shot poison at them and made them sick;
He left behind for us in the seven Sacraments the
medicine with which they will be cured. Baptism
cures earthly lineages of this great sin called original sin, thus returning the earthly lineages to their
earliest states and renewing them. The spiritual
strengthening of faith is that which gives root to,
and bears fruit in, works of faith. Confession
cleanses, prepares and draws the sin out of our
souls. The receiving of the body of Jesus Christ
gives people eternal life.

---

85. oqcimonomahuilico: read *oquimonomahuilico.*

86. tequan, coatl: read t*equancoatl* or perhaps *tequani
coatl* (for both, see Molina 1977, 104v).

87. yotilitztli: read *yoliliztli.*

[40 VERSO]

El Matrimonio, reprime y refrena la concupis-
cencia, y fue constituydo para el augmento de la
propagacion humana.

El Horden Sacerdotal, da poder a los Sacerdotes
para administrar los demas Sacramentos, y comu-
nicarlos a todos los Christianos.

¶ PLATICA PRImera, sobre el Sacramento de el
Baptismo.

HAora vosotros, los que aqui aveis traydo estas
criaturas de Dios, para receuir el agua del Sancto
Baptismo, aduertid que esto estays obligados a
guardar y hazer.

Traeys estos niños, para que los hagamos del
gremio y rebaño del vnico y verdadero Dios, el

[41 RECTO]

qual los saca oy, y libra del poder del demonio,
que por el pecado eran sus esclauos, porque
aunque niños inocentes, vienen maculados del
antiguo pecado original, en que sus padres y
madres los conciben, y aora con el agua del baptismo se laban, y limpian de esta macula en que
nacieron, y quedan vellos, y hermossos ante el
acatamiento de Dios, y para siempre le pertene-
sen, por cuya causa estays, y quedays muy obligados, los que soys sus padres, y padrinos a
enseñarles como an de seruir a Dios, enseñan-
doles las oraciones, y doctrina.

Y aduertid que soleys cometer acerca del
Sacramento del Baptizmo, vn muy graue pecado,
teniendo trato carnal con aquellos con quienes
habeys contrahydo parentesco espiritual, mediante este Sacramento, y cometeys vn horrible
pecado de insesto pues para que de aqui ade-

[40 VERSO]

Marriage curbs and checks lust, and was established for the increase of human propagation.

Priesthood gives priests the authority to
administer the rest of the Sacraments and to
bestow them on all Christians.

¶ FIRST SPEECH, about the Sacrament of
baptism.

NOW you who are here who have brought these
creatures of God to receive the water of holy baptism, note that you are obligated to observe and
do this.

You bring these children so that we [might]
make them [part] of the company and flock of
the only true God,

[41 RECTO]

Who draws them out today and saves them from
the power of the devil, which through sin they
were his slaves, because although they are innocent children they come stained with the ancient
original sin in which their fathers and mothers
conceive them. And now with the water of baptism they are washed and cleansed of this stain in
which they were born, and they remain lovely and
beautiful before the reverence of God and will
belong to Him forever. For this reason you who
are their parents and godparents are and remain
very obligated to teach them how they have to
serve God, teaching them the prayers and [the
Christian] doctrine. And note that you are in the
habit of committing a very grave sin concerning
the Sacrament of baptism, having carnal acts with
those with whom (by means of this Sacrament)
you have contracted spiritual kinship, and you
commit a dreadful sin of incest. Well then, so that
from now on

[40 VERSO]

Temachiotiliztli quiteilhuitia in chicahualiztli. In Nenamictiliztli yc oquimochihuili in quitemacaz in nematiliztli, in ihuicpa in tla[l]ticpacayotl, yhuan inyc quitlaaquilotiz, quicacamayotiz, in tlalticpac tlacamecayotl. O ca yehuatl in chicontetl, Sacramentos yytoloca, auh inic ceceyaca momatiz, in catlehuatl moneltiliz, in acachtopa, in yquac moçeliz ca nican micuiloa.

¶ *TENONOTZAliztli* in etechcopa [sic] in Sacramento, Tequatequiliztli.

IN axcan, in amehuantin, in nican anquihual-huica[que], in itlachichihualtzitzihuan Dios inic quiçelizque, in itlaçomahuizatzin ca nican ca in amomamal in amonahuatil, mochihuaz. Oanquihualhuicaque inic itetzinco tiquinpoaz-que, in huel nelli teotl ca ye icenmayan qnuimomaquixti-[88]

[41 RECTO]

lia in yhuicpa in tlacatecolotl, intltalacoltica,[89] oquinmaceuhca, auh in macihui in pipiltzitzintin ámo tle quimatti, yeçe ca ye catzahuatihuitze in huehue tlatlacolli, in impan quitlacatilia in innanhuan. Auh in axcan ica in Nequatequilizatl, mopapaca mocencahua, quiça in tlatlacolli in ipan tlacati auh oc cepa qualneci in ixpantzinco in Dios, auh ca ye ycenmayan itetzinco pohui, ipampa in huel amomamal mochihua in àmintahuan, in anquimachtizque in quenin quimotlayecoltilizque in Dios anquimititizque in teotlatolli in teoyotl.

Auh nican ca in huel ye anquitlacoa in quemanian inin Sacramento in Teoyotica nehuayolcatiliztli, in anquinnepanoa in teoyotica amohuayolque cenca temamauhti in tlatlacolli anquimotequiuhtia insesto: Auh yc huel pachiuhtiez, in amoyolo, in âmo anmoxolopitlapi-

[40 VERSO]

Extreme unction makes people merit [bodily] vigor. With marriage prudence is made for and given to people regarding [the pleasures of] earthly things, and so that earthly lineages will bear fruit and give forth. [Description of priest-hood missing.] This is the declaration of the seven Sacraments. And inasmuch as each person will have some doubt which will be carried out first when he takes communion, here are written [some guidelines].

¶ [First] *ADMONITORY* speech, about the Sacrament of baptism.

NOW you who have brought here God's little creatures so that they shall receive His precious and esteemed water: here is what your burden of responsibility and obligation will become. You have brought them so that we will assign them to the true God, for He will forever save them

[41 RECTO]

from the devil who through sin made them his subjects. Even though they are little children and know nothing, yet they come dirtied with the ancient sin in which their mothers gave them birth. And now with the water of baptism they are bathed and prepared, the sin in which they were born has come out, and again they are beautiful before God and forever belong to Him. Because of this you who are their parents are very respon-sible for teaching them how to serve God and showing them the divine words and the things pertaining to God.

Here is [how] you sometimes violate this Sacrament [with respect to] spiritual relationships. You have sexual relations with those of your relatives with whom you have established [church-sponsored] spiritual relationships; you are responsible for the very terrifying sin of incest. So that your heart will be content and satisfied and you will not make up foolish things,

---

88. qnuimomaquixti-: read *quinmomaquixti-*.
89. intltalacoltica: read *intlatlacoltica.*

lante no pequeys de ignorancia, sino que sepays lo que contraheys, tened muy entendido, que aquestos niños que aqui traeys, ya son vuestros hijos espirituales y con sus padres habeys contrahydo parentesco espiritual, y este es muy proximo y cercano, y assi mirad lo que hazeis, y abrid los ojos, no os suceda alguna vez cometer algun insesto, y pecado graue, y esto es lo que estays obligados a hazer, y guardar.

¶ *PLATICA SEgunda*, sobre el Sacramento de la Confirmacion.

A Los Obispos, y Arçobispos, les dio Dios poder, y facultad para confirmar, y para que este Sacramento nos de firmeça, y constancia en la Fee, de tal manera, que no aya cosa en el mundo, que nos pueda mudar, ni apartar della sino que tenga, y eche fir-

firmissimas[20] rayzes en nuestro coraçon. De tal suerte que primero nos quiten la vida mil vezes (si fuere posible) que nos apartemos della, ni la dexemos, como hazen, y nos enseñan los Martyres: Y assi estays obligados todos a confirmar a vuestros hijos, y hazerles receuir esta merced y fauor del Cielo (que se llama Confirmacion) teniendo muy gran cuydado quando van los Prelados a vuestros Pueblos para que no quede ninguno sin recebirla, avnque sea ya de edad, y hombre grande. Y aduertid que tambien con este Sacramento, contraheys espiritual parentesco y receuis dones de gracia.

¶ *PLATICA TERcera* sobre el Sacramento de la Confession, y Penitencia.

you do not sin from ignorance, rather that you know what you are getting into, understand well that those children that you bring here are spiritually already your children and you have entered into a spiritual kinship with their parents, and this [kinship] is very near and close. And thus look to what you do and open your eyes. Do not some time let it happen to you that you commit some incest and grave sin. And this is what you are obligated to do and observe.

¶ *SECOND SPEECH*, about the Sacrament of confirmation.

God gave the bishops and the archbishops the power and authority to confirm and so that this Sacrament gives us steadiness and constancy in the faith, to such a degree that there is nothing in the world that can make us change or remove it from us; rather, that it has and puts forth

very firm roots in our heart, in such a way that first they kill us a thousand times (if it were possible) than that we withdraw from it or leave it, as the martyrs do and teach us. And thus you are all obligated to confirm your children and make them receive this mercy and favor of Heaven (which is called confirmation), taking very great care that when the prelates go to your towns that no one remains who hasn't received it, even though he is already of age and a grown man. And note that also with this Sacrament you contract spiritual kinship and you receive gifts of grace.

¶ *THIRD SPEECH*, about the Sacrament of confession and penance.

---

20. firmissimas: first syllable was anticipated on 41v; error by the printer.

[41 VERSO]

quizque, ma yuh xicmatican in axcan ca inin pipiltzi[tzi]ntin oanquinhualhuicaque ca ye amopilhuan teoyotica, auh in intahuan in innanhuan, ca ye oanquimohuayolcaticque, ca çan huel amotech ca, amo hueca amohuayolque: amo [a]mechiztlacahuiz in tlacatecolotl, amo quemanian itla anquimotequichtizque,[90] in amo quali. O ca yehuatl, in axcan anquicaqui, in huel amopial amonahuatil yez.

❡ *TENONOTZA*lliztli in itechcopa in Sacramento teoyotica Techicahuilliztli.

IN yehuantzitzin, tlatocateopixque Obispos, yhuan Arçobispos oquimmomaquilli in Dios in huellitiliztli in nican tlalticpac inic motequail-pilizque quinezcayotia inin Sacramento in teoyotica Techicahualiztli, inic huel chicahuatiez in totlaneltoquiliz, in

[42 RECTO]

atle huel quicuaniz, quixopehuaz in huel itech in toyolo, nelhuayoaz, motlaaquilotiz, inic aca[c]htopa çentzompa timiquizque in amo ticmacahuazque, in yuh quimochihuiliani in Martyres. Auh ca huel amomamal mochihua, in antetahuan in antenanhuan inic mochintin amopilhuan anquinquailpizque yhuan anquinceliztizque in in ilhuicac tetlauhtilli in ittoca Confirmacion, cenca anquimo-cuitlahuizque in yquac hualmohuica in teopixcatlatoque in ipan in amaltepeuh inic mochintin quiçelizque, in ayac mocahuaz, in manel ye huehueintin tlaca, auh ça ye no yuhqui ica inin Sacramento anquiçelia in teoyotica nehuayolcatiliztli yhuan in teoqualnexiliz-mahuiçotl gracia.

❡ *TENONOTZA*liztli 3. in itechcopa in Sacramento Neyolcutilliztli.

[41 VERSO]

know now that these children you have brought already are your children in a spiritual sense, and you have made their fathers and mothers your relatives; near relations, not distant ones. [Do] not let the devil lie to you, [do] not sometime take responsibility for that which is evil. O, this that you are now hearing shall be your charge and obligation!

❡ [Second] *ADMONITORY* speech, concerning the Sacrament of spiritual strengthening.

GOD gave power here on earth to those who are ruler-priests (the bishops and archbishops) so that they will tie up people's heads [with a rib-bon] to signify this Sacrament of spiritual strengthening, and so that our faith will be strong and firm;

[42 RECTO]

nothing will move [or] push it away. [Rather,] it will firmly take root in our hearts and bear fruit, so that first we die 400 times [i.e., die a thousand deaths] (as the martyrs customarily do) than drop it from our grasp. And it becomes the bur-den of responsibility of you fathers and mothers to confirm all your children and to make them receive this heavenly mercy called confirmation. You will take great care when the ruler-priests come to your altepetls that all will receive it, no one will be left out, not even the very old people. And likewise with this Sacrament you contract spiritual relationships and divinely beautiful esteem, grace.

❡ Third *ADMONITORY* speech, concerning the Sacrament of confession.

---

90. anquimotequichtizque: probably to be read *anquimotequiuhtizque.*

[42 VERSO]

CON Que se laban, y limpian todas las maculas del alma, en que se enloda despues del Baptismo, es el Sacramento de la Confession, y penitencia, el qual nuestro Señor IESV Christo dexó consti-tuydo a los Sacerdotes, y ya hemos dicho en otras partes todo lo que pertenece a este Sacramento. Aora solo diremos aqui, lo que esta obligado a hazer el Penitente.

Lo primero y principal ha de tener summo dolor, y contricion de sus pecados, con que ha offendido a Dios no amandole como deue quebrantando sus sanctos mandamientos.

Lo segundo, que no ha de mentir, ni engañar en la confession al Confessor, porque sea verdadera.

Lo tercero, que ha de hazer firmissimo proposito de no offender mas a Dios.

Lo quarto ha de restituyr luego lo que tubiere a su cargo, y quedar libre de todo ello. Con todo lo qual[21]

[43 RECTO]

quedará descargada su alma.

❡ *PLATICA QVARta* del Sanctissimo Sacramento del Altar, verdadero cuerpo y sangre de Nuestro Señor Iesu Christo.

EL manjar de vida eterna, es el cuerpo de nuestro Señor IESV Christo, que se llama Sanctissimo Sacramento, el qual manifiesta, y declara el sumo amor que nos tubo, no queriendo dexarnos otro manjar, sino el mismo, con vn altissimo e inefable mysterio, se quedó acá en el Sanctissimo Sacramento. Y avnque le ven los ojos del cuerpo, que parece pan, ya no es pan lo que queda alli, sino su verdadero cuerpo, solos los accidentes, y apariencias de pan quedan, debaxo de los quales está escondido y oculto. Por dos cosas

[42 VERSO]

IT IS the Sacrament of confession and penance (which our Lord Jesus Christ left established for the priests) with which all the stains of the soul (in which it dirties itself after baptism) is washed and cleansed, and already we have said in other places all that pertains to this Sacrament. Now we will only say here what the penitent is obligated to do.

What is first and foremost [is that] he has to have great pain and contrition for his sins with which he offended God, not loving Him as he should [and] violating His holy commandments.

Secondly, he must not lie nor deceive the confes-sor in confession so that it will be a true [confes-sion].

Thirdly, he has to firmly resolve to offend God no more.

Fourthly, he has to make restitution right away of what he is responsible for, and remain free of all of it. With all of which

[43 RECTO]

his soul will have discharged its obligations.

❡ *FOURTH SPEECH*, about the most holy Sacrament of the Altar, the true body and blood of our Lord Jesus Christ.

THE sustenance of eternal life is the body of our Lord Jesus Christ that is called the most holy Sacrament, which reveals and declares the great love He had for us, not wanting to leave us another sustenance, but Him Himself, Who, with a most high and inexpressible mystery, remained here in the most holy Sacrament. And although the eyes of the body see that it appears to be bread, what remains there is no longer bread but His true body; only the surface and outward appearances of bread remain, beneath which He is hidden and concealed. For two reasons

---

21. qual: indicated (as is logical) at the bottom of 42v as the first word of 43r, but it does not appear there.

[42 VERSO]

INyc mopapaca in yxquich ytliliuhca ycatzahuaca
in toyolia in ipan huetzi in o yuh moquatequi: ca
yehuatl in neyolcuitiliztli in inmac oquimo-
cahuilitehuac in totlaçotemaquixticatzin IESV
Christo in teopixque. Auh ca ye omoteneuh, ca ye
omitto in ixquich ytoloca, ca ça yxquich in nican
ticytozque in huel izquitlamantli quichihuaz in
moyolcuitiani. Inic centlamantli: huel quite-
quipachoz quiyoltonehuaz in itlatlacol, inic
oquimoyolitlacalhui in Dios, in amo oquimo-
tlaçotilli, yhuan inic oquitlaco, oquixopeuh in
izqui yteotenahuatiltzin. Auh inic ontlamantli
amo tle ic iztlacatiz, amo tle ic quimoztlacahuiliz
in teyolcuitiani, inic amo nenquiçaz in
ineyolcuitiliz. Auh inic yetlamantli: ycemmayan
motlacahualtiz quiçemixnahuatiz in tlatlacolli.
Auh inic nauhtlamantli: intla itla ymamal
mochihua, in aço oquitecuilli in teaxca in

[43 RECTO]

tetlatqui, niman motlamamallaçaz, quicahuaz
aoctle ic etixtiez in iyolia.

¶ *TENONOTZAlliztli* 4. in itechcopa in mahuiz-
Sacramento ynacayotzin totlaçotemaquixticatzin
Iesu Christo.

IN cemicac yolilliztlaqualli: ca yehuatl in inacayotzin IESV Christo moteneuhtzinoa Sanctissimo
Sacramento, auh ca quiçennezcayotia in
ihueitetlaçotlalitzin, in amo quimonequilti, in ma
itla oc centlamantli tlaqualli,
otechmocahuilillitehuani, in çan huel yehuatzin
in itech in Sanctissimo Sacramento, ilhuicac
teotlamahuiçoltica, oncan omocauhtzinotehuac,
auh in maçihui in ticyta in yca in totlacatlachializ
in tlaxcalli neçi, ca aocmo tlaxcalli in oncan ca, ca
çan huel yehuatl in inacayotzin, ça ixquich in
tlaxcalnenezcayotl

[42 VERSO]

It is confession that our beloved Savior Jesus
Christ left in the hands of priests with which our
souls are cleansed of the blackness and filth they
fall into after being baptized. Everything there is
to say about it already has been declared and said.
Here we will say all and absolutely everything the
penitent will do. First thing: his sins will very
much trouble and pain him, that he offended
God [by] not loving Him and that he broke and
disdainfully rejected all His divine commandments. Second thing: he will not lie about something; he will not lie about something to his
confessor so that his confession is vainly wasted.
Third thing: he will firmly propose to restrain
himself from sin. Fourth thing: if something
becomes his burden of responsibility—perhaps
he took someone else's goods

[43 RECTO]

and property—then he will relieve himself of that
burden, relinquishing it; nothing shall weigh
down his soul.
¶ Fourth *ADMONITORY* speech, concerning the
esteemed Sacrament of the body of our beloved
Savior Jesus Christ.

THE food of eternal life is the body of Jesus
Christ, called the most holy Sacrament. It thoroughly signifies His great loving charity; He did
not want to have left us any other food but Him
Himself in the most holy Sacrament, where He
stayed through a heavenly and divine miracle.
And even though with our human eyes we see
that it appears to be bread, what exists is no
longer bread but His very body; it is all just the
appearances of bread

[43 VERSO]

quiso su Magestad quedase desta manera, como parece por las diuinas letras. La primera, para que pudiessemos llegar a receuirle, y verle; porque si su diuina Magestad quedara descubierto, y manifiesto no pudiera la capacidad de la naturaleza humana resistir su infinita, é inefable luz, como el Sol, que no le podemos mirar de hito en hito, sino que nos siega y vislumbra la vista material del cuerpo. Y lo segundo, porque avn no meresemos verle acá en la tierra, hasta que por medio del exercicio de nuestras buenas obras, lleg[u]emos a merecer este sumo y soberano bien. Y aunque veys, y os parece que este Celestial pan, se diuide en muchas y diuersas partes, y particulas, en todas, y en cada vna de ellas está nuestro Señor IESV Christo entero; porque solos los accidentes de pan, son los que parecen diuidirse, pero su Sanctissimo

[44 RECTO]

cuerpo, no se diuide, ni parte, sino que todo está entero en todas las Ostias y en cada vna dellas: de la manera que si quebrays vn cristalino Espejo, y lo diuidis en diuersas partes, y pedaços, vereys que en cada pedaço, y parte del Espejo, por pequeña que sea se ve el Sol, sin que se aya quebrado ni diuidido sino que en todas ellas, y en cada vna dellas está entero, refulgente, bello, y hermoso; porque solo el Espejo es el que se quiebra diuide, y haze partes, pero el Sol, no se diuide, ni muda, porque está en el Cielo. De la mesma manera es Nuestro Señor IESV Christo en el Sanctissimo Sacramento, porque avnque se diuiden las Ostias en infinitas partes, siendo vnas pequeñas, y otras grandes, su Sanctissimo cuerpo no se diuide, ni en vnas partes es mas que en otras: sino que en todas, y en cada vna dellas está todo entero, y no está

[43 VERSO]

His Majesty wanted it to remain this way, as is [clearly] seen in the divine scriptures. First so that we might be able to come to receive and see Him, because if His Divine Majesty remained revealed and manifest the [limited] capacity of human nature could not bear His infinite and indescribable light, like the sun at which we cannot stare because it blinds and dazzles the body's physical vision. And second, because we still do not deserve to see Him here on earth until by means of the exercise of our good works we manage to deserve this most high and supreme benefit. And although you see it and it seems to you that this heavenly bread is divided into many and distinct parts and particles, our Lord Jesus is complete in all and every one of them, because only the outward appearance of bread is that which seems divided, but His most holy

[44 RECTO]

body does not divide or split up, but rather is complete in all and each one of the hosts. In the [same] way that if you break a crystalline mirror and divide it into different parts and pieces you will see that the sun can be seen in each piece and part (however small it may be) without it having been broken or divided, but that in all and every one of them it is complete, brilliant, beautiful and lovely, because it is only the mirror that breaks, divides and is made into parts, but the sun does not divide nor change because it is in Heaven. In the same way our Lord Jesus Christ is in the most holy Sacrament, because although the hosts are divided into [an] infinite [number of] parts (some being small and others large) His most holy body is not divided, nor is [there] more in some parts than in others—He is entirely whole in all and each one of them, and He is not

[43 VERSO]

oncan mocauhtiquiça, inic motlapachihuiltitica, inyc motlatitzinotica. Ontlama[n]tli ynic yuhqui oquimonequilti. Mocauhtzinoz, in yuh neztica, in ipan in teotlamachilizamoxtli inyc çentlamantli, ipampa in huel tictocelilizque, yhuan huel tictotilizque, ypampa intla huel techmotititzinozquia, in huel monextitzinozquia, mopantlatzinozquia, ca àmo huel quimonamiquilizquia, in totlacayeliz in iteotilizpepetlaquilitzin. In yuhqui tonalli in ahuel quinamiqui in totlachializ, in çan techixmimictia. Auh inyc ontlamantli, ca yehuatl inic ayamo tolhuil in tictotilizque in nican tlalticpac ipampa huel oc monequi in tlaneltoquiliztica titlacnopilhuizque, auh in manel ye anquitta, in cenca miacan quiça inin ilhuicac tlaxcalli, in cenca miacan motlatlapana, mononoquaquixtia, ca no[hui]yan itech çeçeyacan moçenyetzinotica, moçemacitzino

[44 RECTO]

tica in totemaquixticatzin IESV Christo in tlaxcalnenezcayotl ca yehuatl in neci motlatlapana, mononoqualtlallia,[91] auh in inacayotzin, ca amo quen mochihua, ca no[hui]yan çeçecni ytech in Ostia mocemacitzinotica in yuhqui chipahuac tezcatl intla moteteyni motlatlapana in cenca miacan quiça, ca çeçecni tezcatapalcatitech motaz in tonalli, auh amo quen mochihua in tonalli, amo can tlapani, amo can xelihui, çan huel maçitica inic yahualtic, inic chipahuac, inic tlanexo, inic tonalmeyo, inic mahuiztic, ipampa ca çan ixquich in tezcatl in tlatlapani, teteyni, xexelihui, nononquaquiça, auh in tonalli, ca amo quen mochihua, ca ylhuicatitech yetiuh çan no yuhcatzintli in totlaçotemaquixticatzin IESV Christo in itech moye[t]ztica in Santissimo Sacramento, ca in macihui in cenca miacan quiça, moxexeloa in Ostia in cequi huehuei, in cequi tepi.

[43 VERSO]

left behind there with which He covered Himself and is hidden. He thus wanted that two things remain, as is clear in the book of divine wisdom. The first thing is on account of our being able to receive and see Him, because if He would show Himself [directly] to us, would manifest Himself and appear, our human state of being would not be able to contend with His divine resplendence. It is like our human sight which cannot contend with the sun; it just blinds us [with its great light and clarity]. The second thing is that we do not yet deserve to see Him here on earth because it is very necessary that we obtain that mercy through faith. And even though you see this heavenly bread is in very many parts, broken up and divided separately into many pieces, our Savior Jesus Christ is completely present and whole everywhere in each one of them.

[44 RECTO]

The [surface] appearances of the bread seem to be broken up and separately set down, but His body is undisturbed, He is perfectly complete everywhere in each one of the parts in the host. It is like a clear and beautiful mirror: if it is quite shattered and broken up into a great many parts, the sun can be seen in many places. But the sun is undisturbed, not broken [or] divided anywhere, but very whole in roundness, in beauty, in being full of radiance and sunbeams, in esteem, for it is just all of the mirror that is broken, shattered, divided up and separated, but the sun is undisturbed. Likewise such is our beloved Savior Jesus Christ in Heaven and in the most holy Sacrament, for even though the host is in many parts and divided up—some are large, some are small—

---

91. monononqualtlallia: read *mononoquatlallia*.

en vnas pequeño, y en otras grande como parecen los accidentes, sino que en todas partes, y en cada vna dellas está con todo su poder, grandeza, y hermosura, deidad, y potencia, como está en el Cielo, y todos quantos Christianos ay en el mundo le reciben, y se les comanica[22] Sacramentalmente. Esto es lo que se te ha dicho Christiano: mas aduierte, que para haber de receuir este pan de vida eterna, as de ver primero muy bien lo que hazes, y voluer sobre ti los ojos de tu consideracion, para que no le reciuas indignamente, y recibas juizio, y muerte; porque el que es convidado del Señor de lo criado, no ha de yr a su mesa con macula ninguna: concidere primero, quien le convida, y que manjar come, y con quienes se ha de sentar a la mesa: el que le convida ha de considerar, que es el omnipotente Dios, que puede en vn instante

condenarle: lo que come ha de advertir que no es manjar acá del mundo, sino el verdadero cuerpo de Christo Nuestro Señor, y con quienes se sienta a la mesa, son los Cortesanos Celestiales los Angeles, y Diuinas criaturas; porque avnque no los vemos con los ojos corporales, los de la fee nos los muestran, que vajan del Cielo en infinitas multitudes donde está el Sanctissimo Sacramento, que da y comunica vida eterna, y gloria para siempre, y plenitud de gracia. Por lo qual estays obligados a tener summa reverencia al Sanctissimo Sacramento, y estar muy ciertos que está en la tierra con su summo poder como está acá en el Cielo.

small in some and large in others as [may] outwardly appear. Rather, He is with all His power, grandeur and splendor, divinity and faculties, in all and each one of the parts as He is in Heaven, and all the Christians there are in the world receive Him and He is given to them sacramentally. This is what has been said to you, Christian. But note that in order to receive this bread of eternal life you first have to see very well what you are doing and turn upon yourself the gaze of your own reflection so that you do not unworthily receive Him and receive judgment and death. For he who is invited by the Lord of Creation should not go to His table with any blemish but consider first Who is inviting him and what food he will eat and with whom he will seat himself at the table. He whom He invites has to consider Who God Almighty is, that in an instant He can

condemn him. He has to be aware that what he is eating is not food of the world here but the true body of Christ our Lord, and those with whom he sits down at the table are the heavenly courtiers, the angels and divine creatures, because although we do not see them with the eyes of our bodies, those of our faith reveal them to us, that they descend from Heaven in infinite multitudes wher[ever exists] the most holy Sacrament that gives and bestows eternal life and glory forever and fullness of grace. Because of this you are obligated to hold the most holy Sacrament in the highest reverence and to be very sure that He is here on earth with His supreme power as He is in Heaven.

---

22. comanica: read *comunica*.

[44 VERSO]

tzitzin, yeçe in yehuatzin ca amo no moxelihuitia,
amo motepitonahuitia, amo quen mochiuh-
tzinoa, ca no[hui]yan, çececni moçemacitzinotica, auh ámo cecni tepitzin, cecni hueitzintli,
inic moyetztica, ca no[hui]yan yuh moyetztica, in
mochi ca yhuelitzin, ymahuitzçotzin [sic],
ytlatocayotzi, yteotilitzin in yuhqui ilhuica[c]
moyetztica. Auh mochintin, in ixquichtin
cemanahuac oncate christianos quimoce-
panmacehuitzinoa. O ca yehuatl in in axcan
ticcaqui in titla[l]ticpac tlacatl, auh yece inic
ticmoceliliz inin nemiliztlaxcaltzintli huel cenca
monequi in huel acachtopa timoyeyecoz mixco
mocpac titlachiaz, ámo çan tlapic ticmoma-
catihuetziz, ma nen oncan ticnamic in çemicac
miquiliztli ipampa in aquin ytlacoanotzaltzin
mochihuaz in ilhuicahua, in tlalticpaque huel
cenca monequi in chipahuatiaz átle ic catzahuac,
atle ic tetlaylti mochiuhtiaz in iyo-

[45 RECTO]

lia, huel acachtopa quitztimotlaliz in aquin
quimocoanochilia yhuan in tlen tlaqualli quiqua
yhuan in aquique intloc tlaqua: in quimocoanochilia quilnamiquiz, ca teotl cenhuelitini, auh
çan achitonca intla quimonequilti in mictlan
quimotlaxiliz. Auh in tlen quiqua quilnamiquiz,
ca àmo tlalticpac tlaqualli ca huel yehuatl in
inacayotzin in totlaçotemaquixticatzin. Auh in
innahuac tlaqua ca yehuantin in ilhuicac
tlatocapipiltin Angeles, ca in macihui in àmo
oncan tiquintlaca[y]oytta ca huel melahuac in
yuh techmachtia in teotlaneltoquiliztli, oncan
hualmocemacitimani, hualcenquiçatimani in
campa moyetztica in Santissimo Sacramento, in
quimotemaquilia in yoliliztli in papaquiliztli
cemicac, yhuan in ixquich teoqualnexilizmahuiçotl. Auh ipampa huel cenca monequi,
anquimocemmahuiztilizque, yhuan huel yuh yez
in amo

[44 VERSO]

yet He does not divide up, is not diminished, is
undisturbed, for everywhere and in each part He
is perfectly whole. He is not small in one part,
large in another, for He is everywhere with all His
power, honor, rulership and divinity as He is in
Heaven, and absolutely all the Christians there are
in the world jointly enjoy Him. O, this is what
you, a person of the earth, are hearing now! But
yet, in order to receive this bread of life, it is very
necessary from the very first to test yourself, look
closely at yourself. Do not falsely give it to yourself quickly, do not uselessly encounter eternal
death there, because it is very necessary that he
who will become the invited guest of the Master
of Heaven and earth shall be pure, his soul not
dirtied [or] made disgusting with anything.

[45 RECTO]

From the very first he will ponder Who is inviting
him to the feast, what food he is consuming, and
with whom he is eating. He will remember that
He who invites him is God the Almighty and if
He [so] wished could in a moment cast him into
hell. And he will remember what he is eating, for
it is not earthly food; it is the very body of our
beloved Savior. And he is eating with the angels,
the high-born nobles of Heaven; even though we
cannot humanly see them (as the faith truly and
honestly teaches us) they all come and congregate
wher[ever] the most holy Sacrament (which gives
people life, joy and divinely beautiful esteem,
grace) is. Wherefore we very greatly need to
honor it and will have heartfelt certainty

[45 VERSO]

¶ *PLATICA QVIN*ta, sobre el Sacramento de la Extremavncion.

*HI*jo mio aora te tiene tu Dios y señor en sus prisiones, y quiero consolarte, y animarte con vna palabra, advirtiendote que el Cielo oy te ha hecho vn singularissimo favor y merced, dandote fuerça, y vngiendote nuestra Madre la Yglesia, con el Olio de la gracia, para que puedas pelear, y resistir los enemigos de tu alma, y esforçar, y animar tu cuerpo: tente por muy dichoso, y buen animo. Ya no tengas tu coraçon en las cosas desta vida, pues estás cierto que ya la dexas, y te [a]percibes para la otra: mira si tienes alguna cosa que remuerda a tu conciencia, confiessala, y dexala declarada, no

[46 RECTO]

te engañe el diablo, no te mueras sin dezirla, y vayas desta presente vida a la otra con tu alma manchada con esse pecado; porque como yrás a parecer ante la presencia de Dios. Aora es tiempo hijo mio que te ayudes, y no desconfies de la infinita misericordia de Dios, que por malo y pecador que seas, te ha de perdonar.

¶ *PLATICA SEX*ta, sobre el Sacramento del Orden Sacerdotal.

EL Sexto Sacramento, el Orden Sacerdotal, con el qual eligen, y ordenan a los Sacerdotes para que sean ministros acá en en [sic] el mundo de Nuestro Señor Iesu Christo. A estos se les da todo el poder del Cielo para que puedan comunicar todos los Sacramentos que hemos dicho. A ellos les dio poder acá en la tierra Nuestro Señor para que exerciten el sa-

[45 VERSO]

¶ *FIFTH SPEECH*, about the Sacrament of extreme unction.

MY son, now your God and Lord has you in His shackles, and I want to console and encourage you with a word, drawing your attention to the fact that today Heaven has done you a most singular favor and mercy, our mother the Church giving you strength and anointing you with the oil of grace so that you can fight and resist the enemies of your soul and strengthen and give new life to your body. Consider yourself very fortunate and be strong. Do not any longer set your heart on the things of this life since you are sure that already you are leaving it and preparing yourself for the next. Look if you have something gnawing away at your conscience, confess it and leave it stated. Do not let

[46 RECTO]

the devil deceive you, do not die without saying it and go from this life to the next with your soul blemished with that sin, because how are you going to appear in the presence of God? Now it is time, my son, that you help yourself, and not mistrust the infinite mercy of God, that however bad a man and a sinner you are He has to pardon you.

¶ *SIXTH SPEECH*, about the Sacrament of priesthood.

The sixth Sacrament—the priesthood—with which they elect and ordain the priests in order to be ministers of our Lord Jesus Christ here in the world. All the power of Heaven is given to them so that they can bestow all the Sacraments that we have mentioned. Our Lord has given them power here on earth so that they exercise the practice of the sacrosanct

[45 VERSO]

yolo in ca oncan mocenyetztica in yuhqui ilhuicatl iytec.

¶ *TENONOTZA*liztli 5. in itechcopa in Sacramento Temachiotilliztli.

*N*Otlaçopiltze in axcan omitzmolpili in moteotzin, in motlatocatzin Iesu Christo, ca nican ca cententli ic nimitzellacahua, nimitzyolalia ma yuh quimati in moyolo, ca çenca huei in axcan mitzilhuiltia, in ilhuicatl mitzmoçalhuia in Santa Yglesia, inic huel inhuicpa timocaliz, timochicahuaz, in quiyaochihuaznequi in moyolia ticchicahuaz in monacayo, tictlapaltiliz in mix in moyolo, çenca ximotlaçocamati, auh xicmotili, ca ye oncan, ca ye yxquich, ca ye ticcahua in tlalticpactli, aocmo ytech tictlaliz in moylo ca ye ycemmayan. Auh àço ytla mitztequipachoa, xicitto, xicnex-

[46 RECTO]

titiuh àmo mitztlapololtiz in tlacatecolotl, ámo ipan timiquiz, inyc catzahuatiaz in moyolia quen tineçitiuh in ixpantzinco in Dios, oquic qualcan ximopalehui, auh àmo quen xicchihua in moyolo, ca huei in iteicnoitalitzin in Dios, auh in manel ye cenca miac ticmohuiquililia, ca mitzmocnoitiliz.

¶ *TENONOTZA*liztli 6. in itechcopa in Sacramento Teopixcayotl.

*IN*yc Chiquacentetl Sacramento, yehuatl in Teopixcayotl, quinteochihua in Teopixque, in ixiptlatzitzihuan yezque in nican tlalticpac, in totlaçotemaquixticatzin Iesu Christo. Auh ca yehuatl in cennemactlalillo in ilhuicac huelitiliztli inic quitemacazque quitetlauhtizque in ixquich omoteneuh Sacramentos yehuantin onca in

[45 VERSO]

that He is there in His entirety as He is in Heaven.

¶ Fifth *ADMONITORY* speech, concerning the Sacrament of extreme unction.

O my beloved child, now your God and Ruler Jesus Christ has you in His custody; here, with a word [or two], I will encourage and console you. May you be certain that today Heaven gives you a very great mercy, the holy Church anoints you so that you can do battle and be firm against those who want to wage war on your soul. Make your body strong and your spirits brave, and be very grateful. Look, there it is, it is all over, you are leaving the earth behind; do not any longer set your heart on it for it will be forever [behind you]. But perhaps something is troubling you? Say it, reveal it,

[46 RECTO]

do not let the devil confuse you, do not die in it so that your soul will go [on], dirty and filthy. What will you look like before God? While it is still an appropriate time, help yourself, and do not upset yourself, for God's compassion is great. Even though you owe Him for a great many [things], He will have mercy on you.

¶ Sixth *ADMONITORY* speech, concerning the Sacrament of priesthood.

The sixth Sacrament is priesthood. They ordain the priests who will be the representatives here on earth of our beloved Savior Jesus Christ. It is a gift given to all of them; the heavenly power to give to and bestow on people all the aforementioned Sacraments. They have the

[46 VERSO]

crosancto Mysterio de la Missa, en el qual les dexò sus Diuinas palabras, para que pronunciandolas ellos como las pronunciò nuestro Señor constituyessen luego su verdadero cuerpo en la Ostia, para los que dessean la vida Eterna. Dio tambien su Magestad poder a los Sacerdotes para que en su lugar perdonen, y desaten de los pecados, confessando, absoluiendo atando, y desatando &c. Dioseles facultad tambien para Baptizar, casar, y hazer y communicar las demas obras, y por ser Ministros del mesmo Dios, estays obligados a estimarlos, y tenerlos en lo que son, pues estan en lugar de Dios.

¶ *PLATICA SEPtima*, sobre el Sacramento del Matrimonio.

[47 RECTO]

AORA hijos os junta nuestra madre la Iglesia, y os desposa ya para mientras viuieredes aveys de estar juntos, no mañana ni essotro os aveys de apartar, avnque os arrepintays de lo hecho: Y assi aora con tiempo mirad lo que hazeis, y el yugo que os echais a cargo, si por ventura no es con toda vuestra voluntad, sino que alguno os ha metido, en ello, que el que tal haze, no se carga del pesado yugo que aveis de lleuar, ni tendra vuestro cuydado quando os arrepintays, y lo segundo abrid los ojos, no seais Parientes en algun grado, o parentesco Espiritual, o de consanguinidad, porque no sera valido. O si aveys hecho algun voto, o promesa de casaros con otra, que sea impedimento.

Y aora tu, que ya recibes por tu Esposa esta muger, no te la da la Yglesia para que sea tu esclaua, sino por tu compañera, para que ambos esteys en seruicio

[46 VERSO]

mystery of the Mass (in which he left them His divine words), such that pronouncing them as our Lord pronounced them they then create His true body in the host, destined for those who desire eternal life. His Majesty also gave priests the power to pardon and dissolve sin, confessing, absolving, binding and unbinding, etc., in His place. He also gave them the authority to baptize, marry, and make and bestow the rest of the works, and on account of being ministers of the same God you are obligated to respect them and consider them for what they are, since they are taking God's place.

¶ *SEVENTH SPEECH*, about the Sacrament of marriage.

[47 RECTO]

NOW children, our mother the Church gathers you here and marries you now, for as long as you might live you have to be together; you cannot separate tomorrow nor any other [time] even though you regret what is done. And thus now take some time to consider what you are doing, and the yoke you are assuming as a responsibility. If perhaps it is not totally willingly but because someone [else] has stuck you into it, he who does so is not taking on the heavy yoke that you have to bear nor will he have your worries when you regret it. And second, open your eyes: you cannot be relatives within some degree of spiritual kinship or consanguinity, because [then the marriage] will not be valid. Or if you have made some vow or promise to marry another: that would be an impediment.

And now you who already are receiving this woman as your wife: the Church does not give her to you so that she might be your slave but as your companion, so that you both serve

[46 VERSO]

huelli inic quichihuazque, in ilhuicac tlamahuiçolli Missa yn ipan oquinamocahuilitehuac[92]
in totemaquixticatzin Iesu Christo, in iyotzin in
itlatoltzin ipampa in iquac yehuantin
quitenquixtizque ipan in tlaxcalli Hostia, niman
inacayotzin mochihuaz in Iesu Christo, in intech
monequiz in cemicac yoliliztli quelehuia, yhuan
oquimmocenamaquilli in ihuelitzin inic
teylpizque in itechcopa in tlatlacolli teyolcuitizque,
tecencahuazque, tepapacazque, tequatequizque,
tenamictizque, yhuan quichihuazque in oc cequi
in ilhuicac tlamahuiçolli, auh inic Dios yxiptla-
tzitzihuan cenca mahuiztililozque ymacaxozque,
ca huel yuh momatiz in ca yehuatzin nican
tictotlacanonochilia.

❡ *TENONOTZAliztli 7. in itechcopa in*
Sacramento Nenamictilliztli.

[47 RECTO]

TLa xihualhuiyan nopilhuane, in axcan teoyotica
amechMocetililia in Santa Yglesia anmonamictia,
auh ca nican ca in anquicaqui, ca ye içenimayan[93]
in ammana, ca ámo moztla, huiptla anmocahuaz-
que, in manel anmoyolcuepazque. Auh in axcan
xicytacan, oquic qualcan in tlen anquicellia, in
tlen anquichihua, in acaçomo anmoçeyolocacopa
ámo çatepan anmoxiuhtlatizque ca cenca huei in
tlamamalli, in ye anquimomamaltia. Aço çan aca
amechyolehia,[94] cuix yehuatl amechpatiz intla
mo[z]tla, huiptla oanmaxiuhtlatique,[95] auh inic
ontlamantli, xicytacan, aço quen anmonotza, in
aço Teoyotica, tlapalotica, yeyca ca acan
ompohuiz, in nenamictiliztli anquichihuazque
anoço campa oc cecni Teoyotl oanquiteneuhque,
ca ic teotzoni[96] in nenemictiliztli,[97] auh in axcan
ye ticana çihuatzintli ca àmo motlacauh, ca çan
nepanol am-

[46 VERSO]

power to perform the heavenly miracle of the
Mass in which our Savior Jesus Christ left behind
for them His fine words. Because when they
declare them over the bread of the host then it
becomes the body of Jesus Christ, very necessary
for those who desire eternal life. And He gave to
all of them His power to bind people concerning
sin; confessing people, preparing them, cleansing
and baptizing and marrying them, and they can
perform all the other miracles of Heaven. So that
God's representatives are greatly honored and
fearfully respected, it would be well to understand
that here we speak of Him in human terms.

❡ Seventh *ADMONITORY* speech, concerning the
Sacrament of marriage.

[47 RECTO]

Come, my children, whom today the holy Church
is spiritually making one and are getting married.
Here is what you will understand. You are taking
each other for always and cannot abandon one
another tomorrow or the next day even if you
have a change of heart. Now look while it is still a
good time [to reconsider] what you are receiving
and doing. Perhaps you are not entirely willing;
will you not become tired and impatient with one
another later? For it is a great burden of responsibility that you are taking onto your shoulders.
Perhaps someone just put you up to it? Will he fix
it for you if tomorrow or the day after you are
tired of each other? Second thing is, look: are you
relations, [either] through the church [or]
through blood? Because [in such a case] the marriage you make will count for nothing. Or perhaps somewhere in another place you made
someone a promise of holy matrimony, so that
the [present] marriage is struck down.[98] The
woman you are taking now is not your slave but
you jointly will have

---

92. oquinamocahuilitehuac: read *oquinmocahuilitehuac.*
93. içenimayan: read *içemmayan.*
94. amechyolehia: read *amechyolehua.*
95. oanmaxiuhtlatique: read *oanmoxiuhtlatique.*
96. teotzoni: probably to be read *tzotzoni.*
97. nenemictiliztli: read *nenamictiliztli.*

---

98. *struck down*: tentative translation.

[47 VERSO]

de Dios Nuestro Señor, y viuays vnanimes, y conformes, sin que el diablo trayga las discordias que suele entre vosotros, como os acontece siempre, sino que muy conformes le siruays, y siendo seruido de daros Hijos, crialdos luego con la leche de su Doctrina para que le sepan seruir.

Y vosotros los que os hazeys testigos deste Matrimonio, quiças les encubris algun impedimento, declaraldo luego, porque si no lo declarays incurris en vn muy graue pecado contra Dios, quiça por ventura por averos emborrachado dezis aqui lo que no sabeys; porque ya sabemos quan faciles soys en esto, y assi no os engañe el diablo,

[47 VERSO]

our Lord God. And live as one and in agreement, without the devil bringing the discord that is customary among you and as always happens, but very much in agreement serve Him. And He being pleased to give you children, raise them then with the milk of His doctrine so that they know how to serve Him.

And you who become witnesses to this Marriage: perhaps you are covering up some impediment for them. State it at once, because if you do not state it you fall into a very grave sin against God. Perhaps by chance on account of getting yourselves drunk you are saying here what you do not know, because we already know how prone you are to this. And so do not let the devil deceive you,

[48 RECTO]

porque os aveys de yr al infierno, y todo lo que les sucediere a los contrayentes estará a vuestro cargo. Y assi abrid los ojos.

NOTA
Acerca de algunos terminos improprios
de Lengua Mexicana,
que ha tenido el Credo, y demas Oraciones
de la Doctrina Christiana.
Ponense los propios y naturales.

SVPVESTO *que en las palabras del Credo, y demas Oraciones de la Doctrina Christiana, consiste todo el fundamento de nuestra Sancta Fee Chatholica [sic], hauiendo puesto en esta obra la instruccion de los Sauctos*[23] *Sacramentos, y Platicas para disuadir a los Naturales de sus antiguos reçauios de Ydolatria, y demas raçonamientos para el mejor conocimiento, disposicion è inteligencia del bien que consiguen, de los Sacramentos que se les administran, en vituperio de los vicios y pecados, (particularmente de [a]quellos à que son muy dados) no seria justo dexar passar al-*[24]

[48 RECTO]

because you will have to go to hell, and all that will happen to those contracting matrimony will be your responsibility. And so open your eyes.

NOTE
concerning some improper terms
of the Mexican language
that the Credo and the rest of the prayers
of the Christian doctrine have had.
[Here] are put the appropriate and native ones.

GIVEN *that the entire basis of our holy Catholic faith is contained in the words of the Credo and the rest of the prayers of the Christian doctrine—having put in this work instruction concerning the holy Sacraments and speeches to dissuade the natives from their ancient and evil customs of idolatry, and the other reasonings for the better knowledge, disposition and understanding of the advantage they secure from the Sacraments that are administered to them in condemnation of vices of sin (particularly those to which they are much given)—it would not be right to let pass*

---

23. Sauctos: read *Sanctos.*

24. In anticipation of the following page, *algu-* is written beneath the last word of this page ("passar"), but 48v begins with "[-]gunas." The missing syllable is placed on this page; error by the printshop.

[47 VERSO]

mopiazque, a[n]motlaçotlazque
anquimotlayecoltilizque in Dios amo tle teuhtli
tlaçolli amotzalan amonepantla quitlalitiez in
tlacatecolotl, in iuhqui anchichime anyezque
anmoquaquatiezque, in yuhqui mochipa
anquichihuani, çan paca yocoxca amotlatocazque
in ipan ytlayecoltilocatzin in Dios, auh intla
oamechmomaquilia amapilhuan,[99] anquin-
tlaçotlazque, niman ipan anquinhuapahuazque in
itlayecoltilocatzin.

Auh in amehuantia,[100] in axcan in ipan
antlaneltillia in monamictia, aço itla anquim-
machillia inic ytlacahui, inic tzotzoni in
nenamictiliztli niman xiqualyto çan, yeyca
intlacamo ca ipan anhuetzizque in itlatel-
chihualtzin Dios aço çan oamechtlahuantique
inic nican tlen anquitotihuitze? Acaço nelli? Aço
çan amiztlacati, ca ye amoyeliz inic mochipa
yuhqui anquichihuani, ma ytla ic amechtlapololti,
in tlaca-

[48 RECTO]

tecolotl, ca mictlan anyazque intla ytla ic
tlatlacahuiz in nenamictiliztli amomamal
mochihua in ixquich ic motolinizque in
monamictia huel xitlapocan in amixtelolo.

[47 VERSO]

and love each other. You shall serve God, the devil
not setting down between and among you the
dust and refuse of sin, [for] you will be like dogs
nipping at one another as you always are accustomed to doing. Just go along in life peacefully
and calmly in service to God, and if He gives you
children love them, then raise them in His service.

And you who are now providing verification
for those who are getting married: do you know
of something which is in detriment of, and an
impediment to, the marriage? Then speak up,
because if not you will incur God's disdain. What
do you come to say here: are you just drunk? It is
not true? Or do you just lie? For it is your nature
that you always are accustomed to doing so. Do
not let the devil confuse you with something,

[48 RECTO]

for you will go to hell if the marriage is thus
impeded, and all that which will afflict those who
are getting married will become your burden of
responsibility. Open well your eyes!

[The bilingual portion of Alva's original text ends on 48 recto. The remaining pages of the
Confessionario Menor contain a note to confessors written in Spanish, four prayers written in
Nahuatl, and printing information in Spanish.]

---

99. amapilhuan: read *amopilhuan.*
100. amehuantia: read *amehuantin.*

[48 VERSO]

gunas palabras improprias que hasta el dia de oy an
corrido assi en el Credo como en las demas
Oraciones, poniendo las proprias y naturales, y
aquellas que directamente corresponden a la fuerça
y propriedad de la significacion del romance, siendo
la principal causa desto, como es publico y notorio,
que en los principios de la conuersion de los
Naturales deste nueuo Mundo aquellos primeros
Padres de la Orden de San Francisco (a quienes se
debe el primer trabajo de la Predicacion
Euangelica) para haber de traduzir entonces de
lengua Latina o Castellana, en la Mexicana, fue
forçoso y necessario valerse de algunos Principales
de la Ciudad de Tezcuco, y otras partes que ya
tenian alguna noticia de la Lengua Castellana, y
por no entender la fuerça de la significacion de los
vocablos Castellanos que entonces se les pregunta-
ban, ni los Padres poder estar en tan breue tiempo
en los proprios de su Lengua natural, se pusieron
algunos terminos improprios y equiuocos en las
principales partes y articulos del Credo, y demas
Oraciones, de la Doctrina Christiana, y por no
hauer aduertido en ello, los Ministros que despues
acà a auido an corrido assi hasta el dia de oy, y
como aora ay muchos Indios que entienden la
Lengua Castellana como la propria suya, les causa
muy grande admiracion y nouedad, el ver que
teniendo su lengua natural propriissimos [sic] terminos para significar lo que està improprio en cosas
que tanto importan, los aya tan improprios y
equiuocos, que no significan sino a la contra de lo
que se pretendio significar entonces, de los qual
podran

[48 VERSO]

some [of the] improper words that until today have
been accepted both in the Credo and in the rest of
the prayers, [I am] putting down [here] the proper
and native ones and those that directly correspond
to the natural integrity and propriety of the meaning of the Spanish. The principal cause of this being
(as is public and well known) that at the beginning
of the conversion of the natives of this New World
those first Fathers of the Order of Saint Francis (to
whom is owed the first work of evangelical preaching) in order to have to translate then from the
Latin language or Spanish into Mexican it was
inevitable and necessary to avail themselves of some
leading citizens of the city of Texcoco and other
parts that already had had some acquaintance with
the Spanish language. And on account of not understanding the natural integrity of the Spanish words
that then were asked of them, not even the Fathers
could be in such a brief time properly precise in
their native language, [so] some improper and
ambiguous words were set down in the principal
parts and articles of the Credo and the rest of the
prayers of the Christian doctrine. And on account of
the ministers who afterwards came here not having
become aware of it, [those improper and ambiguous
words] thus have circulated until today. And as now
there are many Indians who understand the
Spanish language like their own, it causes them
great amazement and surprise, their language having native and very appropriate terms for signifying
what is [now] improper in what are things of such
importance, to see that [the terms] are so unsuitable
and ambiguous that they only signify the opposite of
what they then endeavored to signify. About these

[49²⁵ RECTO]

muy bien hablar de esperiencia los ministros muy
versados entre los Naturales, y ellos mesmos pregun-
tados lo dirán, y esto es manifiesto pues vemos que
por la necessidad, priesa y ocupacion que en aquellos tiempos se offreciò, por el infinito numero de
adultos que se Baptizauan, no vuo mas lugar, que
enseñarles las oraciones en Latin, y se ha perseuer-
ado con este manifiesto absurdo è inconuiniente,
hasta el dia de oy, que casi todos los Naturales rezan
en Latin, sin saber lo que se dizen, estando obligados a saber, y entender lo que pertenece al bien de
sus almas, y fee explicita para poderse saluar segun
los Sanctos Concilios, y Cathecismo Catholicos, con
que vuiera sido mas auentaxada su deuocion, y
affecto a las cosas tocantes a la virtud, y Religion
Christiana. Atendiendo pues a todo lo dicho, y a lo
que en adelante podra suceder, siendo Nuestro
Señor seruido que se vaya a dar en el Nueuo
Mexico, con los Reynos de donde vinieron estos
Mexicanos, para que se les enseñe, y predique la
palabra del Euangelio sagrado: con la fuerza de la
razon he tenido animo y osadia sujetandome
quanto a lo primero, de los que mas han versado
esta material (si bien heredada) a escriuir tambien
en esta obra el Credo, y demas Oraciones, con sus
proprios y naturales terminos, saltim donde fueron
necessarios, y porque no vasta esto para dar entera
satisfacion de lo que digo, quiero resoluerlo con sufi-
cientes razones en la forma siguiente.

En el Simbolo de la Fee y Credo VerbiGracia está
puesto en Lengua Mexicana, en lugar de aquellas
palabras Omni-

[49 RECTO]

the ministers who are very conversant with the
Indians could well speak from experience, and questioned they themselves would say it. And this is
manifest, since we see that on account of the necessity, haste and concerns that presented themselves at
that time [and] the infinite number of adults who
were baptized there was no alternative to teaching
them the prayers in Latin. And this manifest absurdity and inconvenience has persisted until today:
almost all the natives pray in Latin without knowing what is being said, [though] being obligated to
know and understand what pertains to the good of
their souls and explicit faith in order to save themselves according to the holy councils and Catholic²⁶
catechism. So their devotion and attachment to the
things bearing on virtue and the Christian religion
would have been much improved [if the prayers
were in their native language(?)]. Keeping in mind
then all that has been said and that in the future
could occur, if our Lord pleases, that [conversions]
may take place in New Mexico, with the kingdoms
from whence the Mexicans came so that the words
of the sacred Gospel may be taught and preached to
them: with the force of reason I have taken heart
and been bold, subjecting myself with respect to the
first, to those who have dealt most with this material (although inherited) also to write in this work
the Credo and the rest of the prayers with their suitable and natural terms, saltim [at least] where they
were necessary. And because this is not enough to
give entire satisfaction about what I am saying, I
want to resolve it with sufficient reasons in the following way.

In the Articles of the Faith and the Credo, for
example, ixquich yhuilli [all His-power/All-
powerful] is put in the Mexican language in place
of the words

---

25. The printshop erroneously placed "48" instead of "49"
at the top of this page.

26. Catholic: in this context refers to both holy councils
and catechism.

[49 VERSO]

potentem, ixquich yhuilli, *que su propria, y natural significacion destos vocablos, y como los Indios los han entendido hasta aora no significan lo mesmo que,* Omnipotentem, *que fue lo que se pretendio significar, sino lo mesmo que si dixeran, tanto poderoso, prueuase, porque este vocablo* ixquich, *significa vna cosa muy finita, y limitada, que signifique cosa finita y limitada es euidente; porque* ixquich, *termina, y limita a su proprio y natural corresponsiuo,* quexquich, *que es lo mesmo que,* quantum, tantum, *y los mesmos Naturales, quando quieren dar a entender, que vna cosa es muy corta y limitada, vsan siempre del termino* ixquich, *como VerbiGracia en el numero, que es el que tiene alguna apariencia, y razon de infinito: para dar ellos a entender que no lo es, si se les pregunta,* quexquich cuix huel acan tlami? Cuix huel acan tzonqulca?[27] *Responden* ca amotzin ca çan tlami ca çan tzonquiça ca çan ixquich in, *y no importan los subsequentes* silicet, oquiyocox in ilhuicatl in tlalticpactli, *para que estos vocablos signifiquen y suenen impropriamente, y aun todo el Peri[o]do en rigor significa lo mesmo que si dixeran,* nicnoneltoquitia in Dios Tetatzin in oquiyocox in ilhuicatl in tlalticpactli, *como si dixeran, creo en Dios Padre, que crio el cielo y la tierra, y no mas; por quanto el officio del aduerbio ò adjectiuo en la oracion particularmente en esta Lengua, dan el complemento a toda la oracion, y hazen variar toda su significacion, como en la que está referida. Esto supuesto, el proprio y natural*

[49 VERSO]

Omnipotentem [All-powerful]. *The suitable and native meaning of these words (as the Indians have understood it until now) does not mean the same as* Omnipotentem, *which is what it was claimed to mean, but the same as if they had said "so much power." This is proved because the word* ixquich [all] *signifies a very finite and limited thing. That it signifies a finite and limited thing is obvious because* ixquich *concludes and limits its own natural and corresponding term* quexquich [how much], *which is the same as* quantum [how much] *and* tantum [are so much]. *And when the natives themselves want to explain that a thing is very brief and limited they always make use of the term* ixquich as, *for example, in numbers, which have some probabillity and likelihood of being infinite. In order for them to explain that it is not [infinite], if they are asked* "quexquich cuix huel acan tlami? Cuix huel acan tzonquiça?" [How much of it is there? Does it nowhere come to an end? Does it nowhere conclude?], *they respond* "Ca amotzin ca çan tlami ca çan tzonquiça ca çan ixquich in" [No, it does come to an end, it does conclude, this is all there is], *and the subsequent words do not matter,* scilicet [namely], oquiyocox in ilhuicatl in tlalticpactli [He created Heaven and earth], *so that these words declare and enunciate an impropriety and the whole sentence strictly means just the same as if they said* "nicnoneltoquitia in Dios Tetatzin in oquiyocox in ilhuicatl in tlalticpactli" [I believe in God the Father Who created Heaven and earth], *as if they said "I believe in God the Father Who created Heaven and earth" and nothing more. Because the task of the adverb or adjective in a sentence (particularly in this language) [is that] they give the complement to the whole sentence and make its entire meaning vary, as in what was referred is reported above. This granted, the proper and native*

---

27. tzonqulca: read *tzonquiça*.

[50 RECTO]

vocablo y termino, y que les da a entender la infinita potencia de Dios, y corresponde propriissimamente [sic] a las palabras Omnipotentem . çenhuellitini Dios, *porque* huellitini *significa lo mismo que potens tan solamente, y la particula çen por via de aduerbio, significa con mayor fuerça y enerjia que omnis, el Todopoderoso, ó infinitamente poderoso, y todos los Atributos de la Diuina Esencia se les dan a entender a los Naturales elegantissimamente el ser infinitas con el termino çen, como VerbiGracia* çentlamantilliçecatzintli, cemicatilliçecatzintli, &c. *Con que queda el entendimiento de todos muy porporcionado a su proprio y natural concepto: Y en aste*[28] *caso le conuiene propriissimamente [sic] la deffinicion de la verdad, que* veritas est adequatio intellectus ad rem. *Esto mesmo se a de entender de los demas terminos que se han puesto en lo restante del Credo, y demas Oraciones, que por escusar prolixidad no refiero aqui, dexandolos para otras mayores, que con el fauor de Dios Nuestro Señor, saldran a luz.*

[50 RECTO]

word and term that gives them to understand the infinite power of God and corresponds most properly to the words Omnipotentem *[is]* çenhuellitini [all-He can] Dios, *because* huellitini [He can] *means the same as* potens [powerful] *only, and the particle* çen [completely] *by way of [its function as] an adverb signifies with greater force and energy than* omnis [all] *the Almighty, or infinitely powerful. And all the attributes of the divine essence are explained most elegantly to the natives as being infinite with the term* çen, *as for example,* çentlamantilliçecatzintli [Master of All Conditions[29]], cemicatilliçecatzintli [Master of Eternity], *etc. And so the understanding of all remains very proportionate to its correct and natural concept. And in this case it most appropriately suits the definition of truth, that* veritas est adequatio intellectus ad rem [truth is an adjustment of intellect with respect to the thing]. *In the same way the rest of the terms that have been put in what remains of the Credo and the remaining prayers are to be explained. To avoid long-windedness I do not list [them] here, leaving them for others [who are] better [than I, whose works] will, by the kindness of God our Lord, be published.*

---

28. aste: read *este.*

29. Tentative translation. See Siméon 1988, 610: "tlamantiliztli. s.v. Forma, manera, estado de una cosa. R. *mani.*" See also the related terms in Molina 1977, 63v: "Forma de materia. yuhcayotl. yuhquiyotl. yuhcatiliztli. tlamantiliztli."

[50 VERSO]

LAS QRATRO[101] ORACIONES.
El Credo.

Nicnoneltoquitia in çenhuellitini Dios Tetatzin in
oquimochihuilli in ilhuicatl in tlalticpactli, no
nicnoneltoquitia in Totecuyo Iesu Christo in çan
huel yçeltzin ypiltzin Dios in iteotlamahuiçolti-
catzinco Spiritu Sancto omonacayotzino: omotla-
catilli ytetzinco in Santa Maria moçemaçitzinotica
çemicac ychpochtli: motlahyyohuilli ytencopa in
Pontio Pilato, † Cruztitech mamaçoaltilloc,
momiquilli tococ motemohui in mictlan, yyelhuitica,[102] mozcallitzino intloc in mimique,
motlecahui in ilhuicac ymayeccampantzinco
omotlallitzinoto in çenhuellitini Dios Tetatzin,
auh ye ompa in hualmehuitiz in quinmotlatzon-
tequillilliquiuih in yolque, yhuan in mimique no
nicnoneltoquitia in Dios Spiritu Sancto Sancta
Yglesia Catholica, yhuan nitlaneltoca in itechcopa
in inneçentlallilliz in sanctome yhuan in itechpa,
tlatlacolpolihuilliztli yhuan ca oc çepa yolihuaz.

[51 RECTO]

El Pater noster.

TOtatzine in ilhuicac timoetztica, ma çenca
yectenehuallo in motocatzin, ma hualauh in
motlatocayotzin ma chihuallo in motlanequill-
litzin in yuh chihuallo in ilhuicac in tlalticpac,
auh ma xitechmomaquilli in axcan in totlaxcal
momoztlaye totech monequiz, auh ma xitech-
mopopolhuillilli in totlatlacol, in yuh tiquin-
popolhuia in techtlatlacalhuia, auh macamo
xitechmocahuilli inic ipan tihuetzizque in
tene[y]ecoltiliztli. Ma in mochihua.

[50 VERSO]

THE FOUR PRAYERS.
The Credo.[103]

I believe in Almighty God the Father Who created
Heaven and earth. I also believe in our Lord Jesus
Christ. Only He is the Son of God Who gave
Himself flesh through the divine miracle of the
Holy Spirit. He was born in Saint Mary, com-
pletely, perfectly and eternally virgin. He suffered
by order of Pontius Pilate, † had His arms
stretched out on the cross, died, was buried,
descended into hell, and after three days stirred
Himself back to life among the dead. He ascended
to Heaven to go sit at the right hand of Almighty
God the Father, and from there He shall come to
judge the living and the dead. I also believe in
God the Holy Spirit and the holy Catholic
Church, and I believe concerning the gathering
together of the saints and concerning the pardon
of sin and that people will come back to life.

[51 RECTO]

The Paternoster.[104]

O our Father Who are in Heaven, may Your name
be greatly praised, may Your kingdom come, may
Your will be done as it is done in Heaven and
earth. And may You give us now our daily tortillas
that we need. And may You pardon us our sins as
we pardon those who offend us. And do not
abandon us so that we fall into temptation. Amen.

---

103. Modern Standard English version: I believe in God,
the Father almighty, creator of heaven and earth. I believe in
Jesus Christ, his only Son, our Lord. He was conceived by the
power of the Holy Spirit and born of the Virgin Mary. He suffered under Pontius Pilate, was crucified, died, and was buried.
He descended to the dead. On the third day he rose again. He
ascended into heaven, and is seated at the right hand of the
Father. He will come again to judge the living and the dead. I
believe in the Holy Spirit, the holy catholic Church, the communion of saints, the forgiveness of sins, the resurrection of the
body, and life everlasting. (Courtesy of Stafford Poole, C.M.)

104. Modern English version: Our Father, who art in
heaven, hallowed be thy name, thy kingdom come, they will be
done on earth as it is in heaven. Give us this day our daily
bread and forgive us our trespasses as we forgive those who
trespass against us. And lead us not into temptation but
deliver us from evil. (Courtesy of Stafford Poole, C.M.)

---

101. Qratro: read *Qvatro.*
102. yyelhuitica: read *yeylhuitica.*

El Aue Maria.

MA ximopaquiltitie Sancta Mariatzine timoçentemilltitica[105] in teoqualnexilizmahuiçotl gracia,
motlantzinco moyetztica in tlatoani Dios, inic
tiçenquizcayectenehualloni tiquinmopanahuillia
in mochintin çihua, auh no çenquizcayectene-
hualloni in ytlaaquillo in moxillantzin Iesus,
Sancta Mariatzine, in titlaçonantzin Dios, ma
topampa ximotlatlauhtilli in ye axcan yhuan in ye
tomiquiztempan, Ma in mochihua.

La Salue.

MA ximopaquiltitie tlatocaçihuapille, in tinantzin
tetlaocollilliztli, nemillitzintle, tzopellicatzintle
tonechixcayellitzine, ma ximopaquiltitie, ca tim-
itzontotzatzillillia in tipilhuan Eua, mohuicco-
patzinco tonelçiçiuhtinemi tichocatinemi in nican
choquizixtlahuacan iho totepantlatocatzine ma ye
cuelle, ma xitech, hualmocnoytilli,[106] auh ma no
xitechhualmotitilli in itlaaquillo moxillantzin
Iesus in çenca yectenehualloni intla otictonquixtique[107] in totlamaçehualiz iho ycnoacatzintle yho
tetlaocollianie, yho tzopellicatzintle Sancta
Mariatzine cemicac ychpochtzintle.

The Ave Maria.[108]

REJOICE, O Saint Mary, you are completely full
of divinely beautiful honor and grace. God the
Ruler is with you. As to being completely and perfectly worthy of praise: you surpass all women.
And also completely and perfectly worthy of
praise is the fruit of your womb Jesus. O Saint
Mary, you are the beloved mother of God. Pray
for us now and at the time of our death. Amen.

The Salve.[109]

REJOICE, O Queen, you the mother are compassion. O life, O sweetness, O our hope, rejoice, for
we the children of Eve cry out to you, here in the
desert of weeping we go about sighing, crying out
towards you. O our intercessor, alas! Let it be that
you take pity on us, and may you also show us
here the fruit of your womb, Jesus, very worthy of
praise, if we carry out our penance. Alas, O merci-
ful one! Alas, O compassionate one! Alas, O sweet
one! O Saint Mary! O Virgin eternal!

108. Modern Standard English version: Hail Mary, full of
grace, the Lord is with thee. Blessed are thou amongst women
and blessed is the fruit of thy womb, Jesus. Holy Mary, Mother
of God, pray for us sinners now and at the hour of our death.
(Courtesy of Stafford Poole, C.M.)

109. Modern Standard English version: Hail, Holy Queen,
mother of mercy, hail our life, our sweetness and our hope. To
thee do we cry, poor banished children of Eve, to thee do we
send up our sighs, mourning, and weeping in this valley of
tears. Turn then, most gracious advocate, thine eyes of mercy
towards us and after this our exile show unto us the fruit of
thy womb, Jesus. O clement, o loving, o sweet Virgin Mary.
(Courtesy of Stafford Poole, C.M.)

105. timoçentemilltitica: read *timoçentemiltitica.*
106. xitech, hualmocnoytilli: read *xitechhualmocnoytilli.*
107. otictonquixtique: probably to be read *otictzonquixtique.*

LAVS DEO

[52 VERSO]

EN MEXICO

En la Imprenta de Francisco Salbago librero,
Impressor del Secreto del Sancto Officio.
En la Calle de San Francisco
Año *M.DC.XXXIIII*

PRAISE GOD

[52 VERSO]

IN MEXICO

in the press of Francisco Sálbago,
bookseller and printer
of the Office of Cases of Faith of the Holy Office.
On the street of Saint Francis.
Year of 1634.

BIBLIOGRAPHY

Augustine. 1958. *On Christian Doctrine*. Indianapolis: The Liberal Arts Press.

———. 1972. *City of God*. Middlesex, U.K.: Penguin.

Alva, Bartolomé de. 1634. *Confessionario mayor y menor en lengua mexicana*. México: Francisco Salbago.

Alva Ixtlilxochitl, Fernando de. 1975–1977. *Obras históricas*. 2 vols. Edited by Edmundo O'Gorman. México: Universidad Nacional Autónoma de México.

Anderson, Arthur J. O. 1993. Old Word-New Word: *Huehuetlatolli* in Sahagún's Sermons. In *Current Topics in Aztec Studies*, edited by Alma Cordy-Collins and Douglas Sharon. San Diego Museum Papers 30. San Diego: San Diego Museum of Man.

Anderson, Arthur J. O., Frances Berdan, and James Lockhart. 1976. *Beyond the Codices: The Nahua View of Colonial Mexico*. Berkeley and Los Angeles: University of California Press.

Anonymous, Order of St. Jerome. 1524. *Arte para bien confesar*. Toledo.

Anunciación, fray Domingo de la. 1565. *Doctrina cristiana en lengua castellana y mexicana*. México: Pédro Ocharte.

"Animal Propheta y dichosa patricida." MS. MM 462, Bancroft Library, University of California at Berkeley.

Anunciación, fray Juan de la. 1575. *Doctrina cristiana en lengua castellana y mexicana*. México: Antonio de Espinosa.

———. 1577. *Sermonario en lengua mexicana*. México: Antonio Ricardo.

Archivo General de la Nación, Bienes Nacionales, 830, exp. 1, Cuenta de los bienes de don Juan de Alva Cortés.

———. 1253, exp. 1, Provisión real, 14 Oct. 1631,

———. 830, exp. 3., fol. 165, Colación e institución canónica, 25 Oct. 1631.

Archivo del Arzobispo de México, Sagrada Mitra, Ordenes Sacros.

Arenas, Pedro de. 1611. *Vocabulario manual en las lenguas castellana y mexicana*. México: Henrico Martínez.

Bautista, fray Juan de. 1600a. *Advertencias para los confesores de los naturales*. 2 vols. México: Melchor Ocharte.

———. 1600b. *Huehuehtlahtolli*. México: [Melchor Ocharte?].

———. 1606. *Sermonario en lengua mexicana*. México: Diego López Dávalos.

Beristaín y Souza, José Mariano. 1883. *Biblioteca septentrional*. vol. 1. Amecameca: Colegio Católico.

Bierhorst, John, ed. and trans. 1992. *History and Mythology of the Aztecs: The Codex Chimalpopoca*. Tucson: University of Arizona Press.

Bloomfield, Morton W. 1967. *The Seven Deadly Sins*. East Lansing, Mich.: Michigan State University Press.

Bossy, John. 1975. The Social History of Confession in the Age of the Reformation, *Transactions of the Royal Historical Society*, 5th ser., 25:21–38.

Boyle, Leonard E. 1974. The Summa for Confessors as a Genre, and Its Religious Intent. In *The Pursuit of Holiness in Late Medieval and Renaissance Religion*, edited by Charles Trinkaus with Heiko Oberman. Leiden: Brill.

———. 1981. The *Summa confessorum* of John of Freiburg and the Popularization of the Moral Teaching of St. Thomas and Some of his Contemporaries. In *Pastoral Care, Clerical Education, and Canon Law, 1200–1400*. London: Variorum Reprints.

Brundage, James. 1987. *Law, Sex, and Christian Society in Medieval Europe*. Chicago: The University of Chicago Press.

Carochi, Horacio. 1645. *Arte de la lengua mexicana*. México: Juan Ruiz.

Camino del cielo. Undated. MS. 1470 in the Ayer Collection, Newberry Library, Chicago.

Celestino Solís, Eustaquio, Armando Valencia R., and Constantino Medina Lima, eds. 1985. *Actas de cabildo de Tlaxcala, 1547–1567*. México: Archivo General de la Nación.

Cervantes, Fernando. 1994. *The Devil in the New World*. New Haven: Yale University Press.

Chimalpahin Quauhtlehuanitzin, Domingo Francisco de San Antón Muñón. 1965. *Die Relationen Chimalpahin's zur Geschichte México's*. Edited by Günter Zimmermann. 2 vols. Hamburg: Cram, De Gruyter & Co.

Ciruelo, Pedro. 1530. *Reprobación de supersticiones y hechicerías*. Alcalá.

———. 1534. *Arte de bien confesar*. Valladolid.

Clavijero, Francisco Javier. 1982. *Historia antigua de México*. México: Porrúa.

Colín, Mario. 1967. *Índice de documentos relativos a los pueblos del Estado de México. Ramo de Mercedes del Archivo General de la Nación*. 2 vols. México: Biblioteca Enciclopedia del Estado de México.

Contreras Gallardo, fray Pedro de. 1638. *Manual de administrar los santos sacramentos*. México: Juan Ruiz.

Covarrubias, fray Pedro. 1521. *Memorial de pecados y aviso de la vida Christiana copiosa . . . provechoso assi para los confessores como para los penitentes*. Sevilla.

Delumeau, Jean. 1990. *Sin and Fear: The Emergence of a Western Guilt Culture, 13th–18th Centuries*. Translated by Eric Nicholson. New York: St. Martin's Press.

———. 1990. *L'aveu et le pardon*. Paris: Fayard.

Doctrina cristiana en lengua española y mexicana. 1548. México: Juan Pablos.

Duggan, Lawrence G. 1984. "Fear and Confession on the Eve of the Reformation," *Archiv für Reformationsgeschichte* 75:153–75.

Durán, fray Diego. 1967. *Historia de las indias de Nueva España e islas de la tierra firme*. Vol. 1. Edited by Ángel María Garibay K. México: Porrúa.

Fernández de Recas, Guillermo. 1961. *Cacicazgos y nobiliario indígena de la Nueva España*. México: Universidad Nacional Autónoma de México.

Galdo Guzmán, fray Diego de. 1642. *Arte mexicano*. México: Por la viuda de Bernardo Calderón.

Gante, fray Pedro de. 1981. *Doctrina cristiana en lengua mexicana*. Photoreproduction of the 1553 edition, with an introduction by Ernesto de la Torre Villar. México: Centro de Estudios Históricos Fray Bernardino de Sahagún.

Gaona, fray Juan de. 1582. *Coloquios de la paz y tranquilidad cristiana en lengua mexicana*. México: Pedro Ocharte.

Garibay K., Ángel María. 1953–1954. *Historia de la literatura náhuatl*. México: Porrúa.

Gerhard, Peter. 1993. *A Guide to the Historical Geography of New Spain*. 2d ed. Norman, Okla.: University of Oklahoma Press.

Gerson, Jean. 1960. *De arte audiendi confessiones*, Edited by Msgr. Pierre Glorieux. Vol. 8 of *Opera omnia*. 10 vols. Paris: Desclée.

———. 1960. *De erroribus circa artem magicam*. Edited by Msgr. Pierre Glorieux. Vol. 10 of *Opera omnia*. 10 vols. Paris: Desclée.

———. 1960. *Examen de conscience selon les péchés capitaux*. Edited by Msgr. Pierre Glorieux. Vol. 7 of *Opera omnia*. 10 vols. Paris: Desclée.

———.1960. *Le miroir de l'âme. 7:193–206*. Edited by Msgr. Pierre Glorieux. Vol. 7 of *Opera omnia*. 10 vols. Paris: Desclée.

Hill, Jane H., and Kenneth C. Hill. 1986. *Speaking Mexicano: Dynamics of Syncretic Language in Central Mexico*. Tucson: University of Arizona Press.

Homza, Lu Ann. 1992. Religious Humanism, Pastoral Reform, and the Pentateuch in Early Modern Spain: Pedro Ciruelo's Journey from Grace to Law. Ph.D. diss., University of Chicago.

Horcasitas, Fernando. 1974. *El teatro náhuatl: épocas novohispana y moderna*. México: Universidad Nacional Autónoma de México.

Hunter, William A. 1960. The Calderonian *Auto Sacramental* El Gran Teatro del Mundo. *Publications*, Tulane University, Middle American Research Institute 27:105–201.

Karttunen, Frances, and James Lockhart. 1976. *Nahuatl in the Middle Years: Language Contact*

Phenomena in Texts of the Colonial Period. University of California Publications in Linguistics 85. Berkeley and Los Angeles: University of California Press.

Karttunen, Frances, and James Lockhart, eds. 1987. *The Art of Nahuatl Speech: The Bancroft Dialogues.* Nahuatl Studies Series, 2. Los Angeles: UCLA Latin American Center.

Karttunen, Frances. 1982. Nahuatl Literacy. In *The Inca and Aztec States, 1400–1800: Anthropology and History,* edited by George A. Collier, Renato I. Rosaldo, and John D. Worth. New York: Academic Press.

———. 1983. *An Analytical Dictionary of Nahuatl.* Austin: The University of Texas Press.

Las Casas, fray Bartolomé de. 1979. *Los indios de México y Nueva España.* México: Porrúa.

León, fray Martín de. 1611. *Camino del cielo.* México: Diego López Dávalos.

———. 1614. *Sermonario en lengua mexicana.* México: Imprenta de Diego López Dávalos por C. Adriano César.

León-Portilla, Ascensión H. de. 1988. *Tepuztlahcuilolli: Impresos en Náhuatl.* México: Instituto de Investigaciones Históricas, Instituto de Investigaciones Filológicas, Universidad Nacional Autónoma de México.

———. 1992. Algunas publicaciones sobre lengua y literatura nahuas. In *Estudios de Cultura Náhuatl,* 22:467–93.

León-Portilla, Miguel. 1981. La embajada de los japoneses en México, 1614. El testimonio en nahuatl del cronista Chimalpahin. In *Estudios de Asia y África,* 16(2):215–41.

Lockhart, James, Frances Berdan, and Arthur J. O. Anderson. 1986. *The Tlaxcalan Actas: A Compendium of the Records of the Cabildo of Tlaxcala (1547–1627).* Salt Lake City: University of Utah Press.

Lockhart, James. 1992. *The Nahuas After the Conquest: A Social and Cultural History of the Indians of Central Mexico, Sixteenth Through Eighteenth Centuries.* Stanford: Stanford University Press.

———. 1993. *We People Here: Nahuatl Accounts of the Conquest of Mexico.* Berkeley and Los Angeles: University of California Press.

Lorra Baquio, Francisco de. 1634. *Manual mexicano de la administración de los santos sacramentos.* México: Diego Gutiérrez.

Mannheim, Bruce. 1991 *The Language of the Inka Since the European Invasion.* Austin: University of Texas Press.

Mansfield, Mary C. 1995. *The Humiliation of Sinners: Public Penance in Thirteenth-Century France.* Ithaca and London: Cornell University Press.

McNeill, John T., and Helen Gadamer, eds. *Medieval Handbooks of Penance.* Records of Civilization: Sources and Studies, 29. New York: Columbia University Press.

McNeill, John T. 1974. *The Celtic Churches, A History* A.D.. *200–1200.* Chicago: University of Chicago Press.

Mendieta, fray Gerónimo de. 1980. *Historia eclesiástica indiana.* México: Porrúa.

Menéndez Pidal, Ramón. 1978. *La lengua de Cristóbal Colón.* Espasa-Calpe, Madrid.

Michaud-Quantin, Pierre. 1959. A propos des premiéres *Summae confessorum.* In *Recherches de theologia ancienne et moderne* 26:265–69.

———. 1962. *Sommes de casuistique et manuels de confession au moyen age (XII–XVI siécles).* Analecta Mediaevalia Namurcensia 13 Louvain: Æditions Nauwelaerts.

Mijangos, fray Juan de. 1624. *Sermonario en lengua mexicana.* México: Juan de Alcázar.

Molina, fray Alonso de. 1552. *Ordinanças.* MS. M-M 455, Bancroft Library, University of California at Berkeley.

———. 1578. Doctrina cristiana en lengua mexicana. México: Pedro Ocharte.

Molina, fray Alonso de. 1984. *Confesionario mayor en lengua mexicana y castellana.* Photoreproduction of the 1569 edition with an introduction by Roberto Moreno. México: Instituto de Investigaciones Filológicas, Instituto de Investigaciones Históricas, Universidad Nacional Autónoma de México.

Nalle, Sara T. 1989. Literacy and Culture in Early Modern Castile. *Past and Present* 125:65–96.

Ozment, Steve. 1975. *The Reformation in the Cities.* New Haven, CT: Yale University Press.

Palau y Dulcet, Antonio. 1948. *Manual del libro hispano-americano.* 28 vols. Barcelona: J.M. Viador.

Paredes, Ignacio de. 1758. *Catecismo mexicano*. México: Biblioteca Mexicana.

———. 1759. *Promptuario manual mexicano*. México: Biblioteca Mexicana.

Pedraza, Juan de. 1568. *Summa de casos de conciencia*. Alcalá.

Peñaforte, Raymund de. 1720. *Summa, textu sacrorum canorum*. Paris.

Pérez, fray Manuel. 1713a. *Arte de el idioma mexicano*. México: Francisco Rivera Calderón.

———. 1713b. *Farol indiano, y guía de curas de indios*. México: Francisco Rivera Calderón.

Peters, Edward. 1985. *Torture*. New York: Basil Blackwell.

Poole, Stafford, C.M. 1995. *Our Lady of Guadalupe: The Origins and Sources of a Mexican National Symbol, 1531–1797*. Tucson and London: University of Arizona Press.

Poschmann, Bernhard. 1968. *Penance and the Anointing of the Sick*. Translated by F. Courtney. London.

Prieras, Sylvester. 1518. *Summa summarum quae Sylvestrina dicitur*. Strausburg.

Rafael, Vicente L. 1988. *Contracting Colonialism: Translation and Christian Conversion in Tagalog Society Under Early Spanish Rule*. Ithaca: Cornell University Press.

Ravicz, Marilyn Ekdahl. 1970. *Early Colonial Religious Drama in Mexico: From Tzompantli to Golgotha*. Washington: The Catholic University Press.

Reyes García, Luis, ed. 1978. *Documentos sobre tierras y señoríos en Cuauhtinchan*. Colección Científica, Fuentes, Historia Social. México: Centro de Investigaciones Superiores, Instituto Nacional de Antropología e Historia.

Rincón, Antonio de. 1595. *Arte mexicano*. México: Pedro Balli.

Ruiz de Alarcón, Hernando. 1987. *Treatise on the Heathen Superstitions that Today Live Among the Indians Native to this New Spain, 1629*. Translated and edited by J. Richard Andrews and Ross Hassig. Norman, Okla.: University of Oklahoma Press.

Rusconi, Roberto. 1972. Manuali milanesi di confessione editi tra il 1474 et il 1523. *Archivum Franciscanum Historicum* 6:107–56.

Sahagún, fray Bernardino de. 1548. *Sermonario*. MS. 1485 in the Ayer Collection. Chicago: Newberry Library.

———. 1583. *Psalmodia christiana*. México: Pedro Ocharte.

———. 1969. *Florentine Codex. Book 6— Rhetoric and Moral Philosophy*. Translated and edited by Charles E. Dibble and Arthur J. O. Anderson. Salt Lake City and Santa Fe, N.M.: University of Utah Press and School of American Research, Santa Fe.

———. 1982. *Historia general de las cosas de Nueva España*. Edited by Ángel María Garibay K. México: Porrúa.

———. 1993a. *Adiciones, apéndice a la postilla y ejercicio cotidiano*. Translated and edited by Arthur J. O. Anderson. México: Universidad Nacional Autonóma de México.

———. [1583] 1993b. *Psalmodia Christiana (Christian Psalmody)*. Translated and edited by Arthur J. O. Anderson. Salt Lake City: University of Utah Press.

Salomon, Frank, and George L. Urioste, eds. and trans. 1991. *The Huarochirí Manuscript*. Austin: University of Texas Press.

Sánchez Antonio, Blanco. 1987. Inventario de Juan de Ayala, gran impresor toledano (1556). *Boletín de la Real Academia Española* 67:207–51.

Sandstrom, Alan R. 1991. *Corn is Our Blood: Culture and Ethnic Identity in a Contemporary Aztec Indian Village*. Norman, Okla.: University of Oklahoma Press.

Schwaller, John Frederick. 1985. *The Origins of Church Wealth in Mexico*. Albuquerque: University of New Mexico Press.

———. 1987a. *Guías de manuscritos en Nahuatl*. México: Universidad Nacional Autónoma de México.

———. 1987b. *The Church and Clergy in Sixteenth-Century Mexico*. Albuquerque: University of New Mexico Press.

Sell, Barry D. 1992a. Church Imprints in Nahuatl as an Example of Cultural Interaction. In *Five Centuries of Mexican History/Cinco siglos de historia de México*, edited by Virginia Guedea and Jaime E. Rodríguez O., Vol. 1. México: Instituto de Investigaciones Dr. José María Luis Mora.

————. 1992b. 'The Good Government of the Ancients': Some Colonial Attitudes About Precontact Nahua Society. *UCLA Historical Journal* 12:152–76.

————. 1993. Friars, Nahuas, and Books: Language and Expression in Colonial Nahuatl Publications. Ph.D. diss., UCLA.

————. 1995. Change and the Consciousness of Change: Later Colonial Observations About Nahuatl and Nahuas. Paper given at the joint meeting of the Pacific Coast Council on Latin American Studies and the Rocky Mountain Council on Latin American Studies, Las Vegas, March 3–5, 1995.

Sell, Barry D., and Larissa Taylor. 1996. He Could Have Made Marvels in This Language: A Nahuatl Sermon by Father Juan de Tovar, S.J. *Estudios de Cultura Náhuatl* 26:211–44.

Siméon, Rémi. 1988. *Diccionario de la lengua nahuatl o mexicana.* México: Siglo Veintiuno.

Spaulding, Karen. 1984. *Huarochirí: An Andean Society Under Inca and Spanish Rule.* Stanford: Stanford University Press.

Talavera, Hernando de. [N.d. (after 1492)] 1911. *Breve forma de confesar.* Edited by Miguel Mir. Nueva Biblioteca de Autores Españoles 1. Madrid: Casa Editorial Bailly.

Teetaert, Amédée, OFM Cap. 1928. La 'Summa de poenitentia' de Saint Raymond de Penyafort. *Ephemerides theologicae lovanienses* 5:54.

Tentler, Thomas N. 1977. *Sin and Confession on the Eve of the Reformation.* Princeton: Princeton University Press.

Thomas of Chobham. 1968. *Thomae de Chobham summae confessorum.* Edited by F. Broomfield. Analecta Mediaevalia Namurcensia 25. Louvain: Editions Nauwelaerts.

Turrini, Miriam. 1991. *La coscienza e le leggi: morale e diritto nei testi per le confessione della prima età moderna.* Annali dell'Istituto storico italo-germanico, monografia 13. Bologna: Società editrice il Mulino.

Vázquez Gastelu, Antonio de. 1726. *Arte de la lengua mexicana.* Puebla: Francisco Javier Morales y Salazar.

Valtanás, fray Domingo de. 1963. *Apologia sobre ciertas materias morales en que hay opinion, y apologia de la comunion frequente.* In *Estudio preliminar y edición.* Edited by Alvaro Huergo, OP, and Pedro Saínz Rodríguez. Barcelona: Juan Flors.

Velázquez, Primo Feliciano. 1975. *Códice Chimalpopoca, Anales de Cuautitlán y Leyenda de los Soles.* 2d ed. México: Universidad Nacional Autónoma de México.

Vetancurt, fray Agustín de. 1982. *Teatro Mexicano: Descripción de los sucesos ejemplares, históricos, y religiosos del Nuevo Mundo de las Indias.* Photoreproduction of the 1698 edition. México: Porrúa.

Vio, Tommaso de (Cajetan). 1581. *Summula Caietani.* Lyon.

Vogel, Cyrille. 1966. *Le pécheur et la pénitence dans l'eglise ancienne.* Paris: Les éditions du Cerf.

————. 1994. "Réflexions de l'historien sur la discipline pénitentielle dans l'eglise latine." In *En Rémission des Péchés,* edited by Alexandre Faivre. Brookfield, VT: Variorum Reprints.

Whittaker, George. 1988. "Aztec Dialectology and the Nahuatl of the Friars." In *The Work of Bernardino de Sahagún: Pioneer Ethnographer of Sixteenth-Century Aztec Mexico,* edited by J. Jorge Klor de Alva, H. B. Nicholson, and Eloise Quiñones Keber. Studies on Culture and Society, Vol. 2. Albany: Institute for Mesoamerican Studies, University of Albany, State University of New York.

INDEX